CST-6 NEW YORK STATE TEACHER CERTIFICATION SERIES

This is your
PASSBOOK for...

Communication and Quantitative Skills Test (CQST)

Test Preparation Study Guide
Questions & Answers

NATIONAL LEARNING CORPORATION®

COPYRIGHT NOTICE

This book is SOLELY intended for, is sold ONLY to, and its use is RESTRICTED to individual, bona fide applicants or candidates who qualify by virtue of having seriously filed applications for appropriate license, certificate, professional and/or promotional advancement, higher school matriculation, scholarship, or other legitimate requirements of education and/or governmental authorities.

This book is NOT intended for use, class instruction, tutoring, training, duplication, copying, reprinting, excerption, or adaptation, etc., by:

1) Other publishers
2) Proprietors and/or Instructors of "Coaching" and/or Preparatory Courses
3) Personnel and/or Training Divisions of commercial, industrial, and governmental organizations
4) Schools, colleges, or universities and/or their departments and staffs, including teachers and other personnel
5) Testing Agencies or Bureaus
6) Study groups which seek by the purchase of a single volume to copy and/or duplicate and/or adapt this material for use by the group as a whole without having purchased individual volumes for each of the members of the group
7) Et al.

Such persons would be in violation of appropriate Federal and State statutes.

PROVISION OF LICENSING AGREEMENTS – Recognized educational, commercial, industrial, and governmental institutions and organizations, and others legitimately engaged in educational pursuits, including training, testing, and measurement activities, may address request for a licensing agreement to the copyright owners, who will determine whether, and under what conditions, including fees and charges, the materials in this book may be used them. In other words, a licensing facility exists for the legitimate use of the material in this book on other than an individual basis. However, it is asseverated and affirmed here that the material in this book CANNOT be used without the receipt of the express permission of such a licensing agreement from the Publishers. Inquiries re licensing should be addressed to the company, attention rights and permissions department.

All rights reserved, including the right of reproduction in whole or in part, in any form or by any means, electronic or mechanical, including photocopying, recording, or by any information storage and retrieval system, without permission in writing from the Publisher.

Copyright © 2025 by
National Learning Corporation

212 Michael Drive, Syosset, NY 11791
(516) 921-8888 • www.passbooks.com
E-mail: info@passbooks.com

PASSBOOK® SERIES

THE *PASSBOOK® SERIES* has been created to prepare applicants and candidates for the ultimate academic battlefield – the examination room.

At some time in our lives, each and every one of us may be required to take an examination – for validation, matriculation, admission, qualification, registration, certification, or licensure.

Based on the assumption that every applicant or candidate has met the basic formal educational standards, has taken the required number of courses, and read the necessary texts, the *PASSBOOK® SERIES* furnishes the one special preparation which may assure passing with confidence, instead of failing with insecurity. Examination questions – together with answers – are furnished as the basic vehicle for study so that the mysteries of the examination and its compounding difficulties may be eliminated or diminished by a sure method.

This book is meant to help you pass your examination provided that you qualify and are serious in your objective.

The entire field is reviewed through the huge store of content information which is succinctly presented through a provocative and challenging approach – the question-and-answer method.

A climate of success is established by furnishing the correct answers at the end of each test.

You soon learn to recognize types of questions, forms of questions, and patterns of questioning. You may even begin to anticipate expected outcomes.

You perceive that many questions are repeated or adapted so that you can gain acute insights, which may enable you to score many sure points.

You learn how to confront new questions, or types of questions, and to attack them confidently and work out the correct answers.

You note objectives and emphases, and recognize pitfalls and dangers, so that you may make positive educational adjustments.

Moreover, you are kept fully informed in relation to new concepts, methods, practices, and directions in the field.

You discover that you are actually taking the examination all the time: you are preparing for the examination by "taking" an examination, not by reading extraneous and/or supererogatory textbooks.

In short, this PASSBOOK®, used directedly, should be an important factor in helping you to pass your test.

NEW YORK STATE TEACHER CERTIFICATION EXAMINATIONS™
INTRODUCTION

GENERAL INFORMATION

About the Testing Program

Those seeking a New York State teaching certificate for the common branch subjects in prekindergarten through grade 6 or for academic subjects in the secondary grades 7 through 12, i.e., English, a language other than English, mathematics, a science (biology, chemistry, earth science, physics), or social studies, must pass the New York State Teacher Certification Examinations (NYSTCE®) as part of the requirements for certification.

Those seeking a New York State teaching certificate in other areas may need to achieve qualifying scores on the NYSTCE® as indicated in the table which follows.

The New York State Teacher Certification Examinations™ program consists of the

- Liberal Arts and Sciences Test (LAST)
- Elementary and Secondary Assessment of Teaching Skills Written (ATS-W)
- Content Specialty Tests (CSTs)
- Language Proficiency Assessments (LPAs)
- Assessment of Teaching Skills - Performance (ATS-P) (Video)

These exams provide an objective basis of competency and skill for teaching in New York State.

For the requirements, check the summary table of testing requirements which follows.

Test Development

The New York State Teacher Certification Examinations™ are criterion referenced and objective based. A criterion-referenced test is designed to measure a candidate's knowledge and skills in relation to an established standard rather than in relation to the performance of other candidates. The purpose of these exams is to certify candidates who have demonstrated requisite knowledge and skills necessary for a public school teacher.

> The New York State Teacher Certification Examination C"NYSTCE.") program was developed and is administered by the New York State Education Department ("NYSED® ") and National Evaluation Systems, Inc. ("NES"), and this test preparation guide was neither developed in connection with these organizations, nor is it endorsed by them. The NES® and NYSTCE®names and logos are registered service marks of. National Evaluation Systems, Inc. for use with testing services and related products.

An individual's performance on a test is evaluated against an established standard. The passing score for each test is established by the New York State Commissioner of Education based on the professional judgments and recommendations of New York State educators. Examinees who do not pass a test may retake it at any of the subsequent scheduled test administrations.

Description of the Tests

The following is a description of the tests within the NYSTCE® program.

Liberal Arts and Sciences Test (LAST). The Liberal Arts and Sciences Test consists of multiple-choice test questions and a written assignment. Candidates are asked to demonstrate conceptual and analytical skills, critical-thinking and communication skills, and multicultural awareness. The test covers scientific and mathematical processes, historical and social scientific awareness, artistic expression and the humanities, communication skills, and written n analysis and expression. The Liberal Arts and Sciences Test is required for a provisional certificate.

Elementary and Secondary Versions of the Assessment of Teaching Skills - Written (ATS-W). There are two versions of the Assessment of Teaching Skills - Written (ATS-W). The elementary ATS-W should be taken by individuals seeking a PreK-6, common branch subject teaching certificate. The secondary ATS-W should be taken by individuals seeking a certificate for a secondary academic subject. Individuals seeking a certificate in other titles may take either the elementary or the secondary ATS-W. The ATS-W is required for a provisional certificate.

The elementary and secondary versions of the Assessment of Teaching Skills - Written consists of multiple-choice test questions and a written assignment. These tests address knowledge of the learner, instructional planning and assessment, instructional delivery, and the professional environment.

Content Specialty Tests (CSTs). There are currently 21 Content Specialty Tests. For a complete list of test titles, see the list that follows.

The Content Specialty Tests (except Japanese, Russian, Mandarin, Cantonese, Hebrew, and Greek) contain multiple-choice test questions. The CSTs for languages other than English also include audiotaped listening and speaking components and writing components. The CSTs are required for a permanent certificate.

Language Proficiency Assessments (ELPA-C, ELPA-N, TLPAs). The Language Proficiency Assessments are required for ESOL certificates and for bilingual education extension certificates in New York State.

Assessment of Teaching Skills - Performance (ATS-P) (video). The Assessment of Teaching Skills - Performance (ATS-P) (video) is one requirement for individuals seeking a permanent New York State teaching certificate in specified areas. For this assessment, candidates are required to prepare a videotape of their instruction with students who are part of their regular teaching assignments in grades PreK through 12. The teaching skills assessed by the ATS-P (video) are defined by the five objectives in the Instructional Delivery subarea of the Assessment of Teaching Skills test framework.

From the official announcement for instructional purposes

TESTS

Test (Test Code)

Liberal Arts and Sciences Test (LAST) (01)
Elementary Assessment of Teaching Skills - Written (ATS-W) (90)
Secondary Assessment of Teaching Skills - Written (ATS-W) (91)
Elementary Education (02)
English (03)
Mathematics (04)
Social Studies (05)
Biology (06)
Chemistry (07)
Earth Science (08)
Physics (09)
Early Childhood (21)
Latin (10)
Cantonese (11)
French (12)
German (13)
Greek (14)
Hebrew (15)
Italian (16)
Japanese (17)
Mandarin (18)
Russian (19)
Spanish (20)
English to Speakers of Other Languages (ESOL) (22)
English Language Proficiency Assessment for Classroom Personnel (ELPA-C) (23)
English Language Proficiency Assessment for Nonclassroom Personnel (ELPA-N) (25)
Target Language Proficiency Assessment - Spanish (24)
Target Language Proficiency Assessment other than Spanish

NEW YORK STATE TEACHER CERTIFICATION TESTING REQUIREMENTS

(Commissioner's Regulation) Teaching Certificates	Current Requirements		Projected Requirements
(8 NYCRR 80.15) PreK-6, Common Branch Subjects	LAST ATS-W CST (Elementary Education) ATS-P	Provisional Provisional Permanent Permanent	Same as current requirements
7-9 Extension	Same as base certificate, PLUS: CST in academic subject	Permanent	
Early Childhood Annotation (PreK-3)	CST in annotation	Permanent	
(8 NYCRR 80.16) 7-12 Academic Subjects, e.g., English, Language other than English, Mathematics, Science (Biology, Chemistry, Earth Science, Physics), Social Studies	LAST ATS-W CST (in academic subject) ATS-P	Provisional Provisional Permanent Permanent	Same as current requirements
5-6 Extension	Same as base certificate		
(8 NYCRR 80.9) Bilingual Education [Extension]	Same as base certificate, PLUS: LPA in English (oral)* LPA in Target Language (oral & written)*	Prov./Perm. Prov./Perm.	Same as current requirements
(8 NYCRR 80.10) English to speakers of other languages (ESOL)	LAST* ATS-W* LPA in English (oral)* CST* (ESOL) ATS-P*	Provisional Provisional Provisional Permanent Permanent	Same as current requirements
(8 NYCRR 80.5) Occupational Subjects, e.g. Agricultural Subjects, Business/Distributive Education, Health Occupations, Trade Subjects, Technical Subjects, Home Economics Subjects	Baccalaureate-based certificates: LAST + ATS-W or NTE Core Battery Associate & non-degree-based certificate titles: ATS-W or NTE Core Battery	Provisional Permanent	Baccalaureate-based certificates: LAST Provisional ATS-W Provisional CST Permanent ATS-P Permanent Associate & non-degree-based certificate titles: ATS-W Provisional ATS-P Permanent

NEW YORK STATE TEACHER CERTIFICATION TESTING REQUIREMENTS

(Commissioner's Regulation) Teaching Certificates	Current Requirements		Projected Requirements	
(8 NYCRR 80.6) Special Education, e.g. Special Education, Blind/ Partially Sighted, Deaf/ Hearing Impaired <hr> Speech/Hearing Handicapped	LAST & ATS-W or NTE Core Battery	Provisional	Same as for PreK-6 or 7-12 certificate, PLUS: Special Education Supplement to ATS-W Special Education supplement to ATS-P	Provisional Permanent
(8 NYCRR 80.7) Reading	LAST & ATS-W or NTE Core Battery	Provisional	Same as for PreK-6 or 7-12 certificate, PLUS: CST in Reading	Permanent
(8 NYCRR 80.8) School Media Specialist	LAST + ATS-W or NTE Core Battery	Provisional	LAST ATS-W CST ATS-P	Provisional Provisional Permanent Permanent
(8 NYCRR 80.17) Special Subjects, e.g. Art, Business/Distributive Education, Dance, Health, Home Economics, Music, Physical Education, Recreation, Speech, Technology Education	LAST + ATS-W or NTE Core Battery	Provisional	LAST ATS-W CST ATS-P	Provisional Provisional Permanent Permanent

LAST = Liberal Arts & Sciences Test
ATS-W = Assessment of Teaching Skills - Written
CST = Content Specialty Test
ATS-P = Assessment of Teaching Skills - Performance (video)
LPA = Language Proficiency Assessment

FOR FURTHER INFORMATION

If you have questions regarding which test(s) you must take, contact the teacher certification contact person at your college or:

NEW YORK STATE EDUCATION DEPARTMENT
OFFICE OF TEACHING
CULTURAL EDUCATION CENTER
ALBANY, N.Y. 12230

TELEPHONE: (518) 474-3901
9:00-11:45 A.M., 12:45-4:30 P.M. Eastern Time

Relay center telephone number for the deaf within New York State: 1-800-622-1220

Nationwide AT&T Relay Operator for the Deaf: 1-800-855-2880 (TTY)

If you have questions regarding the Test Registration, Administration Procedures, Admission Ticket, or Score Report, contact:

NYSTCE
NATIONAL EVALUATION SYSTEMS, INC.
30 GATEHOUSE ROAD
P.O. BOX 660
AMHERST, MA 01004-9008

TELEPHONE: (413) 256-2882
9:00 A.M. - 5:00 P.M. Eastern Time

Telephone number for the deaf: (413) 256-8032 (TTY)

NEW YORK STATE TEACHER CERTIFICATION EXAMINATIONS

FIELD 80: COMMUNICATION AND QUANTITATIVE SKILLS TEST (CQST)
TEST FRAMEWORK

Reading
Writing
Mathematics

SUBAREA I—READING

0001 Understand the meaning of general vocabulary words.

For example:

- determining the meaning of commonly encountered words presented in context
- identifying appropriate synonyms or antonyms for words
- recognizing the correct use of commonly misused pairs of words (e.g., their/there, to/too)

0002 Understand the stated main idea of a reading passage.

For example:

- identifying the stated main idea of a passage
- identifying the topic sentence of a passage
- recognizing introductory and summary statements of a passage
- selecting an accurate restatement of the main idea of a passage

0003 Understand the sequence of ideas in a reading passage.

For example:

- identifying the order of events or steps described in a passage
- organizing a set of instructions into their proper sequence
- identifying cause-and-effect relationships described in a passage

0004 Interpret textual and graphic information.

For example:

- interpreting information from tables, line graphs, bar graphs, and pie charts
- recognizing appropriate representations of written information in graphic or tabular form
- recognizing differences between fact and opinion

FIELD 80: COMMUNICATION AND QUANTITATIVE SKILLS TEST (CQST)
TEST FRAMEWORK

SUBAREA II—WRITING

0005 Understand the standard use of verbs.

For example:

- identifying standard subject-verb agreement (e.g., number, person)
- identifying verb tense (e.g., present, past)
- recognizing consistency of verb tense (e.g., verb endings)

0006 Understand the standard use of pronouns and modifiers.

For example:

- identifying agreement (e.g., number, gender, person) between a pronoun and its antecedent
- using possessive pronouns (e.g., its vs. it's), relative pronouns (e.g., that, which), and demonstrative pronouns (e.g., this, that)
- using comparative and superlative modifiers (e.g., good/better/best)

0007 Understand standard sentence structure and punctuation.

For example:

- distinguishing between sentence fragments and complete sentences
- distinguishing between run-on sentences and correctly divided sentences
- identifying correct and incorrect punctuation

0008 Understand the standard use of capitalization and spelling.

For example:

- identifying standard capitalization at the beginning of sentences
- identifying standard capitalization of proper words and titles
- recognizing standard spelling of commonly encountered words presented in context

FIELD 80: COMMUNICATION AND QUANTITATIVE SKILLS TEST (CQST)
TEST FRAMEWORK

SUBAREA III—MATHEMATICS

0009 Understand number concepts.

For example:

- identifying the place value of digits (e.g., hundreds, tens, ones, tenths)
- identifying correctly rounded numbers (e.g., to the nearest ten)
- identifying equivalent weights and measures in different units (e.g., feet and inches, quarts and pints, kilograms and grams)
- estimating the solution to a measurement problem (e.g., height, distance, perimeter)

0010 Understand the addition and subtraction of whole numbers.

For example:

- solving problems involving the addition of whole numbers
- solving problems involving the subtraction of whole numbers
- applying principles of addition and subtraction of whole numbers to solve problems encountered in everyday life

0011 Understand multiplication and division of whole numbers.

For example:

- solving problems involving the multiplication of whole numbers
- solving problems involving the division of whole numbers
- applying principles of multiplication and division of whole numbers to solve problems encountered in everyday life

0012 Understand operations involving fractions, decimals, and percents.

For example:

- solving problems involving fractions (e.g., recipes)
- solving problems involving decimals (e.g., money)
- solving problems involving percents (e.g., grades, discounts)
- solving problems involving conversions between fractions, decimals, and percents

HOW TO TAKE A TEST

You have studied long, hard and conscientiously.

With your official admission card in hand, and your heart pounding, you have been admitted to the examination room.

You note that there are several hundred other applicants in the examination room waiting to take the same test.

They all appear to be equally well prepared.

You know that nothing but your best effort will suffice. The "moment of truth" is at hand: you now have to demonstrate objectively, in writing, your knowledge of content and your understanding of subject matter.

You are fighting the most important battle of your life—to pass and/or score high on an examination which will determine your career and provide the economic basis for your livelihood.

What extra, special things should you know and should you do in taking the examination?

I. YOU MUST PASS AN EXAMINATION

A. WHAT EVERY CANDIDATE SHOULD KNOW
Examination applicants often ask us for help in preparing for the written test. What can I study in advance? What kinds of questions will be asked? How will the test be given? How will the papers be graded?

B. HOW ARE EXAMS DEVELOPED?
Examinations are carefully written by trained technicians who are specialists in the field known as "psychological measurement," in consultation with recognized authorities in the field of work that the test will cover. These experts recommend the subject matter areas or skills to be tested; only those knowledges or skills important to your success on the job are included. The most reliable books and source materials available are used as references. Together, the experts and technicians judge the difficulty level of the questions.
Test technicians know how to phrase questions so that the problem is clearly stated. Their ethics do not permit "trick" or "catch" questions. Questions may have been tried out on sample groups, or subjected to statistical analysis, to determine their usefulness.
Written tests are often used in combination with performance tests, ratings of training and experience, and oral interviews. All of these measures combine to form the best-known means of finding the right person for the right job.

II. HOW TO PASS THE WRITTEN TEST

A. BASIC STEPS

1) Study the announcement

How, then, can you know what subjects to study? Our best answer is: "Learn as much as possible about the class of positions for which you've applied." The exam will test the knowledge, skills and abilities needed to do the work.

Your most valuable source of information about the position you want is the official exam announcement. This announcement lists the training and experience qualifications. Check these standards and apply only if you come reasonably close to meeting them. Many jurisdictions preview the written test in the exam announcement by including a section called "Knowledge and Abilities Required," "Scope of the Examination," or some similar heading. Here you will find out specifically what fields will be tested.

2) Choose appropriate study materials

If the position for which you are applying is technical or advanced, you will read more advanced, specialized material. If you are already familiar with the basic principles of your field, elementary textbooks would waste your time. Concentrate on advanced textbooks and technical periodicals. Think through the concepts and review difficult problems in your field.

These are all general sources. You can get more ideas on your own initiative, following these leads. For example, training manuals and publications of the government agency which employs workers in your field can be useful, particularly for technical and professional positions. A letter or visit to the government department involved may result in more specific study suggestions, and certainly will provide you with a more definite idea of the exact nature of the position you are seeking.

3) Study this book!

III. KINDS OF TESTS

Tests are used for purposes other than measuring knowledge and ability to perform specified duties. For some positions, it is equally important to test ability to make adjustments to new situations or to profit from training. In others, basic mental abilities not dependent on information are essential. Questions which test these things may not appear as pertinent to the duties of the position as those which test for knowledge and information. Yet they are often highly important parts of a fair examination. For very general questions, it is almost impossible to help you direct your study efforts. What we can do is to point out some of the more common of these general abilities needed in public service positions and describe some typical questions.

1) General information

Broad, general information has been found useful for predicting job success in some kinds of work. This is tested in a variety of ways, from vocabulary lists to questions about current events. Basic background in some field of work, such as sociology or economics, may be sampled in a group of questions. Often these are principles which have become familiar to most persons through exposure rather than through formal training. It is difficult to advise you how to study for these questions; being alert to the world around you is our best suggestion.

2) Verbal ability

An example of an ability needed in many positions is verbal or language ability. Verbal ability is, in brief, the ability to use and understand words. Vocabulary and grammar tests are typical measures of this ability. Reading comprehension or paragraph interpretation questions are common in many kinds of civil service tests. You are given a paragraph of written material and asked to find its central meaning.

IV. KINDS OF QUESTIONS

1. Multiple-choice Questions

Most popular of the short-answer questions is the "multiple choice" or "best answer" question. It can be used, for example, to test for factual knowledge, ability to solve problems or judgment in meeting situations found at work.

A multiple-choice question is normally one of three types:
- It can begin with an incomplete statement followed by several possible endings. You are to find the one ending which best completes the statement, although some of the others may not be entirely wrong.
- It can also be a complete statement in the form of a question which is answered by choosing one of the statements listed.
- It can be in the form of a problem – again you select the best answer.

Here is an example of a multiple-choice question with a discussion which should give you some clues as to the method for choosing the right answer:

When an employee has a complaint about his assignment, the action which will best help him overcome his difficulty is to
- A. discuss his difficulty with his coworkers
- B. take the problem to the head of the organization
- C. take the problem to the person who gave him the assignment
- D. say nothing to anyone about his complaint

In answering this question, you should study each of the choices to find which is best. Consider choice "A" – Certainly an employee may discuss his complaint with fellow employees, but no change or improvement can result, and the complaint remains unresolved. Choice "B" is a poor choice since the head of the organization probably does not know what assignment you have been given, and taking your problem to him is known as "going over the head" of the supervisor. The supervisor, or person who made the assignment, is the person who can clarify it or correct any injustice. Choice "C" is, therefore, correct. To say nothing, as in choice "D," is unwise. Supervisors have and interest in knowing the problems employees are facing, and the employee is seeking a solution to his problem.

2. True/False

3. Matching Questions

Matching an answer from a column of choices within another column.

V. RECORDING YOUR ANSWERS

Computer terminals are used more and more today for many different kinds of exams.

For an examination with very few applicants, you may be told to record your answers in the test booklet itself. Separate answer sheets are much more common. If this separate answer sheet is to be scored by machine – and this is often the case – it is highly important that you mark your answers correctly in order to get credit.

VI. BEFORE THE TEST

YOUR PHYSICAL CONDITION IS IMPORTANT

If you are not well, you can't do your best work on tests. If you are half asleep, you can't do your best either. Here are some tips:

1) Get about the same amount of sleep you usually get. Don't stay up all night before the test, either partying or worrying—DON'T DO IT!
2) If you wear glasses, be sure to wear them when you go to take the test. This goes for hearing aids, too.
3) If you have any physical problems that may keep you from doing your best, be sure to tell the person giving the test. If you are sick or in poor health, you relay cannot do your best on any test. You can always come back and take the test some other time.

Common sense will help you find procedures to follow to get ready for an examination. Too many of us, however, overlook these sensible measures. Indeed, nervousness and fatigue have been found to be the most serious reasons why applicants fail to do their best on civil service tests. Here is a list of reminders:

- Begin your preparation early – Don't wait until the last minute to go scurrying around for books and materials or to find out what the position is all about.
- Prepare continuously – An hour a night for a week is better than an all-night cram session. This has been definitely established. What is more, a night a week for a month will return better dividends than crowding your study into a shorter period of time.
- Locate the place of the exam – You have been sent a notice telling you when and where to report for the examination. If the location is in a different town or otherwise unfamiliar to you, it would be well to inquire the best route and learn something about the building.
- Relax the night before the test – Allow your mind to rest. Do not study at all that night. Plan some mild recreation or diversion; then go to bed early and get a good night's sleep.
- Get up early enough to make a leisurely trip to the place for the test – This way unforeseen events, traffic snarls, unfamiliar buildings, etc. will not upset you.
- Dress comfortably – A written test is not a fashion show. You will be known by number and not by name, so wear something comfortable.
- Leave excess paraphernalia at home – Shopping bags and odd bundles will get in your way. You need bring only the items mentioned in the official notice you received; usually everything you need is provided. Do not bring reference books to the exam. They will only confuse those last minutes and be taken away from you when in the test room.

- Arrive somewhat ahead of time – If because of transportation schedules you must get there very early, bring a newspaper or magazine to take your mind off yourself while waiting.
- Locate the examination room – When you have found the proper room, you will be directed to the seat or part of the room where you will sit. Sometimes you are given a sheet of instructions to read while you are waiting. Do not fill out any forms until you are told to do so; just read them and be prepared.
- Relax and prepare to listen to the instructions
- If you have any physical problem that may keep you from doing your best, be sure to tell the test administrator. If you are sick or in poor health, you really cannot do your best on the exam. You can come back and take the test some other time.

VII. AT THE TEST

The day of the test is here and you have the test booklet in your hand. The temptation to get going is very strong. Caution! There is more to success than knowing the right answers. You must know how to identify your papers and understand variations in the type of short-answer question used in this particular examination. Follow these suggestions for maximum results from your efforts:

1) Cooperate with the monitor

The test administrator has a duty to create a situation in which you can be as much at ease as possible. He will give instructions, tell you when to begin, check to see that you are marking your answer sheet correctly, and so on. He is not there to guard you, although he will see that your competitors do not take unfair advantage. He wants to help you do your best.

2) Listen to all instructions

Don't jump the gun! Wait until you understand all directions. In most civil service tests you get more time than you need to answer the questions. So don't be in a hurry. Read each word of instructions until you clearly understand the meaning. Study the examples, listen to all announcements and follow directions. Ask questions if you do not understand what to do.

3) Identify your papers

Civil service exams are usually identified by number only. You will be assigned a number; you must not put your name on your test papers. Be sure to copy your number correctly. Since more than one exam may be given, copy your exact examination title.

4) Plan your time

Unless you are told that a test is a "speed" or "rate of work" test, speed itself is usually not important. Time enough to answer all the questions will be provided, but this does not mean that you have all day. An overall time limit has been set. Divide the total time (in minutes) by the number of questions to determine the approximate time you have for each question.

5) Do not linger over difficult questions

If you come across a difficult question, mark it with a paper clip (useful to have along) and come back to it when you have been through the booklet. One caution if you do this – be sure to skip a number on your answer sheet as well. Check often to be sure that you have not lost your place and that you are marking in the row numbered the same as the question you are answering.

6) Read the questions

Be sure you know what the question asks! Many capable people are unsuccessful because they failed to read the questions correctly.

7) Answer all questions

Unless you have been instructed that a penalty will be deducted for incorrect answers, it is better to guess than to omit a question.

8) Speed tests

It is often better NOT to guess on speed tests. It has been found that on timed tests people are tempted to spend the last few seconds before time is called in marking answers at random – without even reading them – in the hope of picking up a few extra points. To discourage this practice, the instructions may warn you that your score will be "corrected" for guessing. That is, a penalty will be applied. The incorrect answers will be deducted from the correct ones, or some other penalty formula will be used.

9) Review your answers

If you finish before time is called, go back to the questions you guessed or omitted to give them further thought. Review other answers if you have time.

10) Return your test materials

If you are ready to leave before others have finished or time is called, take ALL your materials to the monitor and leave quietly. Never take any test material with you. The monitor can discover whose papers are not complete, and taking a test booklet may be grounds for disqualification.

VIII. EXAMINATION TECHNIQUES

1) Read the general instructions carefully. These are usually printed on the first page of the exam booklet. As a rule, these instructions refer to the timing of the examination; the fact that you should not start work until the signal and must stop work at a signal, etc. If there are any special instructions, such as a choice of questions to be answered, make sure that you note this instruction carefully.

2) When you are ready to start work on the examination, that is as soon as the signal has been given, read the instructions to each question booklet, underline any key words or phrases, such as least, best, outline, describe and the like. In this way you will tend to answer as requested rather than discover on reviewing your paper that you listed without describing, that you selected the worst choice rather than the best choice, etc.

3) If the examination is of the objective or multiple-choice type – that is, each question will also give a series of possible answers: A, B, C or D, and you are called upon to select the best answer and write the letter next to that answer on your answer paper – it is advisable to start answering each question in turn. There may be anywhere from 50 to 100 such questions in the three or four hours allotted and you can see how much time would be taken if you read through all the questions before beginning to answer any. Furthermore, if you

come across a question or group of questions which you know would be difficult to answer, it would undoubtedly affect your handling of all the other questions.

4) If the examination is of the essay type and contains but a few questions, it is a moot point as to whether you should read all the questions before starting to answer any one. Of course, if you are given a choice – say five out of seven and the like – then it is essential to read all the questions so you can eliminate the two that are most difficult. If, however, you are asked to answer all the questions, there may be danger in trying to answer the easiest one first because you may find that you will spend too much time on it. The best technique is to answer the first question, then proceed to the second, etc.

5) Time your answers. Before the exam begins, write down the time it started, then add the time allowed for the examination and write down the time it must be completed, then divide the time available somewhat as follows:
   - If 3-1/2 hours are allowed, that would be 210 minutes. If you have 80 objective-type questions, that would be an average of 2-1/2 minutes per question. Allow yourself no more than 2 minutes per question, or a total of 160 minutes, which will permit about 50 minutes to review.
   - If for the time allotment of 210 minutes there are 7 essay questions to answer, that would average about 30 minutes a question. Give yourself only 25 minutes per question so that you have about 35 minutes to review.

6) The most important instruction is to read each question and make sure you know what is wanted. The second most important instruction is to time yourself properly so that you answer every question. The third most important instruction is to answer every question. Guess if you have to but include something for each question. Remember that you will receive no credit for a blank and will probably receive some credit if you write something in answer to an essay question. If you guess a letter – say "B" for a multiple-choice question – you may have guessed right. If you leave a blank as an answer to a multiple-choice question, the examiners may respect your feelings but it will not add a point to your score. Some exams may penalize you for wrong answers, so in such cases only, you may not want to guess unless you have some basis for your answer.

7) Suggestions
   a. Objective-type questions
      1. Examine the question booklet for proper sequence of pages and questions
      2. Read all instructions carefully
      3. Skip any question which seems too difficult; return to it after all other questions have been answered
      4. Apportion your time properly; do not spend too much time on any single question or group of questions
      5. Note and underline key words – all, most, fewest, least, best, worst, same, opposite, etc.
      6. Pay particular attention to negatives
      7. Note unusual option, e.g., unduly long, short, complex, different or similar in content to the body of the question
      8. Observe the use of "hedging" words – probably, may, most likely, etc.

9. Make sure that your answer is put next to the same number as the question
10. Do not second-guess unless you have good reason to believe the second answer is definitely more correct
11. Cross out original answer if you decide another answer is more accurate; do not erase until you are ready to hand your paper in
12. Answer all questions; guess unless instructed otherwise
13. Leave time for review

b. Essay questions
   1. Read each question carefully
   2. Determine exactly what is wanted. Underline key words or phrases.
   3. Decide on outline or paragraph answer
   4. Include many different points and elements unless asked to develop any one or two points or elements
   5. Show impartiality by giving pros and cons unless directed to select one side only
   6. Make and write down any assumptions you find necessary to answer the questions
   7. Watch your English, grammar, punctuation and choice of words
   8. Time your answers; don't crowd material

8) Answering the essay question

Most essay questions can be answered by framing the specific response around several key words or ideas. Here are a few such key words or ideas:

M's: manpower, materials, methods, money, management
P's: purpose, program, policy, plan, procedure, practice, problems, pitfalls, personnel, public relations

a. Six basic steps in handling problems:
   1. Preliminary plan and background development
   2. Collect information, data and facts
   3. Analyze and interpret information, data and facts
   4. Analyze and develop solutions as well as make recommendations
   5. Prepare report and sell recommendations
   6. Install recommendations and follow up effectiveness

b. Pitfalls to avoid
   1. Taking things for granted – A statement of the situation does not necessarily imply that each of the elements is necessarily true; for example, a complaint may be invalid and biased so that all that can be taken for granted is that a complaint has been registered
   2. Considering only one side of a situation – Wherever possible, indicate several alternatives and then point out the reasons you selected the best one
   3. Failing to indicate follow up – Whenever your answer indicates action on your part, make certain that you will take proper follow-up action to see how successful your recommendations, procedures or actions turn out to be
   4. Taking too long in answering any single question – Remember to time your answers properly

EXAMINATION SECTION

EXAMINATION SECTION

TEST 1

DIRECTIONS: Each question or incomplete statement is followed by several suggested answers or completions. Select the one that BEST answers the question or completes the statement. *PRINT THE LETTER OF THE CORRECT ANSWER IN THE SPACE AT THE RIGHT.*

Questions 1-3.

DIRECTIONS: Questions 1 through 3 are to be answered on the basis of the following passage.

When you look at a large factory, you probably do not think about the trees growing in the park. But green plans are a special kind of factory all their own. Using nothing more than water and sunlight green plants have the unique ability to produce their own food. At the same time, they also make it possible for other living things to exist.

All of this work is done by their leaves. Special cells in the leaves absorb energy from sunlight. This light energy reacts with water that the plant has absorbed from the ground and splits the water into two chemicals. One chemical, oxygen, is released into the air. The other chemical, hydrogen, helps produce sugars that enable the plant to grow new stems, leaves, blossoms, and seeds.

By making their own food, plants accomplish several things. They keep themselves alive. They grow the seeds needed to reproduce. They produce the pollen that enables other plants of their kind to reproduce. Meanwhile, the oxygen released into the air makes it possible for other living things to survive.

Human beings have created factories that make wonderful products for us to use and enjoy. But the "living factories" that nature has created produce something even more special—life.

1. Read the sentence below, taken from the first paragraph of the passage: 1.____
   Using nothing more than water and sunlight, green plants have the unique ability to produce their own food.
   Select the word that has the opposite meaning of the word unique as it is used in the above sentence.
   A. interesting   B. distinctive   C. common   D. unusual

2. Which sentence BEST expresses the main idea of the passage? 2.____
   A. Most of the living things on Earth depend upon green plants.
   B. Green plants are a very special kind of living factory.
   C. Leaves do the most important work for green plants.
   D. Human factories and nature's factories have a lot in common.

1

3. According to the passage, what happens FIRST when sunlight falls on plant leaves?
   A. The plant produces new stems, leaves, and blossoms.
   B. Special cells in the leaves absorb energy in the sun's rays.
   C. Sugars in the leaves are released that feed the plant.
   D. The leaves absorb water from the ground.

4. The pie chart shown at the right shows the monthly expenses for a company. Which of the following is the BEST approximation of the percentage of expenses spent on raw materials?
   A. 15%
   B. 25%
   C. 33%
   D. Insurance

5. In which sentence is the CORRECT verb form used?
   A. Mathematics continue to be a difficult subject for many high school students.
   B. All of the runners is expected to do well in the race.
   C. Which of the seniors have been selected as class president?
   D. The film consists primarily of interviews with world-famous scientists.

6. Which sentence is constructed CORRECTLY?
   A. All of the students in the class did his part to make the play a big success.
   B. Ms. Jones is one of those teachers who are always trying to make her classes more interesting.
   C. Last year, Ms. Jones encouraged the students in her drama class to produce one-act plays.
   D. Ms. Jones hopes the auditorium will have their own stage lights next year.

7. Which sentence is punctuated INCORRECTLY?
   A. According to the curriculum guidelines, students need to learn about the working world.
   B. Working with local businesses is valuable; it provides an interesting and rewarding experience.
   C. Farmers and merchants, as well as health workers, are involved in the program.
   D. Students get actual working experience; while also attending classes.

8. Which underlined word in the sentence below is spelled CORRECTLY?
   The realisation that they were facing an outbreak of typhoid was an ominous development with potentially ghastly consaquences.
   A. realisation   B. ominnous   C. ghastly   D. consaquences

9. 0.07 is equal to
   A. 7/100   B. 1/7   C. 7/10   D. 10/7

10. Select the number that is missing in the following problem: 1,806 - ___ = 358.
    A. 1,448   B. 1,756   C. 2,164   D. 2,774

11. Which number is a multiple of 7?
    A. 27   B. 48   C. 52   D. 63

12. What is 4% of 400?
    A. 16   B. 64   C. 100   D. 160

KEY (CORRECT ANSWERS)

1. C   7. D
2. B   8. C
3. B   9. A
4. C   10. A
5. D   11. D
6. C   12. A

EXAMINATION SECTION
TEST 1

DIRECTIONS: Each question or incomplete statement is followed by several suggested answers or completions. Select the one that BEST answers the question or completes the statement. *PRINT THE LETTER OF THE CORRECT ANSWER IN THE SPACE AT THE RIGHT.*

Questions 1-3.

DIRECTIONS: Questions 1 through 3 are to be answered on the basis of the following passage.

The ordinary form of mercury thermometer is used for temperatures ranging from -40°F to 500°F. For measuring temperatures below -40°F, thermometers filled with alcohol are used. These are, however, not satisfactory for use at high temperatures. When a mercury thermometer is used for temperatures above 500°F, the space above the mercury is filled with some inert gas, usually nitrogen or carbon dioxide, placed in the thermometer under pressure. As the mercury rises, the gas pressure is increased, so that it is possible to use these thermometers for temperatures as high as 1,000°F. This is the limit, however, as the melting point of glass is comparatively low. For temperatures exceeding 800°F, some form of pyrometer is generally used. The simplest of these is the metallic or mechanical pyrometer. This consists of two metals having different rates of expansion, such as iron and brass attached to each other at one end and with the other ends free. By a system of levers and gears, the expansion of the metals is made to move a hand over a dial graduated in degrees. This should not be used for temperatures exceeding 1,000°F to 1,200°F.

1. According to the passage, what chiefly determines the upper temperature at which mercury thermometers can be used?
   A. Weight of mercury   B. Gas pressure
   C. Melting point of glass D. Amount of gas
   E. Rates of expansion

   1.____

2. What topic is treated in this passage?
   A. Manufacturing of thermometers   B. Mercury thermometers
   C. Temperatures   D. Temperature ranges
   E. Measuring temperatures

   2.____

3. With what, besides mercury, would a thermometer be filled if it were designed to be used for measuring temperatures of about 500°F?
   A. Pyrometer   B. Inert gas   C. Iron and brass
   D. Gas   E. Alcohol

   3.____

Questions 4-6.

DIRECTIONS: Questions 4 through 6 are to be answered on the basis of the following passage.

Our ignorance of the complex subject of social insurance was and remains colossal. For years American business leaders delighted in maligning the British social insurance schemes. Our industrialists condemned them without ever finding out what they were about. Even our universities displayed no interest. Contrary to the interest in this subject taken by organized labor abroad, our own labor movement bitterly opposed the entire program of social insurance up to a few years ago. Since the success of any reform depends largely upon a correct public understanding of the principles involved, the adoption of social insurance measures presented peculiar difficulties for the United States under our Federal type of government of limited powers, our constitutional and judicial handicaps, our long conditioning to individualism, the traditional hostility to social reform by both capital and labor, the general inertia, and our complete lack of trained administrative personnel without which even the best law can be ineffective. Has not bitter experience taught us that far more important than the passage of a law, which is at best only a declaration of intention, is a ready public opinion prepared to enforce it?

4. According to this writer, what attitude have we shown in this country toward social insurance? 4.____
   A. We have been extremely doubtful that it will work, but have been willing to give it a chance.
   B. We have opposed it on the grounds of a careful study of its defects.
   C. We have shown an unintelligent and rather blind antagonism toward it.
   D. We have been afraid that it would not work under our type of government.
   E. We have resented it because of the extensive propaganda in favor of it.

5. To what does the phrase, "our long conditioning to individualism," refer? 5.____
   A. Our habit of depending upon ourselves
   B. Our increasing dependence on the Federal Government
   C. Our long established district of "big business"
   D. Our policies of high protective tariff
   E. Our unwillingness to accept reforms

6. Which of the following ideas is expressed in this passage? 6.____
   A. The surest way to cure a social evil is to get people to pass a law against it.
   B. Legislation alone cannot effect social reforms
   C. The American people are seriously uninformed about all social problems.
   D. Our type of government makes social reform practically impossible.
   E. Capital and labor retard social progress.

Questions 7-9.

DIRECTIONS: Questions 7 through 9 are to be answered on the basis of the following poem.

Loveliest of trees, the cherry now
Is hung with bloom along the bough,
And stands about the woodland ride
Wearing white for Eastertide.

Now, of my threescore years and ten,
Twenty will not come again,
And take from seventy springs a score,
It only leaves me fifty more.

And since to look at things in bloom
Fifty springs are little room,
About the woodlands I will go
To see the cherry hung with snow.

7. How old was the poet when he wrote this poem? 7.____
   A. 20 B. 40 C. 50
   D. 70 E. One cannot tell

8. Which of the following words is used as a descriptive figure of speech rather than in its usual meaning? 8.____
   A. "snow" (last line) B. "twenty" (sixth line)
   C. "woodlands" (next to last line) D. "bloom" (second line)
   E. "bough" (second line)

9. What feeling does the poet express in this passage? 9.____
   A. Delight in beauty B. Religious faith
   C. Anticipation of death D. Enjoyment of old age
   E. Worship of nature

Questions 10-13.

DIRECTIONS: In answering Questions 10 through 13, select the word with the MOST *opposite* meaning as the word provided.

10. Nebulous 10.____
    A. Disgruntled B. Clear C. Fringed
    D. Stricken E. Striped

11. Benign 11.____
    A. Democratic B. Indignant C. Regal
    D. Mottled E. Malignant

12. Callous 12.____
    A. Desperate B. Worn C. Sensitive
    D. Calamitous E. Hollow

13. Desist 13.____
    A. Persevere B. Arise C. Assist
    D. Destroy E. Mitigate

Questions 14-15.

DIRECTIONS: In answering Questions 14 and 15, select the answer with the two words whose relationship is most similar to that of the pair of words provided.

14. Elm : Tree 14.____
    A. Dollar : Dime B. Money : Currency C. Map : Leaves
    D. Oak : Maple E. Dollar : Money

15. Doctor : Disease 15.____
    A. Miser : Money B. Illness : Prescription
    C. Sheriff : Crime D. Theft : Punishment
    E. Intern : Hospital

Questions 16-17.

DIRECTIONS: In answering Questions 16 and 17, read the sentence provided and choose the word which, when added in the blank, would BEST complete the sentence.

16. The simplest animals are those whose bodies are simplest in structure and which do the things done by all living animals, such as eating, breathing, moving, and feeling, in the most _____ way. 16.____
    A. haphazard B. bizarre C. primitive
    D. advantageous E. unique

17. You may inquire how the expert on fossil remains is able to trace descent through teeth, which seem _____ pegs upon which to hang whole ancestries. 17.____
    A. interesting B. reliable C. specious
    D. inadequate E. academic

Questions 18-20.

DIRECTIONS: Questions 18 through 20 are to be answered on the basis of the following graph.

NUMBER OF YOUNGSTERS ATTENDING EIGHT-YEAR ELEMENTARY SCHOOLS AND FOUR-YEAR HIGH SCHOOLS IN THE UNITED STATES FROM 1980 TO 2020

18. In which census year does the graph show high school attendance to have been the GREATEST?
    A. 1980   B. 1990   C. 2000   D. 2010   E. 2020

19. In which year does the graph show the ratio of elementary school to high school youngsters per grade to have been the LEAST?
    A. 1980   B. 1990   C. 2000   D. 2010   E. 2020

20. Which of the following statements is BEST supported by the data of the graph?
    A. Not all graduates of elementary schools eventually graduate from high school.
    B. The number of youngsters in school is a function of the national birth rate.
    C. There were more elementary school than high school youngsters per grade in any one census year.
    D. High school attendance is becoming inversely related to elementary school attendance.
    E. An increase or decrease in elementary school attendance from one census year to another is always accompanied by a corresponding increase or decrease in high school attendance.

21. If two erasers cost 45 cents, how many erasers can be bought for $2.70?
    A. 6   B. 12   C. 15   D. 18   E. 20

22. A stick 35 inches long is to be cut so that one piece is ¼ as long as the other. How many inches long must the shorter piece be?
    A. 5   B. 7   C. 10   D. 12   E. 15

23. 32 is 2/7 of what number?
    A. 9 1/7   B. 14   C. 64   D. 112   E. 224

24. The area of triangle XYZ is 60 square inches. If XY is perpendicular to YZ and YZ = 8 inches, how many inches long is XZ?
    A. 13
    B. 15
    C. 17
    D. 10
    E. 21

25. Lumber is frequently priced in terms of 1,000 board feet. If the price of a certain kind and grade of lumber is $36 per 1,000 board feet, what is the cost of 1,750 board feet of this lumber?
    A. $45   B. $54   C. $63   D. $72   E. Not given

26. The approximate volume of a high round-top haystack may be determined by the following formula: V = (.52M - .44W)WL. In this formula, W and L represent the stack's width and length. M is the "over" measurement obtained by throwing a rope over the stack and measuring the distance over the stack from a point on the ground on one side of the stack to the corresponding point on the opposite side. A stack of alfalfa which is 4 months old has an average width of 20 feet and is 40 feet long. Its "over" measurement is 40 feet.
What is the approximate number of tons of alfalfa in the stack if alfalfa that has settled for more than 90 days runs around 480 cubic feet per ton?
    A. 20   B. 30   C. 40   D. 50   E. 60

26.____

27. Part of a former income tax paid to the federal government was known as the "normal tax." This tax was defined as 4 percent of the balance that remained after 10 percent of the net income had been subtracted from the "surtax net income." Mr. Brown's net income was $40,000 and his "surtax net income" was $17,000.
How much normal tax did he pay?
    A. $520   B. $1,532   C. $1,700   D. $2,300   E. Not given

27.____

28. In a park the radius of a pool is twice the radius of a circular flower bed. The area of the pool is how many times the area of the flower bed?
    A. 1/4   B. 1/2   C. 2   D. 4   E. 8

28.____

29. On each month's bill, the light and power company charges 8 cents per kilowatt-hour for the first 50 kilowatt-hours and 5 cents per kilowatt-hour for the remainder.
What is his bill?
    A. $4.00   B. $6.30   C. $7.80   D. $8.58   E. Not given

29.____

30. You have a nickel, dime, quarter, and fifty-cent piece. A clerk shows you several articles, each a different price and any one of which you could purchase with your coins without receiving change.
What is the LARGEST number of articles he could have shown you?
    A. 8   B. 10   C. 13   D. 15   E. 21

30.____

KEY (CORRECT ANSWERS)

1.	C	11.	E	21.	B
2.	E	12.	C	22.	B
3.	B	13.	A	23.	D
4.	C	14.	E	24.	C
5.	A	15.	C	25.	C
6.	B	16.	C	26.	A
7.	A	17.	D	27.	A
8.	A	18.	D	28.	D
9.	A	19.	D	29.	C
10.	B	20.	C	30.	D

EXAMINATION SECTION
TEST 1

DIRECTIONS: Each question or incomplete statement is followed by several suggested answers or completions. Select the one that BEST answers the question or completes the statement. *PRINT THE LETTER OF THE CORRECT ANSWER IN THE SPACE AT THE RIGHT.*

1. A court order requiring a person to appear in court as a witness is a(n)
   A. enjoinder
   B. impanelment
   C. requiem
   D. subpoena

2. A common substance made from animal fat and lye is
   A. baking soda
   B. floor wax
   C. laundry soap
   D. Vaseline

3. Contour plowing is important because it
   A. reduces soil erosion
   B. increases soil productivity
   C. enables part of the land to remain wooded
   D. permits the growth of two crops at the same time

4. Unintentional killing of a human being is
   A. assault
   B. manslaughter
   C. mayhem
   D. first-degree murder

5. The fact that gases will conduct electricity under some circumstances is demonstrated by the
   A. aurora borealis
   B. carbon filament incandescent lamp
   C. tungsten filament incandescent lamp
   D. neon tube

6. A meal consisting of spaghetti, boiled potatoes, green beans, hot biscuits, and butter is not well balanced because it contains too much
   A. protein   B. starch   C. sugar   D. fat

7. To prevent the indefinite imprisonment of a client without a hearing, an attorney obtains a writ of
   A. attainder
   B. certiorari
   C. habeas corpus
   D. mandamus

8. Foods such as sugar, rice, and potatoes are the principle sources of
   A. carbohydrates
   B. fats
   C. proteins
   D. minerals

9. Pakistan is in
   A. Asia   B. Africa   C. Europe   D. Australia

10. The liberator of Colombia was
    A. Bolivar   B. Cortes   C. da Gama   D. Sandino

11. In the metric system, the unit of volume nearest to one quart is one
    A. cubic centimeter
    B. liter
    C. cubic meter
    D. kilometer

12. Which of the following is due entirely to heredity?
    A. Eye color   B. Insanity   C. Body weight   D. Cancer

13. Voting qualifications in the United States are established by
    A. county boards of election
    B. election district supervisors
    C. municipal laws
    D. state laws

14. The gas used MOST for extinguishing fires is
    A. ammonia
    B. carbon dioxide
    C. chlorine
    D. hydrogen peroxide

15. The Panama Canal Zone is a(n)
    A. independent nation
    B. foreign territory
    C. lease to the United States
    D. colon of Panama

16. A person who prefers to let a state of affairs remain unchanged is
    A. conservative   B. liberal   C. radical   D. reactionary

17. Which of the following liquids is the BEST conductor of electricity?
    A. Alcohol
    B. Kerosene
    C. Water containing dissolved salt
    D. Water containing dissolved sugar

18. Why should all pork be well cooked before it is eaten?
    A. To kill bacteria
    B. To make it more digestible
    C. To soften the connective fibers
    D. To kill parasitic worms

19. Who was sent by France to rule Mexico?
    A. Boulanger   B. Cartier   C. Juarez   D. Maximilian

20. Chemically pure water is obtained by
    A. aeration   B. boiling   C. distillation   D. filtration

21. The Zambezi River is on the continent of
    A. South America
    B. Africa
    C. Australia
    D. Asia

22. Women in the United States have had the constitutional right to vote since
    A. 1789   B. 1865   C. 1898   D. 1920

23. In which of these is the fuel burned outside of the engine? 23.____
    A. Diesel engine B. Gas turbine
    C. Four-cycle gasoline engine D. Steam turbine

24. Which of the following actions is regulated by the autonomic nervous system? 24.____
    A. Walking B. Eating
    C. Rate of heartbeat D. Learned habits

25. Reshaping election districts for the benefit of the controlling political party is called 25.____
    A. eminent domain B. filibustering
    C. gerrymandering D. logrolling

KEY (CORRECT ANSWERS)

1.	D	11.	B
2.	C	12.	A
3.	A	13.	D
4.	B	14.	B
5.	D	15.	C
6.	B	16.	A
7.	C	17.	C
8.	A	18.	D
9.	A	19.	D
10.	A	20.	C

21. B
22. D
23. D
24. C
25. C

TEST 2

DIRECTIONS: Each question or incomplete statement is followed by several suggested answers or completions. Select the one that BEST answers the question or completes the statement. *PRINT THE LETTER OF THE CORRECT ANSWER IN THE SPACE AT THE RIGHT.*

1. Which of the following is a mixture?
   A. Air   B. Copper   C. Sugar   D. Water

2. Longitude is reckoned from the
   A. Tropic of Cancer   B. Tropic of Capricorn
   C. prime meridian   D. international date line

3. The author of *Common Sense* was
   A. Benjamin Franklin   B. Nikolai Lenin
   C. Karl Marx   D. Thomas Paine

4. The specific gravity of a liquid can be measured by a
   A. barometer   B. hydrometer
   C. viscosimeter   D. fathometer

5. Alfalfa is frequently planted in fields from which wheat has been harvested in order to replenish the supply of
   A. phosphates   B. sulphates   C. calcium   d. nitrates

6. Which was viewed by labor unions as inimical to their interests?
   A. Fair Labor Standards Act   B. Taft-Hartley Act
   C. Railway Labor Act   D. Norris-LaGuardia Act

7. A material which contains no water is
   A. allotropic   B. amorphous   C. amphoteric   D. anhydrous

8. The continent having the GREATEST population is
   A. Africa   B. Asia   C. Europe   D. North America

9. Which tax ignores relative ability to pay?
   A. Income tax   B. Inheritance tax
   C. Land tax   D. Poll tax

10. In the metric system, a liter of water weighs almost exactly one
   A. milligram   B. gram   C. kilogram   D. metric ton

11. The green scum that forms on ponds during the summer is caused by the presence of
   A. fungi   B. bacteria   C. protozoa   D. algae

12. Amnesty is a form of
   A. decline   B. dominance   C. pardon   D. rebellion

13. The atomic number of an element corresponds to its number of
    A. electrons   B. neutrons   C. mesons   D. orbits

14. The earth rotates toward the
    A. north   B. south   C. east   D. west

15. Insurrection means
    A. rebellion
    B. assassination
    C. invasion
    D. arrogance

16. As a meteorite approaches the earth, the characteristic LEAST changed will be its
    A. temperature   B. weight   C. velocity   D. density

17. Material for building protoplasm is furnished by
    A. proteins
    B. carbohydrates
    C. minerals
    D. fats

18. The act of inciting rebellion against the government is
    A. interdiction   B. deviation   C. sedition   D. subvention

19. Which of the following chemicals has the GREATEST importance for industry?
    A. Carbon tetrachloride
    B. Hydrochloric acid
    C. Sulphuric acid
    D. Zinc oxide

20. To study the physical characteristics of a country, the BEST map to use is called
    A. outline   B. political   C. geological   D. topographic

21. In the United States government, revenue bills originate in the
    A. Bureau of the Budget
    B. House of Representatives
    C. Senate
    D. Treasury Department

22. The temperature at which the present amount of moisture in the air will condense is called the
    A. relative humidity
    B. percentage of saturation
    C. wet-bulb temperature
    D. dew point

23. The FIRST experimental work of scientific consequence in the field of heredity was done by
    A. Pasteur   B. Mendel   C. De Vries   D. Lamarck

24. A strong exponent of the doctrine of "States' rights" was
    A. John Calhoun
    B. Horace Greeley
    C. George Washington
    D. Daniel Webster

3 (#2)

25. The chemical bond in which two atoms share an electron with each other is called
    A. covalence
    B. coordinate valence
    C. electrovalence
    D. multiple valence

25.____

KEY (CORRECT ANSWERS)

1. A
2. C
3. D
4. B
5. D

6. B
7. D
8. B
9. D
10. C

11. D
12. C
13. A
14. D
15. A

16. C
17. A
18. C
19. C
20. A

21. B
22. D
23. B
24. A
25. A

TEST 3

DIRECTIONS: Each question or incomplete statement is followed by several suggested answers or completions. Select the one that BEST answers the question or completes the statement. *PRINT THE LETTER OF THE CORRECT ANSWER IN THE SPACE AT THE RIGHT.*

1. Among South American countries, the LARGEST producer of copper is 1._____
   A. Argentina   B. Brazil   C. Chile   D. Ecuador

2. Dutch farmers who colonized the Transvaal were called 2._____
   A. Boers
   B. Neanderthalers
   C. Tatars
   D. Walloons

3. Which of the following petroleum products is MOST volatile? 3._____
   A. Asphalt   B. Fuel oil   C. Gasoline   D. Kerosene

4. If the semicircular canals of the ear are damaged, a person has difficulty in 4._____
   A. discriminating differences in sound
   B. maintaining equal pressure on the eardrum
   C. maintaining his balance
   D. coordinating the movements of his body

5. Germany was unified under Prussia's domination by 5._____
   A. Bismarck II
   B. Frederick II
   C. Martin Luther
   D. von Hindenburg

6. Which is the chemical symbol for gold? 6._____
   A. Ag   B. Au   C. Gd   D. Sc

7. The SMALLEST of the following seas is the 7._____
   A. Mediterranean
   B. Red
   C. Caribbean
   D. Bering

8. Which is a manifesto? 8._____
   A. Bill of lading
   B. Declaration of purposes
   C. Final warning
   D. Trade agreement

9. When an automobile accelerates, the stress on the driveshaft connecting the engine to the rear wheels is 9._____
   A. bending   B. compression   C. tension   D. torsion

10. In certain areas, iodine is frequently added to the drinking water in order to prevent 10._____
    A. cholera   B. goiter   C. diphtheria   D. typhoid fever

11. The LAST successful invasion of England occurred in which century? 11._____
    A. Fourth   B. Eighth   C. Eleventh   D. Thirteenth

12. The man credited with determining the relationship between temperature and volume of a gas is
    A. Arrhenius   B. Charles   C. Lavoisier   D. Moseley

13. The state producing the MOST iron ore is
    A. Michigan   B. Pennsylvania
    C. Alabama   D. Minnesota

14. The first great civilizations appeared in
    A. Australia   B. Central Europe
    C. the Near East   D. Northern Asia

15. The unit of electrical resistance is the
    A. ampere   B. ohm   C. volt   D. watt

16. The fluid that collects in a blister on the heel is
    A. bacterial toxins   B. lymph
    C. blood antibodies   D. water

17. Which of the following men obtained for his country "a window to the West"?
    A. Alfred the Great   B. Charles Martel
    C. Thomas Masaryk   D. Peter the Great

18. Which of the following elements has a negative valence?
    A. Aluminum   B. Hydrogen   C. Oxygen   D. Sodium

19. Washington, D.C. is approximately the same latitude as
    A. Lisbon   B. Paris   C. Geneva   D. London

20. The right to vote is called
    A. electorate   B. franchise   C. polling   D. votary

21. The loudness of sound is measured in
    A. decibels   B. Doppler units
    C. overtones   D. vibrations per second

22. A fungus that lives on decaying organic material would be called a
    A. scavenger   B. parasite   C. saprophyte   D. symbiont

23. The Marshall Plan was put into effect through the
    A. Economic Cooperation Administration
    B. North Atlantic Treaty Organization
    C. U.N. Economic and Social Council
    D. International Atomic Development Authority

24. When phosphorus is burned in oxygen to form two molecules of P_2O_5, how many atoms of phosphorus are needed?
    A. One   B. Two   C. Three   D. Four

25. On which scale of temperature is zero degrees the COLDEST? 25.____
    A. Centigrade   B. Fahrenheit   C. Kelvin   D. Reaumur

KEY (CORRECT ANSWERS)

1. C
2. A
3. C
4. C
5. A

6. B
7. B
8. B
9. D
10. B

11. C
12. B
13. D
14. C
15. B

16. C
17. D
18. C
19. A
20. B

21. A
22. B
23. A
24. D
25. C

EXAMINATION SECTION
TEST 1

DIRECTIONS: Each question or incomplete statement is followed by several suggested answers or completions. Select the one that BEST answers the question or completes the statement. *PRINT THE LETTER OF THE CORRECT ANSWER IN THE SPACE AT THE RIGHT.*

Questions 1-3.

DIRECTIONS: In answering Questions 1 through 3, select the word or phrase that is closest in meaning to the word in italics.

1. *cumulative*
    A. additive B. clumsy C. cumbersome
    D. incorrect E. secretive

2. *epigram*
    A. chemical term B. exclamation C. outer skin
    D. pithy saying E. tombstone

3. *avid*
    A. eager B. glowing C. indifferent
    D. lax E. potent

Questions 4-5.

DIRECTIONS: In each group of five words, select the one that is misspelled.

4. A. collaborator B. gaudey C. habilitation
    D. logician E. suavity

5. A. adversary B. beneficiary C. cemetery
    D. desultory E. estuery

Questions 6-7.

DIRECTIONS: In each group of five sentences, select the one which is INCORRECT.

6. A. All things considered, he did unusually well.
    B. The poor boy takes everything too seriously.
    C. Our club sent two delegates, Ruth and I, to Oswego.
    D. I like him better than her.
    E. His eccentricities continually make good newspaper copy.

7. A. Between you and me, I think Henry is wrong.
    B. This is the more interesting of the two books.
    C. This is the most carefully written letter of all.
    D. During the opening course I read not only four plays but also three historical novels.
    E. This assortment of candies, nuts, and fruits are excellent.

8. A handkerchief is a major prop in
    A. HAMLET
    B. JULIUS CAESAR
    C. MACBETH
    D. OTHELLO
    E. THE MERCHANT OF VENICE

9. Which writer is CORRECTLY described?
    A. Archibald MacLeish – poet; former Librarian of Congress
    B. E.E. Cumming – novelist; editor of THE ATLANTIC MONTHLY
    C. John Milton – poet; member of Parliament under Charles I
    D. Stephen Crane – novelist; author of historical romances
    E. William Butler Yeats – poet; a founder of the Drury Lane Theatre

10. The small dipper seems to turn about the North Star once each day because
    A. all stars move in great circles on the celestial sphere
    B. the earth turns on its axis
    C. the North Star is the last star in the handle of the dipper
    D. the planets revolve around the sun
    E. the solar system rotates about a fixed star

11. Respiration is to carbon dioxide as photosynthesis is to
    A. carbon dioxide   B. chlorophyll   C. oxygen
    D. starch   E. sunlight

12. A yellow tulip viewed through a piece of blue glass looks
    A. black   B. white   C. yellow   D. blue   E. green

13. The abolition of slavery in the United States was contemporary with the
    A. emancipation of slaves in the British Empire
    B. founding of Liberia as a home for Black settlers
    C. freeing of the serfs in Russia
    D. limitation of slavery in Brazil
    E. uprising of the peasants in France

14. Which group of countries is entirely behind the *iron curtain*?
    A. Austria, Albania, Czechoslovakia
    B. Austria, Hungary, Czechoslovakia
    C. Estonia, Finland, Poland
    D. Rumania, Yugoslavia, Bulgaria
    E. Rumania, Poland, Hungary

15. The type of society that existed in Japan before it was opened to the rest of the world may BEST be described as
    A. communistic   B. uncivilized   C. socialistic
    D. fascist   E. feudal

15.____

16.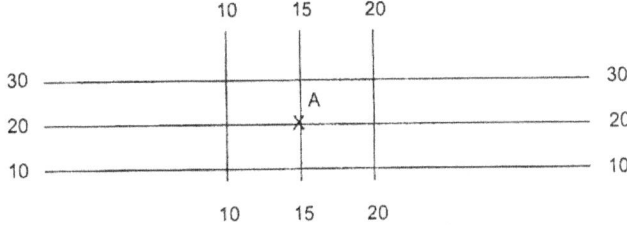

What is the latitude of point A on the above map scale?
    A. 15° east   B. 20° east   C. 15° north
    D. 20° north   E. 20° south

16.____

17. If f(x) is a symbol that represents an algebraic expression in x, then f(a) is the value of the same expression when a is substituted for x.
    If $f(x) = \frac{2x^2 - x}{x+6}$, then f(-5) equals
    A. 55   B. 45   C. -25   D. -5   E. 5

17.____

18. The shorter leg of a right triangle is 6 and the median to the hypotenuse is 5. How long is the other leg of the triangle?
    A. 6   B. $6\sqrt{5}$ C. $6\sqrt{3}$ D. 8   E. 10

18.____

19. The width of the ring (shaded portion of the figure) is percent of the entire area is the area of the shaded portion?
    A. 25%   B. 50%   C. 66 2/3%   D. 75%   E. 80%

19.____

20. Which type of architecture makes extensive use of the flying buttress?
    A. Egyptian   B. Gothic   C. Greek
    D. Renaissance   E. Romanesque

20.____

21. A painting or drawing in a single hue is called a
    A. lithograph   B. mezzotint   C. monochrome
    D. monoprint   E. monotype

21.____

22. Famous incidental music for Shakespeare's A MIDSUMMER NIGHT'S DREAM was written by
    A. Donizetti   B. Dvorak   C. Gretry
    D. Mendelssohn   E. Offenbach

22.____

23. In music, a suite is a(n)
    A. ballad   B. musical instrument   C. sacred song
    D. set of dances   E. operetta

23.____

24. The term value, when used of a color, refers to
    A. the degree of its darkness or lightness
    B. its intensity
    C. its hue
    D. its texture
    E. the variety of its pattern

25. In painting, emphasis on inner emotions, sensations, or ideas rather than actual appearances is called
    A. impressionism
    B. futurism
    C. expressionism
    D. cubism
    E. transcendentalism

KEY (CORRECT ANSWERS)

1.	A	11.	C
2.	D	12.	A
3.	A	13.	C
4.	B	14.	E
5.	E	15.	E
6.	C	16.	D
7.	E	17.	A
8.	D	18.	D
9.	A	19.	D
10.	B	20.	B

21. C
22. D
23. D
24. A
25. C

EXAMINATION SECTION
TEST 1

DIRECTIONS: Each question or incomplete statement is followed by several suggested answers or completions. Select the one that BEST answers the question or completes the statement. *PRINT THE LETTER OF THE CORRECT ANSWER IN THE SPACE AT THE RIGHT.*

Questions 1-10.

DIRECTIONS: In answering Questions 1 through 10, select the alternative that means the *same as* or the *opposite* of the word in italics.

1. *acquire*
   - A. judge
   - B. identify
   - C. surrender
   - D. educate
   - E. happen

   1.____

2. *begrudge*
   - A. envy
   - B. hate
   - C. annoy
   - D. obstruct
   - E. punish

   2.____

3. *obsolete*
   - A. fatal
   - B. modern
   - C. distracting
   - D. untouched
   - E. broken

   3.____

4. *inflexible*
   - A. weak
   - B. righteous
   - C. harmless
   - D. unyielding
   - E. secret

   4.____

5. *nominal*
   - A. just
   - B. slight
   - C. cheerful
   - D. familiar
   - E. ceaseless

   5.____

6. *debt*
   - A. insane
   - B. artificial
   - C. skillful
   - D. determined
   - E. humble

   6.____

7. *censure*
   - A. focus
   - B. exclude
   - C. baffle
   - D. portray
   - E. praise

   7.____

8. *nebulous*
   - A. imaginary
   - B. spiritual
   - C. distinct
   - D. starry-eyed
   - E. unanswerable

   8.____

9. *impart*
   - A. hasten
   - B. adjust
   - C. gamble
   - D. address
   - E. communicate

   9.____

10. *terminate*
    A. gain
    B. graduate
    C. harvest
    D. start
    E. paralyze

Questions 11-20.

DIRECTIONS: In answering Questions 11 through 20, select the word which, if inserted in the blank space, agrees MOST closely with the thought of the sentence.

11. Every good story is carefully contrived; the elements of the story are _____ to fi with one another in order to make an effect on the reader.
    A. read
    B. learned
    C. emphasized
    D. reduced
    E. planned

12. Their work was commemorative in character and consisted largely of _____ erected upon the occasion of victories.
    A. towers
    B. tombs
    C. monuments
    D. castles
    E. fortresses

13. Before criticizing the work of an artist, one needs to _____ the artist's purpose.
    A. understand
    B. reveal
    C. defend
    D. correct
    E. change

14. Because in the administration it hath respect not to the group but to the _____, our form of government is called a democracy.
    A. courts
    B. people
    C. majority
    D. individual
    E. law

15. Deductive reasoning is that form of reasoning in which the conclusion must necessarily follow if we accept the premise as true. In deduction, it is _____ for the premise to be true and the conclusion false.
    A. impossible
    B. inevitable
    C. reasonable
    D. surprising
    E. unlikely

16. Mathematics is the product of thought operating by means of _____ for the purpose of expressing general laws.
    A. reasoning
    B. symbols
    C. words
    D. examples
    E. science

17. No other man loss so much, so _____, so absolutely, as the beaten candidate for high public office.
    A. bewilderingly
    B. predictably
    C. disgracefully
    D. publicly
    E. cheerfully

18. Many television watchers enjoy stories which contain violence. Consequently, those television producers who are dominated by rating systems aim to _____ the popular taste.
    A. raise B. control C. gratify
    D. ignore e. lower

    18.____

19. The latent period for the contractile response to direct stimulation of the muscle has quite another and shorter value, encompassing only a utilization period. Hence, it is that the term *latent period* must be _____ carefully each time that it is used.
    A. checked B. timed C. introduced
    D. defined E. selected

    19.____

20. A man who cannot win honor in his own _____ will have a very small chance of winning it from posterity.
    A. right B. field C. country
    D. way E. age

    20.____

Questions 21-35.

DIRECTIONS: In answering Questions 21 through 35, select the word that BEST completes the analogy.

21. Albino is to color as traitor is to
    A. patriotism B. treachery C. socialism
    D. integration E. liberalism

    21.____

22. Senile is to infantile as supper is to
    A. snack B. breakfast C. dinner
    D. daytime E. evening

    22.____

23. Snow shovel is to sidewalk as eraser is to
    A. writing B. pencil C. paper
    D. desk E. mistake

    23.____

24. Lawyer is to court as soldier is to
    A. battle B. victory C. training
    D. rifle E. discipline

    24.____

25. Faucet is to water as mosquito is to
    A. swamp B. butterfly C. cistern
    D. pond E. malaria

    25.____

26. Astronomy is to geology as steeplejack is to
    A. mailman B. surgeon C. pilot
    D. miner E. skindiver

    26.____

27. Chimney is to smoke as guide is to
    A. snare   B. compass   C. hunter
    D. firewood   E. wild game

28. Prodigy is to ability as ocean is to
    A. water   B. waves   C. ships
    D. icebergs   E. current

29. War is to devastation as microbe is to
    A. peace   B. flea   C. dog
    D. germ   E. pestilence

30. Blueberry is to pea a sky is to
    A. storm   B. world   C. star
    D. grass   E. purity

31. Pour is to spill as lie is to
    A. deception B. misstatement C. falsehood
    D. perjury   E. fraud

32. Disparage is to despise as praise is to
    A. dislike   B. adore   C. acclaim
    D. advocate   E. compliment

33. Wall is to mortar as nation is to
    A. family   B. people   C. patriotism
    D. geography E. boundaries

34. Servant is to butter as pain is to
    A. cramp   B. hurt   C. illness
    D. itch   E. anesthesia

35. Fan is to air as newspaper is to
    A. literature B. reporter   C. information
    D. subscription E. reader

36. A set of papers is arranged and numbered from 1 to 49. If the paper numbered 3 is drawn first and every ninth paper thereafter, what will be the number of the last paper drawn?
    A. 45   B. 46   C. 47   D. 48   E. 49

37. Which quantity can be measured *exactly* from a tank of water by using only a 10-pint can and an 8-pint can? _____ pint(s)
    A. 1   B. 6   C. 3   D. 7   E. 5

38. If city R has more fires than city S, and city T has more fires than cities P and S combined, then the number of fires in city
    A. P must be less than in city T
    B. T must be less than in city R
    C. T must be greater than in city R
    D. R must be greater than in city P
    E. S must be greater than in city T

39. The average of three numbers is 25.
    If one of the numbers is increased by 4, the average will remain unchanged if each of the other two numbers is reduced by
    A. 1   B. 2   C. 2/3   D. 4   E. 1 1/3

40.
    ```
                    1
                  1   1
                1   2   1
              1   3   3   1
            1   4   6   4   1
          1   5  10   X   5   1
    ```
    Above are the first six rows of a triangular array constructed according to a fixed law.
    What number does the letter X represent?
    A. 8   B. 10   C. 15   D. 20   E. 5

41. If all A are C and no C are B, it necessarily follows that
    A. all B are C   B. all B are A   C. no A are B
    D. no C are A   E. some B are A

42. What number is missing in the series 7, ____, 63, 189?
    A. 9   B. 11   C. 19   D. 21   E. 24

43. A clock that gains one minute each hour is synchronized at noon with a clock that loses two minutes an hour.
    How many minutes apart will the minute hands of the two clocks be at midnight?
    A. 0   B. 12   C. 14   D. 24   E. 30

44. The pages of a typewritten report are numbered by hand from 1 to 100.
    How many times will it be necessary to write the numeral 5?
    A. 10   B. 11   C. 12   D. 19   E. 20

45. The number 6 is called a *perfect* number because it is the sum of all its integral divisors except itself.
    Another *perfect* number is
    A. 12   B. 16   C. 24   D. 28   E. 36

KEY (CORRECT ANSWERS)

1. C	11. E	21. A	31. B	41. C
2. A	12. C	22. B	32. B	42. D
3. B	13. A	23. C	33. C	43. D
4. D	14. D	24. A	34. A	44. E
5. B	15. A	25. E	35. C	45. D
6. C	16. B	26. D	36. D	
7. E	17. D	27. C	37. B	
8. C	18. C	28. A	38. A	
9. E	19. D	29. E	39. B	
10. D	20. E	30. D	40. B	

EXAMINATION SECTION

TEST 1

ENGLISH USAGE

DIRECTIONS: This section is based on passages which contain expressions that are inappropriate in standard written English. You are to decide how these expressions can be made appropriate and effective.

The passages are presented in a spread-out format in which various words, phrases, and punctuation have been underlined and numbered. In the right-hand column, opposite each underlined portion, you will find a set of responses numbered to correspond to that of the underlined portion. Each set of responses contains a NO CHANGE option and three alternatives to the underlined version.

Since your judgment about the appropriateness and effectiveness of a response will depend on your perceptions of the passage as a whole, the author's purpose and the type of audience, first read through the entire passage quickly. Then, reread the passage slowly and carefully. As you come to each underlined portion during your second reading, look at the alternatives in the right-hand column and decide which of the four words or phrasings is BEST for the given context. Since your response will often depend on your reading several of the sentences surrounding the underlined portion, make sure you have read ahead far enough to make the best choice.

If you think that the original version (the one in the passage) is best, indicate A in the corresponding space at the right. If you think that an alternative version is best, indicate the letter corresponding to the alternative that you have chosen as best.

In every case, consider ONLY the underlined words, phrases, and punctuation marks; you can assume that the rest of the passage is correct as written.

Thor Heyerdahl became famous for a unique sailing expedition, which he later described in KON-TIKI. Having developed a theory that the original Polynesians had sailed or drifted to the South Sea Islands from South America, <u>it then had to be</u> tested. After careful study, he built a raft
               1

1. A. NO CHANGE
   B. he set out to test it
   C. it was decided that it must be tested
   D. the theory was then to be tested

1.____

that was as authentic as possible. Using only primitive equipment, he and five other men sailed into the South Seas from <u>Peru, which he judged to be in the same</u> general
               2
area as the land of

2. A. NO CHANGE
   B. Peru, being judged as
   C. Peru, which had been
   D. Peru judged as being

2.____

33

the original Polynesians. As a result, <u>his group and him</u> will long be remembered not
only as thorough scientists but also as courageous men.

    Heyerdahl's courage was first tested in Ecuador. His search for trees <u>that was large enough</u> for the expeditionary raft
sent him to Quito, a city high in the Andes. There, he and his companions were warned about headhunters and bandits on the <u>trail. Feeling undaunted,</u> they
hired a driver and jeep from the U.S. <u>Embassy, going on with</u> their dangerous task

<u>After the raft was done,</u> Heyerdahl made final preparations for the expedition. Even before his crew came aboard,

<u>the courage which Heyerdahl possessed</u> was tested again. As the raft was being towed out of the harbor, it drifted under the stern of a tug. Heyerdahl had to struggle to save it.

<u>Dangers at sea</u> were present, but Heyerdahl and his men did not show fear. Instead they developed games that were actually tests of courage. Although man-eating fish were nearby, the men swam to relieve

3. A. NO CHANGE
   B. him and his group
   C. his group and himself
   D. he and his group

4. A. NO CHANGE
   B. which would be of sufficient size
   C. of adequate size
   D. of certainly sufficient size

5. A. NO CHANGE
   B. trail. Undaunted, they
   C. trail, but they were undaunted, and
   D. trail; undaunted they

6. A. NO CHANAGE
   B. Embassy; and went on with
   C. Embassy and proceeded with
   D. Embassy, and kept on

7. A. NO CHANGE
   B. When the raft was ready
   C. The raft was speedily completed and
   D. The raft having been

8. A. NO CHANGE
   B. Heyerdahls' manly courage
   C. Heyerdahl's courage
   D. the courage of this man

9. A. NO CHANGE
   B. (Do not begin new paragraph) At sea, dangers
   C. (Begin new paragraph) Dangers, at sea
   D. (Begin new paragraph) At sea, dangers

3._____

4._____

5._____

6._____

7._____

8._____

9._____

their <u>tension, maintaining</u> that the fish were
         10
not dangerous unless a man had already
been cut or scratched. One game consisted
of luring sharks within reach,

catching them, <u>and then they would yank it</u>
                           11
onto the raft.

<u>Being on the raft,</u> the sharks thrashed about
      12
and snapped viciously at the men. Another
game was even more dangerous: two men
would paddle away on a rubber dinghy until

they could catch <u>only</u> an occasional glimpse
                          13
of the raft, then they would have to paddle
violently to return.

The final portion of the voyage was the most
thrilling. As the raft neared Raoia, it was
carried rapidly toward the reef, where the
waves beat it <u>very bad.</u> Almost miraculously
                       14
the

men survived, <u>only to find themselves</u> on a
                              15
deserted island. At last their struggle with
the sea had ended. They radioed Rarotonga
and set up camp to await rescue,

Thor Heyerdahl's expedition on the Kon-Tiki
did not necessarily prove his migration theory,
but it did prove that hardy pioneers with
courage, determination, and luck <u>could make
the same trip,</u> even with very primitive
    16
equipment.

10. A. NO CHANGE
    B. tension. Maintaining
    C. tension. He maintained
    D. tension, because it was maintained

11. A. NO CHANGE
    B. then to yank it
    C. and then to yank them up
    D. and yanking them

12. A. NO CHANGE
    B. At that point,
    C. Once there,
    D. A that time,

13. A. NO CHANGE
    B. (Place after *until*)
    C. (Place after *they*)
    D. OMIT

14. A. NO CHANGE
    B. mercilessly
    C. very violent
    D. without any mercy

15. A. NO CHANGE
    B. and only found themselves
    C. only to find themselves
    D. but only found themselves to be

16. A. NO CHANGE
    B. could now do the same trip
    C. could do the same
    D. could have accomplished this the same,

10._____

11._____

12._____

13._____

14._____

15._____

KEY (CORRECT ANSWERS)

1.	B	6.	C	11.	D	16.	A
2.	A	7.	B	12.	C		
3.	D	8.	C	13.	A		
4.	C	9.	D	14.	B		
5.	B	10.	A	15.	C		

TEST 2

MATHEMATICS USAGE

DIRECTIONS: Each question or incomplete statement is followed by several suggested answers or completions. Select the one that BEST answers the question or completes the statement. *PRINT THE LETTER OF THE CORRECT ANSWER IN THE SPACE AT THE RIGHT.*

1. Two wells pump oil continuously. One produces 4,000 barrels of oil per day, which is 33 1/3% more than other well produces.
   How many barrels of oil are produced daily by the two wells?
   A. 5333 1/3 B. 6666 2/3 C. 7000
   D. 8333 1/3 E. 9000

   1.____

2. If a car travels a miles in b minutes, how many minutes will it take to travel c miles?
   A. c/a B. c/b C. c/ab D. ab/c E. cb/a

   2.____

3. In the figure at the right, what is the sum of the angles labeled x and y?
   A. 90°
   B. 100°
   C. 130°
   D. 140°
   E. None of the above

   3.____

4. A man purchased 100 shares of stock at $5 a share.
   If each share rose 10 cents the first month, decreased 8 cents the second month, and gained 3 cents the third month, what was the value of the man's investment at the end of the third month?
   A. $505 B. $520 C. $525
   D. $1,545 E. None of the above

   4.____

5. $\Delta \times \theta = \theta$
   $\theta \times \Delta = \theta$
   $\Delta \times \Delta = \Delta$
   The above multiplication scheme uses symbols other than the usual numerals. Δ corresponds to which base-10 numeral?
   A. 0 B. 1 C. 2 D. 5 E. 10

   5.____

6. What is the length, in inches, of a 144 arc in a circle whose circumference is 60 inches?
   A. 24 B. 12/π C. 12π D. 36 E. 36/π

   6.____

7. What does x equal in the equation $\frac{1}{x} = \frac{1}{5} \cdot \frac{1}{x}$?

   7.____

8. In the universe of all people, let circle M represent all Mary's friends, circle B all Bill's friends, and circle P all Pete's friends.
What is represented by the shaded portion of the figure?
All the people who are
   A. friends of Mary, Bill, and Pete
   B. friends of Mary and Pete
   C. friends of Mary and Pete, but not of Bill
   D. friends of Pete, but not of Bill
   E. not friends of Bill

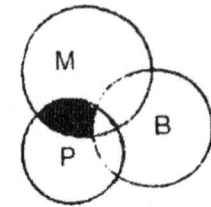

9. A ship sailing due north past an island travels a course that is 12 miles from the island at its closest point.
If a gun on shore has a firing range of 13 miles, for how many miles will the ship remain within range of the gun?
   A. 1   B. 5   C. 9
   D. 10   E. None of the above

10. What is the area of the unshaded sector of circle O shown at the right?
   A. $\dfrac{\pi r}{8}$
   B. $\dfrac{\pi r^2}{2}$
   C. $\dfrac{\pi r^2}{4}$
   D. $\dfrac{\pi r^2}{8}$
   E. $\dfrac{\pi r^2}{45}$

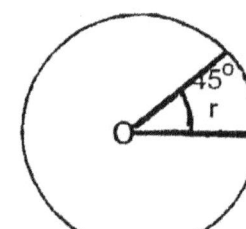

11. What set of values for x and y(x,y) satisfy the following equations: 3y = x + 4, 6x + 2y = 16?
   A. (-2,2)   B. (2,-2)   C. (-2,2)
   D. (2,2)   E. None of the above

12. What is the value of the following expression $\dfrac{A^4 p^{+3} \cdot A^3 p^{+4}}{A^2 p^{+2}}$?

   A. A^{9P+9} B. A^{6P+6} C. A^{3P+3} D. A^{-3P-3} E. A^{5P+5}

KEY (CORRECT ANSWERS)

1.	C	7.	D
2.	E	8.	C
3.	A	9.	D
4.	A	10.	D
5.	B	11	D
6.	A	12.	E

TEST 3

SOCIAL STUDIES READING

DIRECTIONS: This test measures your ability to comprehend, analyze, and evaluate reading, materials in such social studies fields as history, political science, economics, sociology, anthropology, and psychology.

To answer these questions, you will have to draw on your background in social studies, as well as on your ability to understand new material.

In addition to the questions based on reading passages, there are some questions that test your general background knowledge in social studies.

Read the passage through once. Then return to it as often as necessary to answer the questions. *PRINT THE LETTER OF THE CORRECT ANSWER IN THE SPACE AT THE RIGHT.*

Questions 1-5.

DIRECTIONS: Questions 1 through 5 are to be answered on the basis of the following passage.

Over the past several decades, the growth of the United States economy has been marked by expansion of metropolitan areas and by "regionalization" of production—that is, a more even geographical distribution of industries over the United States. Such rapid growth causes drastic changes in the geographical structure of metropolitan areas. Manufacturing industries, which were initially attracted to the core of the city by the proximity of the railroads, a steady labor supply, and the economic advantages of mass production, are now moving toward peripheral locations.

No single explanation can be given for this trend toward suburbanization, but as cities have grown, the supply of undeveloped land has decreased. The advantages of the central metropolis continue to attract economic activity, but congestion in the central city and the development of production techniques which demand more space have tended to push industry into the suburbs. The net result has been a pattern of geographical specialization within metropolitan regions. The central city increasingly becomes geared to white-collar and service activities, and the periphery attracts manufacturing, transportation, and other blue-collar job activities.

The development of residential areas has followed industrial movement to some extent, but suburban living (undoubtedly desired for its amenities) is still largely reserved for those who can afford it. Consequently, the central city has been losing middle- and upper-income families to the suburbs. Now people can live in dispersed residential locations; rising incomes and the proliferation of automobiles have made this both economically and technically feasible. However, this "urban sprawl" creates serious financial problems. Since tax-paying industry has fled to the suburbs, the central city has had to bear the cost of public assistance payments and other welfare service for low-income groups.

When housing developers began building on a large scale, many suburbs rapidly doubled and tripled in size. This new population required more schools and teachers, more fire and police protection, and sizable expenditures for water and sewer lines and roads. Frequently, these towns were entirely dependent on property taxes for their revenues.

To meet ever-increasing expenses and broaden their tax base, some communities have tried to attract new industry. However, when town officials found themselves competing intensely for these industries, they often conceded partial exemption from property taxes to new industry in order to bargain more favorably. As a result, an area often found its tax base weakened rather than strengthened by winning new industry. As a consequence of all these changes, both the suburbs and the central city are entangled in thorny financial problems.

1. According to the author, a rise in wages earned by employees of service industries will PRINCIPALLY tend to
    A. *increase* the physical separation between zones of residence and zones of work
    B. *decrease* the tax revenues of the suburbs
    C. *decrease* the tax revenues of the metropolitan areas
    D. *increase* the work force in the periphery

2. The MOST efficient way to solve the financial problems of a metropolitan area would be to
    A. *cut* personal taxes in central cities
    B. *cut* personal taxes in the suburbs
    C. *decrease* public expenditures in central cities
    D. *place* the entire area under one fiscal authority

3. Which of the following problems should be given FIRST consideration on the basis of the changing urban structure outlined in the passage?
    A. Commuter traffic between areas of residence and areas of work
    B. Highway passenger traffic between two metropolitan areas
    C. Congestion due to heavy truck traffic in downtown areas
    D. The centralization of railroad freight stations in downtown areas

4. The author would consider the giant modern city *essentially* a by-product of the
    A. invention of the internal combustion engine
    B. development of monopolistic industries
    C. Industrial Revolution
    D. capitalist system

5. If the trend outlined in paragraph three continues, the centers of large American cities are more likely than the suburbs to have a HIGH percentage of
    A. small-scale manufacturing firms   B. large-scale factories
    C. railroad stations   D. banks and insurance companies

Questions 6-9.

DIRECTIONS: Questions 6 through 9 are to be answered on the basis of the following passage.

(In 1845, congressional leaders debated the annexation of Texas. The issues considered were many and complex, as the following excerpts from the debate illustrate.)

Speaker 1:
    In annexing Texas, we do not adopt its war with Mexico, if any such exists. In annexation, we will not abide by Texas law; Texas will abide by ours. The United States are not to be merged in Texas, but Texas in them. When we purchased Louisiana from France, France was at war; we did not assume the French war. Mexico, however, may regard annexation as an act of extreme unfriendliness and make it the pretext for declaring war on the United States.

Speaker 2:
    Since the landing of the Pilgrims, our people have moved forward, acquiring territory, unfurling the banner of liberty and equality, creating a power (more potent than that of armies), before which the nations of this continent will continue to give way. No nation can withstand the impact of this principle of enlightened liberty. Under this principle—though I regret to say, sometimes backed by the sword—we have been a progressive, but peaceful, people.

Speaker 3:
    The Anglo-Saxon race, like a mighty flood, has swept over the continent. Some say the flood ought to stop at the Del Norte. I can tell them that it will not. In fifty years it will cover Mexico; in a hundred, Argentina.

Speaker 4:
    The question of admitting Texas seems to make many apprehensive about the balance of political power. Let them look at the complexion of the House. Let them look also at the map and see the broad expanse of land in the north and northwest which is yet to be made into states where slavery can never exist. In addition, by rejecting Texas, we ensure the spread of slavery. Admit Texas, and the Rio Bravo constitutes the limits of this institution. Reject her, and slavery will not stop until its standard waves in triumph over Mexico.

Speaker 5:
    Those who advocate annexation contend that the federal government is one of limited powers. Yet they ask that Congress assume the important power of adding a foreign nation to our own. We are referred to the provision in the Constitution that authorizes Congress to admit new states. History shows that this clause was intended only to confer on Congress the power of admitting new states created from territory already belonging to the United States.

Speaker 6:
    This is the true cause of most of the opposition: fear that an influence opposed to the interests of the manufacturers would be added to the national councils. —

6. Which speaker's argument seems to stem DIRECTLY from a belief in the inevitability of historical events?
   A. 5   B. 4   C. 3   D. 1

1.____

7. Which of the following is TRUE of Speaker 2's description of the United States' method of acquiring new territory as *peaceful*?
   It
   A. is contradicted by other parts of his statement
   B. is supported by U.S. success in acquiring territories
   C. supports a Marxist interpretation of history
   D. is an accurate but unsupported statement

7.____

8. What EARLIER action of Congress was based on the principle of *balance of power* to which Speaker 4 refers?
   The
   A. Northwest Ordinance   B. Judiciary Act
   C. Missouri Compromise   D. Great Compromise

8.____

9. The argument of which speaker implies that United States territory should be limited to that acquired by an agreement?
   A. 5   B. 3   C. 2   D. 1

9.____

Questions 10-15.

DIRECTIONS: Questions 10 through 15 are NOT based on a reading passage. You are to answer these questions on the basis of your background in social studies.

10. Andrew Jackson's term as President is noteworthy LARGELY because during that period
    A. peaceful relations were established with the Plains Indians
    B. the common man came too have more of a say in government
    C. a national bank was established, resulting in this country's first stable currency
    D. women received the right to vote for the first time

10.____

11. The 80-day injunction provision of the Taft-Hartley Act was included for what purpose?
    To
    A. provide a cooling-off period allowing labor and management additional time to resolve disputes
    B. permit the unions to arrange for a survey of membership opinion regarding a strike
    C. permit management to update the profit-loss picture for the forthcoming quarter
    D. give government negotiators the time to make a decision about whether a strike would be advisable

11.____

12. Which of the following might anthropologists find SIMILAR in purpose to the rain dance of the Pueblo Indians?
    A. The playing of the national anthem before sporting events
    B. Traditional country folk dancing
    C. Studies carried out by a college of agriculture to improve the yield of wheat
    D. A prayer meeting in an American church

12.____

13. The MOST significant advance of the Charter of the United Nations over the Covenant of the League of Nations is the
    A. article providing for an international police force to prevent aggression
    B. provision granting veto power to the five permanent members of the Security Council
    C. belief in the maintenance of world peace by international cooperation
    D. establishment of a council with authority to formulate plans for the reduction of armaments

13.____

14. The MAIN purpose of the Bill of Rights is to
    A. prevent presidents from telling states what to do
    B. enlarge the scope of the powers of the federal government
    C. reduce the power of the Supreme Court to declare acts of Congress unconstitutional
    D. limit the power of the federal government to abuse individual freedom

14.____

15. When Western Europe was cut off from some of its Middle Eastern oil by the Suez crisis in 1956, MOST of the petroleum deficit was made up by the United States and
    A. Canada
    B. Eastern Europe
    C. Indonesia
    D. Venezuela

15.____

KEY (CORRECT ANSWERS)

1.	A	6.	C	11.	A
2.	D	7.	A	12.	D
3.	A	8.	C	13.	A
4.	C	9.	A	14.	D
5.	D	10.	B	15.	D

TEST 4

NATURAL SCIENCES READING

DIRECTIONS: This test measures your ability to understand, analyze, and evaluate passages on scientific topics and descriptions of experiments in such fields as biology, chemistry, physics, and physical science.

To answer these questions, you will have to draw on your scientific background as well as on your ability to understand new material.

In addition to the questions based on reading passages, there are some questions that test your general background knowledge in the sciences.

Read the passage through once. Then return to it as often as necessary to answer the questions. *PRINT THE LETTER OF THE CORRECT ANSWER IN THE SPACE AT THE RIGHT.*

Questions 1-5.

DIRECTIONS: Questions 1 through 5 are to be answered on the basis of the following passage.

As the cells that make up different tissues and organs differ in structure and function, so also do they differ in their response to radiation. The law of Bergonie and Tribondeau states that the radiosensitivity of a tissue is directly proportional to its reproductive capacity and inversely proportional to its degree of specialization. In other words, immature, rapidly-dividing cells will be most harmed by radiation. In addition, three other factors are important: undernourished cells are less sensitive than normal ones, the higher the metabolic rate in a cell the lower its resistance to radiation and cells are more sensitive to radiation at specific stages of division.

Radiation alters the electrical charges of the atoms in the irradiated material, breaking the valence bonds holding the molecules together. For example, radiation passing through a cell is most likely to strike water molecules. The breakdown products from these molecules may combine with oxygen to form bleaches, which in turn can break down protein molecules in the cell. One class of these proteins comprises the enzymes that not only play a role in nearly all biochemical reactions but also control cell division. Such inhibition of cell division may permit cells to grow to an abnormal size; when such a cell dies, there is no replacement to fill the void in the tissue. If the cell has been altered so that its daughter cells are genetically different from the parent cell, the daughter cells may die before they reproduce themselves; they may continue to grow without dividing or they may divide at a higher or lower rate than the parent cell.

Because of these possible effects, doctors and scientists have been concerned about the exposure of humans to radiation. A study of the effects of radiation on the human body indicates that the following organ and tissue groups are most affected by radioactivity: (1) blood and bone marrow, (2) lymphatic system, (3) skin and hair follicles, (4) alimentary canal, (5) adrenal glands, (6) thyroid gland, (7.) lungs, (8) urinary tract, (9) liver and gallbladder, (10) bone,

(11) eyes, and (12) reproductive organs. Although no permissible level for exposure of humans to radiation has been established, data reported in 1957 indicate that 25 roentgens cause no observable reaction, 50 roentgens produce nausea and vomiting, 400 to 500 roentgens give the individual a fifty-fifty chance of survival without medical care, and 650 roentgens are lethal.

1. In the first paragraph, the metabolic rate of a cell refers to the cell's
   A. chemical activities
   B. degree of specialization
   C. stage of division
   D. maturity

2. Why is muscle tissue relatively unaffected by radiation? It(s)
   A. cells contain no water
   B. is highly specialized
   C. is protected by the bony skeleton
   D. cells have a unique method of reproduction

3. If radiation can cause cancer as implied in the second paragraph, then which of the following BEST justifies the use of radiation in treating cancer?
   A. Cancer tissue is highly specialized, hence very sensitive to radiation.
   B. Only the cancer cells receive the radiation.
   C. Cancer cells divide relatively rapidly.
   D. The patient may die anyway, and desperate measures are appropriate in such instances.

4. Which of the following would the author probably consider the MOST serious long-range effect of exposure to radiation on human populations?
   A. Possible destruction of natural resources essential to survival
   B. Hereditary changes that might occur in the population
   C. The world's population increasing at a higher rate than the world's food supply
   D. The daughters of people exposed to radiation dying before they can have children

5. Why would a man in outer space be in GREATER danger from radiation than a man on earth?
   A. He would not be shielded from cosmic rays by the earth's atmosphere.
   B. The reduced pressure in a space vehicle inhibits cell division.
   C. Biochemical reactions essential to life cannot occur in outer space.
   D. In a weightless condition, cells are more vulnerable to radiation.

Questions 6-9.

DIRECTIONS: Questions 6 through 9 are to be answered on the basis of the following passage.

A series of experiments was designed to determine how bats are able to fly at night without colliding with obstacles. Bats were released in a closed room across which were strung fine wires adapted to register every time they were touched by one of the bats. The bats were released in the room under the following conditions:

Experiment 1:
The room was well illuminated.

Experiment 2:
The room was completely darkened.

Experiment 3:
The room was darkened, and the bats' eyes were sealed with soft black wax.

Experiment 4:
The room was darkened, the bats' eyes were waxed closed, and numerous small radar transmitters were set in operation throughout the room.

Experiment 5:
The radar transmitters were replaced with loudspeakers which emitted high-frequency sound waves. The room was dark, and the bats' eyes were waxed closed.

Experiment 6:
The lights were turned on, and the bats, without wax on their eyes, were released while the loudspeakers were still producing high-frequency sounds.

On the basis of these experiments, the following observations were made:

In Experiments 1 through 4, the bats did not collide with the wires.

In Experiment 5, the bats seemed confused and frequently collided with the wires.

In Experiment 6, the bats were initially confused and collided with the wires; however, the number of collisions soon decreased.

6. Which conclusion, if any, can be drawn from Experiment 1?
   A. Bats need light to see where they are going.
   B. Bats need sound waves in order to avoid obstacles.
   C. Bats can see in the dark,
   D. None of the above

6.____

7. Which conclusion, if any, can be drawn from Experiment 4?
   A. Bats evidently use some sort of radar to guide themselves.
   B. The presence of radar waves has no apparent effect on the bats.
   C. The presence of radar waves confuses the bats by obstructing their natural means of locating obstacles.
   D. None of the above

7.____

8. Which experiment or group of experiments listed below shows that bats can ordinarily fly safely without using their eyes?
   A. 3 only   B. 1 and 2   C. 1 and 3   D. 1, 2, 3

8.____

9. Which of the following is TRUE about the statement: *Bats are nocturnal animals because daylight interferes with their ability to avoid obstacles.*
   The statement
   A. agrees with the data
   B. is contradicted by the data
   C. cannot be judged without more data
   D. is an experimental assumption

Questions 10-13.

DIRECTIONS: Questions 10 through 13 are NOT based on a reading passage. You are to answer these questions on the basis of your background in the natural sciences.

10. The emergence of new strains of houseflies capable of withstanding the poisonous effects of the chemical DDT is an example of
    A. adaptation
    B. the Mendelian law
    C. implementation
    D. regeneration

11. What is the MAIN difference between a gas and a liquid?
    A. Molecular weight
    B. Shape of the particles
    C. Geometric arrangement of the molecules
    D. Average distance between the molecules

12. How were the coral reefs of tropical seas formed? By
    A. the accumulation of the remains of small marine animals
    B. the erosion of islands by wind and sea
    C. the accumulation of salts and minerals precipitated by the sea
    D. undersea earthquakes

13. A warm breeze may seem cool to a bather who has just come out of the water because
    A. water is a good conductor of heat
    B. moisture from the air condenses on the skin and cools it
    C. the evaporation of water from the wet skin absorbs heat
    D. water is denser than air

KEY (CORRECT ANSWERS)

1.	A	6.	D	11.	D
2.	B	7.	B	12.	A
3.	C	8.	A	13.	C
4.	B	9.	B		
5.	A	10.	A		

READING COMPREHENSION
UNDERSTANDING AND INTERPRETING WRITTEN MATERIAL
EXAMINATION SECTION
TEST 1

DIRECTIONS: Read the following passages, and select the MOST appropriate word from the five alternatives provided for each deleted word. *PRINT THE LETTER OF THE CORRECT ANSWER IN THE SPACE AT THE RIGHT.*

PASSAGE I

Bridges are built to allow a continuous flow of highway and railway traffic across water lying in their paths. But engineers cannot forget the fact that river traffic, too, is essential to or economy. The role of 1 is important. To keep these vessels moving freely, bridges are built high enough, when possible, to let them pass underneath. Sometimes, however, channels must accommodate very tall ships. It may be uneconomical to build a tall enough bridge. The 2 would be too high. To save money, engineers build movable bridges.

1. A. wind   B. boats   C. weight   1.____
   D. wires   E. experience

2. A. levels   B. cost   C. standards   2.____
   D. waves   E. deck

In the swing bridge, the middle part pivots or swings open. When the bridge is closed, this section joins the two ends of the bridge, blocking tall vessels. But this section 3. When swung open, it is perpendicular to the ends of the bridge, creating two free channels for river traffic. With swing bridges, channel width is limited by the bridge's piers. The largest swing bridge provides only a 75-meter channel. Such channels are sometimes too 4. In such cases, a bascule bridge may be built.

3. A. stands   B. floods   C. wears   3.____
   D. turns   E. supports

4. A. narrow   B. rough   C. long   4.____
   D. deep   E. straight

Bascule bridges are drawbridges with two arms that swing upward. They provide an opening as wide as the span. They are also versatile. These bridges are not limited to being fully opened or fully closed. They can be 5 in many ways. They can be fixed at different angles to accommodate different vessels.

5. A. approached B. crossed   C. lighted   5.____
   D. planned   E. positioned

49

In vertical lift bridges, the center remains horizontal. Towers at both ends allow the center to be lifted like an elevator. One interesting variation of this kind of bridge was built during World War II. A lift bridge was desired, but there were wartime shortages of the steel and machinery needed for the towers. It was hard to find enough 6. An ingenious engineer designed the bridge so that it did not have to be raised above traffic. Instead it was 7. It could be submerged seven meters below the river surface. Ships sailed over it.

6. A. work   B. material   C. time   6.____
   D. power   E. space

7. A. burned   B. emptied   C. secured   7.____
   D. shared   E. lowered

PASSAGE II

Before anesthetics were discovered, surgery was carried out under very severe time restrictions. Patients were awake, tossing and screaming in terrible pain. Surgeons were forced to hurry in order to constrain suffering and minimize shock. 8 was essential. Haste, however, did not make for good outcomes in surgery. No surprise then, that the 9 were often poor.

8. A. Blood   B. Silence   C. Speed   8.____
   D. Water   E. Money

9. A. quarters   B. teeth   C. results   9.____
   D. materials   E. families

The discovery of anesthetics happened, in part, by accident. During the early 1800's, nitrous oxide and ether were used for entertainment. At "either frolics" in theaters, volunteers would breathe these gases, become lightheaded, and run around the stage laughing and dancing. By chance, a Connecticut dentist saw such a 10. One volunteer banged his leg against a sharp edge. But he did not 11. He paid no attention to his wound, as though he felt nothing. This gave the dentist the idea of using gas to kill pain,

10. A. show   B. machine   C. face   10.____
    D. source   E. growth

11. A. dream   B. recover   C. succeed   11.____
    D. agree   E. notice

At first, using the "open drip method," ether and chloroform were filtered through a cotton pad placed over the mouth and nose. This direct dose was difficult to regulate and irritating to the nose and throat. Patients would hold their breath, cough, or gag. This made it impossible for them to relax, let alone sleep. Consequently, surgery was often 12. It couldn't begin until the patient had quieted and the anesthesia had taken hold.

12. A. delayed   B. required   C. blamed   12.____
    D. observed   E. repeated

Today's procedures are safer and more accurate. In the "closed method," a fixed amount of gas is released from sealed bottles into an inhalator bag when the patient exhales. He inhales this gas through tubes with his next breath. In this way, the gas is 13. The system carefully regulates how much gas reached the patient.

13. A. heated B. controlled C. cleaned 13.____
    D. selected E. wasted

For dentistry and minor operations, patients need not be asleep. Newer anesthetics can be used which deaden nerves only in the affected part of the body. These 14 anesthetics offer several advantages. For instance, since the anesthesia is fairly light and patients remain awake, they can cooperate with their doctors.

14. A. local B. natural C. ancient
    D. heavy E. three

PASSAGE III

An indispensable element in the development of telephony was the continual improvement of telephone station instruments, those operating units located at the clients premises. Modern units normally consist of a transmitter, receiver, and transformer. They also contain a bell or equivalent summoning device, a mechanism for controlling the unit's connection to the client's line, and various associated items, like dials. All of these 15 have changed over the years. The transmitter, especially, has undergone enormous refinement during the last century.

15. A. parts B. costs C. services 15.____
    D. models E. routes

Bell's original electromagnetic transmitter functioned likewise as receiver, the same instrument being held alternately to mouth and ear. But having to 16 the instrument this way was inconvenient. Suggestions understandably emerged for mounting the transmitter and receiver onto a common handle, thereby creating what are now known as handsets. Transmitter and receiver were, in fact, later 17 his way. Combination handsets were produced for commercial utilization late in the nineteenth century, but prospects for their acceptance were uncertain as the initial quality of transmissions with the handsets was disappointing. But 18 transmissions followed. With adequately high transmission standards attained, acceptance of handsets was virtually assured.

16. A. store B. use C. test 16.____
    D. strip E. clean

17. A. grounded B. marked C. covered 17.____
    D. priced E. coupled

18. A. shorter B. fewer C. better 18.____
    D. faster E. cheaper

Among the most significant improvements in transmitters has been the enormous amplification (up to a thousandfold) of speech sounds. This increased 19 has benefited telecommunications enormously. Nineteenth century telephone conversations frequently were only marginally audible whereas nowadays even murmured conversations can be transmitted successfully, barring unusual atmospheric or electronic disturbances.

19. A. distance B. speed C. market 19.____
    D. volume E. number

Vocal quality over nineteenth century instruments was distorted, the speaker not readily identifiable. By comparison, current sound is characterized by considerably greater naturalism. Modern telephony produces speech sounds more nearly resembling an individual's actual voice. Thus, it is easier to 20 the speaker. A considerable portion of this improvement is attributable to practical applications of laboratory investigations concerning the mechanisms of human speech and audition. These 21 have exerted a profound influence. Their results prompted technical innovations in modern transmitter design which contributed appreciably to the excellent communication available nowadays.

20. A. time B. help C. bill 20.____
    D. stop E. recognize

21. A. studies B. rates C. materials 21.____
    D. machines E. companies

PASSAGE IV

The dramatic events of December 7, 1941, plunged this nation into war. The full 22 of the war we cannot even now comprehend, but one of the effects stands out in sharp relief —the coming of the air age. The airplane, which played a relatively 23 part in World War I, has already soared to heights undreamed of save by the few with mighty vision.

In wartime the airplane is the 24 on wings and the battleship that flies. To man in his need it symbolizes deadly extremes; friend or foe; deliverance or 25.

It is a powerful instrument of war revolutionizing military strategy, but its peacetime role is just as 26. This new master of time and space, fruit of man's inventive genius, has come to stay, smalling the earth and smoothing its surface.

To all of us, then, to youth, and to 27 alike comes the winged challenge to get ourselves ready—to 28 ourselves for living in an age which the airplane seems destined to mold.

22. A. destruction B. character C. history 22.____
    D. import E. picture

23. A. important B. dull C. vast 23.____
    D. unknown E. minor

24. A. giant B. ant C. monster 24.____
    D. artillery E. robot

25. A. ecstasy B. bombardment C. death 25.____
    D. denial E. survival

26.	A. revolting	B. revolutionary	C. residual	26.____
	D. reliable	E. regressive		
27.	A. animals	B. nations	C. women	27.____
	D. men	E. adult		
28.	A. distract	B. engage	C. determine	28.____
	D. deter	E. orient		

PASSAGE V

Let us consider how voice training may contribute to 29 development and an improved social 30.

In the first place, it has been fairly well established that individuals tend to become what they believe 31 people think them to be.

When people react more favorably toward us because our voices 32 the impression that we are friendly, competent, and interesting, there is a strong tendency for us to develop those 33 in our personality.

If we are treated with respect by others, we soon come to have more respect for 34.

Then, too, one's own consciousness of having a pleasant, effective voice of which he does not need to be ashamed contributes materially to a feeling of poise, self-confidence, and a just pride in himself.

A good voice, like good clothes, can do much for an 35 that otherwise might be inclined to droop.

29.	A. facial	B. material	C. community	29.____
	D. personality	E. physical		
30.	A. adjustment	B. upheaval	C. development	30.____
	D. bias	E. theories		
31.	A. some	B. hostile	C. jealous	31.____
	D. inferior	E. destroy		
32.	A. betray	B. imply	C. destroy	32.____
	D. transfigure	E. convey		
33.	A. detects	B. qualities	C. techniques	33.____
	D. idiosyncrasies	E. quirks		
34.	A. others	B. their children	C. their teachers	34.____
	D. ourselves	E. each other		
35.	A. mind	B. heart	C. brain	35.____
	D. feeling	E. ego		

PASSAGE VI

How are symphony orchestras launched, kept going, and built up in smaller communities? Recent reports from five of them suggest that, though the 36 changes, certain elements are fairly common. One thing shines out; 37 is essential.

Also, aside from the indispensable, instrumentalists who play, the following personalities, either singly, or preferably in 38 seem to be the chief needs; a conductor who wants to conduct so badly he will organize his own orchestra if it is the only way he can get one; a manager with plenty of resourcefulness in rounding up audiences and finding financial support; an energetic community leader, generally a woman, who will take up locating the orchestra as a 39; and generous visiting soloists who will help draw those who are 40 that anything local can be used.

36. A. world   B. pattern   C. reason   36._____
    D. scene   E. cast

37. A. hatred   B. love   C. enthusiasm   37._____
    D. participation E. criticism

38. A. combination B. particular   C. isolation   38._____
    D. sympathy   E. solitary

39. A. chore   B. duty   C. hobby   39._____
    D. delight   E. career

40. A. convinced   B. skeptical   C. happy   40._____
    D. unhappy   E. unsure

KEY (CORRECT ANSWERS)

1.	B	11.	E	21.	A	31.	E
2.	B	12.	A	22.	D	32.	E
3.	D	13.	B	23.	E	33.	B
4.	A	14.	A	24.	D	34.	D
5.	E	15.	A	25.	C	35.	E
6.	B	16.	B	26.	B	36.	B
7.	E	17.	E	27.	E	37.	C
8.	C	18.	C	28.	E	38.	A
9.	C	19.	D	29.	D	39.	C
10.	A	20.	E	30.	A	40.	B

READING COMPREHENSION
UNDERSTANDING AND INTERPRETING WRITTEN MATERIAL
EXAMINATION SECTION
TEST 1

DIRECTIONS: Each question or incomplete statement is followed by several suggested answers or completions. Select the one that BEST answers the question or completes the statement. *PRINT THE LETTER OF THE CORRECT ANSWER IN THE SPACE AT THE RIGHT.*

1. The National Assessment of Educational Progress recently released the results of the first statistically valid national sampling of young adult reading skills in the United States. According to the survey, ninety-five percent of United States young adults (aged 21-25) can read at a fourth-grade level or better. This means they can read well enough to apply for a job, understand a movie guide or join the Army. This is a higher literacy rate than the eighty to eighty-five percent usually estimated for all adults. The study also found that ninety-nine percent can write their names, eighty percent can read a map or write a check for a bill, seventy percent can understand an appliance warranty or write a letter about a billing error, twenty-five percent can calculate the amount of a tip correctly, and fewer than ten percent can correctly figure the cost of a catalog or understand a complex bus schedule.
   Which statement about the study is BEST supported by the above passage?
   A. United States literacy rates among young adults are at an all-time high.
   B. Forty percent of young people in the United States cannot write a letter about a billing error.
   C. Twenty percent of United States teenagers cannot read a map.
   D. More than ninety percent of United States young adults cannot correctly calculate the cost of a catalog order.

   1.____

2. It is now widely recognized that salaries, benefits, and working conditions have more of an impact on job satisfaction than on motivation. If they aren't satisfactory, work performance and morale will suffer. But even when they are high, employees will not necessarily be motivated to work well. For example, THE WALL STREET JOURNAL recently reported that as many as forty or fifty percent of newly hired Wall Street lawyers (whose salaries start at upwards of $50,000) quit within the first three years, citing long hours, pressures, and monotony as the prime offenders. It seems there's just not enough of an intellectual challenge in their jobs. An up and coming money-market executive concluded: *Whether it was $1 million or $100 million, the procedure was the same. Except for the tension, a baboon could do my job.* When money and benefits are adequate, the most important additional determinants of job satisfaction are: more responsibility, a sense of achievement, recognition, and a chance to advance. All of these factors have a more significant influence on employee motivation and performance. As a footnote, several studies have found that the absence of these non-monetary factors can lead to serious stress-related illnesses.

   2.____

Which statement is BEST supported by the above passage?
- A. A worker's motivation to perform well is most affected by salaries, benefits, and working conditions.
- B. Low pay can lead to high levels of job stress.
- C. Work performance will suffer if workers feel they are not paid well.
- D. After satisfaction with pay and benefits, the next most important factor is more responsibility.

3. The establishment of joint labor-management production committees occurred in the United States during World War I and again during World War II. Their use was greatly encouraged by the National War Labor Board in World War I and the War Production Board in 1942. Because of the war, labor-management cooperation was especially desired to produce enough goods for the war effort, to reduce conflict, and to control inflation. The committees focused on how to achieve greater efficiency, and consulted on health and safety, training, absenteeism, and people issues in general. During the second world war, there were approximately five thousand labor-management committees in factories, affecting over six million workers. While research has found that only a few hundred committees made significant contributions to productivity, there were additional benefits in many cases. It became obvious to many that workers had ideas to contribute to the running of the organization, and that efficient enterprises could become even more so. Labor-management cooperation was also extended to industries that had never experienced it before. Directly after each war, however, few United States labor-management committees were in operation.

   Which statement is BEST supported by the above passage?
   - A. The majority of United States labor-management committees during the second world war accomplished little.
   - B. A major goal of United States labor-management committees during the first and second world wars was to increase productivity.
   - C. There were more United States labor-management committees during the second world war than during the first world war.
   - D. There are few United States labor-management committees in operation today.

4. Studies have found that stress levels among employees who have a great deal of customer contact or a great deal of contact with the public can be very high. There are many reasons for this. Sometimes stress results when the employee is caught in the middle—an organization wants things done one way, but the customer wants them done another way. The situation becomes even worse for the employee's stress levels when he or she knows was to more effectively provide the service, but isn't allowed to, by the organization. An example is the bank teller who is required to ask a customer for two forms of identification before he or she can cash a check, even though the teller knows the customer well. If organizational mishaps occur or if there are problems with job design, the employee may be powerless to satisfy the customer, and also powerless to protect himself or herself from the customer's wrath. An example of this is the waitress who is forced to serve poorly prepared food. Studies have also found,

however, that if the organization and the employee design the positions and the service encounter well, and encourage the use of effective stress management techniques, stress can be reduced to levels that are well below average.
Which statement is BEST supported by the above passage?
- A. It is likely that knowledgeable employees will experience greater levels of job-related stress.
- B. The highest levels of occupational stress are found among those employees who have a great deal of customer contact.
- C. Organizations can contribute to the stress levels of their employees by poorly designing customer contact situations.
- D. Stress levels are generally higher in banks and restaurants.

5. It is estimated that approximately half of the United States population suffers from varying degrees of adrenal malfunction. When under stress for long periods of time, the adrenals produce extra cortisol and norepinephrine. By producing more hormones than they were designed to comfortably manufacture and secrete, the adrenals can *burn out* over time and then decrease their secretion. When this happens, the body loses its capacity to cope with stress, and the individual becomes sicker more easily and for longer periods of time. A result of adrenal malfunction may be a diminished output of cortisol. Symptoms of diminished cortisol output include any of the following: craving substances that will temporarily raise serum glucose levels such as caffeine, sweets, soda, juice, or tobacco; becoming dizzy when standing up too quickly; irritability; headaches; and erratic energy levels. Since cortisol is an anti-inflammatory hormone, a decreased output over extended periods of time can make one prone to inflammatory disease such ass arthritis, bursitis, colitis, and allergies. (Many food and pollen allergies disappear when adrenal function is restored to normal.) The patient will have no reserve energy, and infections can spread quickly. Excessive cortisol production, on the other hand, can decrease immunity, leading to frequent and prolonged illnesses.
Which statement is BEST supported by the above passage?
- A. Those who suffer from adrenal malfunction are most likely to be prone to inflammatory diseases such as arthritis and allergies.
- B. The majority of Americans suffer from varying degrees of adrenal malfunction.
- C. It is better for the health of the adrenals to drink juice instead of soda.
- D. Too much cortisol can inhibit the body's ability to resist disease.

6. Psychologist B.F. Skinner pointed out long ago that gambling is reinforced either by design or accidentally, by what he called a variable ratio schedule. A slot machine, for example, is cleverly designed to provide a payoff after it has been played a variable number of times. Although the person who plays it and wins while playing receives a great deal of monetary reinforcement, over the long run the machine will take in much more money than it pays out. Research on both animals and humans has consistently found that such variable reward schedules maintain a very high rate of repeat behavior, and that this behavior is particularly resistant to extinction.

Which statement is BEST supported by the above passage?
- A. Gambling, because it is reinforced by the variable ratio schedule, is more difficult to eliminate than most addictions.
- B. If someone is rewarded or wins consistently, even if it is not that often, he or she is likely to continue that behavior.
- C. Playing slot machines is the safest form of gambling because they are designed so that eventually the player will indeed win.
- D. A cat is likely to come when called if its owner has trained it correctly,

7. Paper entrepreneurialism is an offshoot of scientific management that has become so extreme that it has lost all connection to the actual workplace. It generates profits by cleverly manipulating rules and numbers that only in theory represent real products and real assets. At its worst, paper entrepreneurialism involves very little more than imposing losses on others for the sake of short-term profits. The others may be taxpayers, shareholders who end up indirectly subsidizing other shar holders, consumers, or investors. Paper entrepreneurialism has replaced product entrepreneurialism, is seriously threatening the United States economy, and is hurting our necessary attempts to transform the nation's industrial and productive economic base. An example is the United States company that complained loudly in 1979 that it did not have the $200 million needed to develop a video-cassette recorder, though demand for them had been very high. The company, however, did not hesitate to spend $1.2 billion that same year to buy a mediocre finance company. The video recorder market was handed over to other countries, who did not hesitate to manufacture them. 7.____

    Which statement is BEST supported by the above passage?
    - A. Paper entrepreneurialism involves very little more than imposing losses on others for the sake of short-term profits.
    - B. Shareholders are likely to benefit most from paper entrepreneurialism.
    - C. Paper entrepreneurialism is hurting the United States economy.
    - D. The United States could have made better video-cassette recorders than the Japanese but we ceded the market to them in 1979.

8. The *prisoner's dilemma* is an almost 40-year-old game-theory model psychologists, biologists, economists, and political scientists use to try to understand the dynamics of competition and cooperation. Participants in the basic version of the experiment are told that they and their *accomplice* have been caught red-handed. Together, their best strategy is to cooperate by remaining silent. If they do this, each will get off with a 30-day sentence. But either person can do better for himself or herself. If you double-cross your partner, you will go scot free while he or she serves ten years. The problem is, if you each betray the other, you will both go to prison for eight years, not thirty days. No matter what your partner chooses, you are logically better off choosing betrayal. Unfortunately, your partner realizes this too, and so the odds are good that you will both get eight years. That's the dilemma. (The length of the prison sentences is always the same for each variation.) Participants at a recent symposium on behavioral economics at Harvard University discussed the many variations on the game that have been used 8.____

over the years. In one standard version, subjects are paired with a supervisor who pays them a dollar for each point they score. Over the long run, both subjects will do best if they cooperate every time. Yet in each round, there is a great temptation to betray the other because no one knows what the other will do. The best overall strategy for this variation was found to be *tit for tat*, doing unto your opponent as he or she has just done unto you. It is a simple strategy, but very effective. The partner can easily recognize it and respond. It is retaliatory enough not to be easily exploited, but forgiving enough to allow a pattern of mutual cooperation to develop.
Which statement is BEST supported by the above passage?
- A. The best strategy for playing *prisoner's dilemma* is to cooperate and remain silent.
- B. If you double-cross your partner, and he or she does not double-cross you, your partner will receive a sentence of eight years.
- C. When playing *prisoner's dilemma*, it is best to double-cross your partner.
- D. If you double-cross your partner, and he or she double-crosses you, you will receive an eight-year sentence.

9. After many years of experience as the vice president and general manager of a large company, I feel that I know what I'm looking for in a good manager. First, the manager has to be comfortable with himself or herself, and not be arrogant or defensive. Secondly, he or she has to have a genuine interest in people. There are some managers who love ideas—and that's fine—but to be a manager, you must love people, and you must make a hobby of understanding them, believing in them and trusting them. Third, I look for a willingness and a facility to manage conflict. Gandhi defined conflict as a way of getting at the truth. Each person brings his or her own grain of truth and the conflict washes away the illusion and fantasy. Finally, a manager has to have a vision, and the ability and charisma to articulate it. A manager should be seen as a little bit crazy. Some eccentricity is an asset. People don't want to follow vanilla leaders. They want to follow chocolate-fudge-ripple leaders.
Which statement is BEST supported by the above passage?
- A. It is very important that a good manager spend time studying people.
- B. It is critical for good managers to love ideas.
- C. Managers should try to minimize or avoid conflict.
- D. Managers should be familiar with people's reactions to different flavors of ice cream.

10. Most societies maintain a certain set of values and assumptions that make their members feel either good or bad about themselves, and either better or worse than other people. In most developed countries, these values are based on the assumption that we are all free to be what we want to be, and that differences in income, work, and education are a result of our own efforts. This may make us believe that people with more income work that is more skilled, more education, and more power are somehow *better* people. We may view their achievements as proof that they have more intelligence, more motivation, and more initiative than those with lower status. The myth tells us that power, income, and education are freely and equally available to all, and that our

failure to achieve them is due to our own personal inadequacy. This simply is not the case.

The possessions we own may also seem to point to our real worth as individuals. The more we own, the more worthy of respect we may feel we are. Or, the acquisition of possessions may be a way of trying to fulfill ourselves, to make up for the loss of community and/or purpose. It is a futile pursuit because lost community and purpose can never be compensated for by better cars or fancier houses. And too often, when these things fail to satisfy, we believe it is only because we don't have enough money to buy better quality items, or more items. We feel bad that we haven't been successful enough to get all that we think we need. No matter how much we do have, goods never really satisfy for long. There is always something else to acquire, and true satisfaction eludes many, many of us.
Which statement is BEST supported by the above passage?
   A. The author would agree with the theory of *survival of the fittest*.
   B. The possessions an individual owns are not a proper measure of his or her real worth.
   C. Many countries make a sincere attempt to ensure equal access to quality education for their citizens.
   D. The effect a society's value system has on the lives of its members is greatly exaggerated.

11. *De nihilo nihil* is Latin for *nothing comes from nothing*. In the first century, the Roman poet Persius advised that if anything is to be produced of value, effort must be expended. He also said, *In nihilum nil posse revorti*—anything once produced cannot become nothing again. It is thought that Persius was parodying Lucretius, who expounded the 500-year-old physical theories of Epicurus. *De nihilo nihil* can also be used as a cynical comment, to negatively comment on something that is of poor quality produced by a person of little talent. The implication here is: *What can you expect from such a source?*
Which statement is BEST supported by the above passage?
   A. *In nihilum nil posse revorti* can be interpreted as meaning, *If anything is to be produced of value, then effort must be expended.*
   B. *De nihilo nihil* can be understood in two different ways,
   C. Lucretius was a great physicist.
   D. Persius felt that Epicurus put in little effort while developing his theories.

11.____

12. A Cornell University study has found that less than one percent of the billion pounds of pesticides used in this country annually strike their intended targets. The study found that the pesticides, which are somewhat haphazardly applied to 370 million acres, or about sixteen percent of the nation's total land area, end up polluting the environment and contaminating almost all 200,000 species of plants and animals, including humans. While the effect of indirect contamination on human cancer rates was not estimated, the study found that approximately 45,000 human pesticide poisonings occur annually, including about 3,000 cases admitted to hospitals and approximately 200 fatalities.

12.____

Which statement is BEST supported by the above passage?
A. It is likely that indirect pesticide contamination affects human health.
B. Pesticides are applied to over one-quarter of the total United States land area.
C. If pesticides were applied more carefully, fewer pesticide-resistant strains of pests would develop.
D. Human cancer rates in this country would drop considerably if pesticide use was cut in half.

13. The new conservative philosophy presents a unified, coherent approach to the world. It offers to explain much of our experience since the turbulent 1960s, and it shows what we've learned since about the dangers of indulgence and permissiveness. But it also warns that the world has become more ruthless, and that as individuals and as a nation, we must struggle for survival. It is necessary to impose responsibility and discipline in order to defeat those forces that threaten us. This lesson is dramatically clear, and can be applied to a wide range of issues.
Which statement is BEST supported by the above passage?
A. The 1970s were a time of permissiveness and indulgence.
B. The new conservative philosophy may help in imposing discipline and a sense of responsibility in order to meet the difficult challenges facing this country.
C. The world faced greater challenges during the second world war than it faces at the present time.
D. More people identify themselves today as conservative in their political philosophy.

13.____

14. One of the most puzzling questions in management in recent years has been how usually honest, compassionate, intelligent managers can sometimes act in ways that are dishonest, uncaring, and unethical. How could top-level managers at the Manville Corporation, for example, suppress evidence for decades that proved beyond all doubt that asbestos inhalation was killing their own employees? What drove the managers of a Midwest bank to continue to act in a way that threatened to bankrupt the institution, ruin its reputation, and cost thousands of employees and investors their jobs and their savings? It's been estimated that about two out of three of America's five hundred largest corporations have been involved in some form of illegal behavior. There are, of course, some common rationalizations used to justify unethical conduct: believing that the activity is in the organization's or the individual's best interest, believing that the activity is not *really* immoral or illegal, believing that no one will ever know, or believing that the organization will sanction the behavior because it helps the organization. Ambition can distort one's sense of *duty*.
Which statement is BEST supported by the above passage?
A. Top-level managers of corporations are currently involved in a plan to increase ethical behavior among their employees.
B. There are many good reasons why a manager may act unethically.
C. Some managers allow their ambitions to override their sense of ethics,
D. In order to successfully compete, some organizations may have to indulge in unethical or illegal behavior from time to time.

14.____

15. Some managers and supervisors believe that they are leaders because they occupy positions of responsibility and authority. But leadership is more than holding a position. It is often defined in management literature as *the ability to influence the opinions, attitudes and behaviors of others.* Obviously, there are some managers that would not qualify as leaders, and some leaders that are not *technically* managers. Research has found that many people overrate their own leadership abilities. In one recent study, seventy percent of those surveyed rated themselves in the top quartile in leadership abilities, and only two percent felt they were below average as leaders.
Which statement is BEST supported by the above passage?
   A. In a recent study, the majority of people surveyed rated themselves in the top twenty-five percent in leadership abilities.
   B. Ninety-eight percent of the people surveyed in a recent study had average or above-average leadership skills.
   C. In order to be a leader, one should hold a management position.
   D. Leadership is best defined as the ability to be liked by those one must lead.

15.____

KEY (CORRECT ANSWERS)

1.	D	6.	B	11.	B
2.	C	7.	C	12.	A
3.	B	8.	D	13.	B
4.	C	9.	A	14.	C
5.	D	10.	B	15.	A

READING COMPREHENSION
UNDERSTANDING AND INTERPRETING WRITTEN MATERIAL
EXAMINATION SECTION
TEST 1

DIRECTIONS: Each question or incomplete statement is followed by several suggested answers or completions. Select the one that BEST answers the question or completes the statement. *PRINT THE LETTER OF THE CORRECT ANSWER IN THE SPACE AT THE RIGHT.*

Questions 1-3.

DIRECTIONS: Questions 1 through 3 are to be answered SOLELY on the basis of the following passage.

Every organization needs a systematic method of checking its operations as a means to increase efficiency and promote economy. Many successful private firms have instituted a system of audit or internal inspections to accomplish these ends. Law enforcement organizations, which have an extremely important service to *sell*, should be no less zealous in developing efficiency and economy in their operations. Periodic, organized, and systematic inspections are one means of promoting the achievement of these objectives. The necessity of an organized inspection system is perhaps greatest in those law enforcement groups which have grown to such a size that the principal officer can no longer personally supervise or be cognizant of every action taken. Smooth and effective operation demands that the head of the organization have at hand some tool with which he can study and enforce general policies and procedure and also direct compliance with day-to-day orders, most of which are put into execution outside his sight and hearing. A good inspection system can serve as that tool.

1. The central thought of the above passage is that a system of inspections within a police department
    A. is unnecessary for a department in which the principal officer can personally supervise all official actions taken
    B. should be instituted at the first indication that there is any deterioration in job performance by the force
    C. should be decentralized and administered by first-line supervisory officers
    D. is an important aid to the police administrator in the accomplishment of law enforcement objectives

1.____

2. The MOST accurate of the following statements concerning the need for an organized inspection system in a law enforcement organization is: It is
    A. never needed in an organization of small size where the principal officer can give personal supervision
    B. most needed where the size of the organization prevents direct supervision by the principal officer
    C. more needed in law enforcement organizations than in private firms
    D. especially needed in an organization about to embark upon a needed expansion of services

2.____

3. According to the above passage, the head of the police organization utilizes the internal inspection system
   A. as a tool which must be constantly re-examined in the light of changing demands for police service
   B. as an administrative technique to increase efficiency and promote economy
   C. by personally visiting those areas of police operation which are outside his sight and hearing
   D. to augment the control of local commanders over detailed field operations

Questions 4-10.

DIRECTIONS: Questions 4 through 10 are to be answered SOLELY on the basis of the following passage.

Job evaluation and job rating systems are intended to introduce scientific procedures. Any type of approach, when properly used, will give satisfactory results. The Point System, when properly validated by actual use, is more likely to be suitable for general use than the ranking system. In many aspects, the Factor Comparison Plan is a point system tied to money values. Of course, there may be another system that combines the ranking system with the point system, especially during the initial stages of the development of the program. After the program has been in use for some time, the tendency is to drop off the ranking phase and continue the use of the point system.

In the ranking system of rating of jobs, every job within the plant is arranged in some order, either from the one with the simplest qualifications to the one with maximum requirements, or in the reverse order. This system should be preceded by careful job analysis and the writing of accurate job descriptions before the rating process is undertaken. It is possible, of course, to take the jobs as they are found in the business enterprise and use the names as they are without any attempt at standardization, and merely rank them according to the general overall impression of the raters. Such a procedure is certain to fall short of what may reasonably be expected of job rating. Another procedure that is in reality merely a modification of the simple rating described above is to establish a series of grades or zones and arrange all he jobs in the plant into groups within these grades and zones. The practice in most common use is to arrange all the jobs in the plant according to their requirements by rating them and then to establish the classification or groups.

The actual ranking of jobs may be done by one individual, several individuals, or a committee. If several individuals are working independently on the task, it will usually be found that, in general, they agree but that their rankings vary in certain details. A conference between the individuals, with each person giving his reasons why he rated one way or another, usually produces agreement. The detailed job descriptions are particularly helpful when there is disagreement among raters as to the rating of certain jobs. It is not only possible but desirable to have workers participate in the construction of the job description and in rating the job.

4. The MAIN theme of this passage is
   A. the elimination of bias in job rating
   B. the rating of jobs by the ranking system
   C. the need or accuracy in allocating points in the point system
   D. pitfalls to avoid in selecting key jobs in the Factor Comparison Plan

5. The ranking system of rating jobs consists MAINLY of
   A. attaching a point value to each ratable factor of each job prior to establishing an equitable pay scale
   B. arranging every job in the organization in descending order and then following this up with a job analysis of the key jobs
   C. preparing accurate job descriptions after a job analysis and then arranging all jobs either in ascending or descending order based on job requirements
   D. arbitrarily establishing a hierarchy of job classes and grades and then fitting each job into a specific class and grade based on the opinions of unit supervisors

6. The above passage states that the system of classifying jobs MOST used in an organization is to
   A. organize all jobs in the organization in accordance with their requirements and then create categories or clusters of jobs
   B. classify all jobs in the organization according to the titles and rank by which they are currently known in the organization
   C. establish a pre-arranged series of grades or zones and then fit all jobs into one of the grades or zones
   D. determine the salary currently being paid for each job and then rank the jobs in order according to salary

7. According to the above passage, experience has shown that when a group of raters is assigned to the job evaluation task and each individual rates independently of the others, the raters GENERALLY
   A. *agree* with respect to all aspects of their rankings
   B. *disagree* with respect to all or nearly all aspects of the rankings
   C. *disagree* on overall ratings, but agree on specific rating factors
   D. *agree* on overall rankings, but have some variance in some details

8. The above passage states that the use of a detailed job description is of special value when
   A. employees of an organization have participated in the preliminary step involved in actual preparation of the job description
   B. labor representatives are not participating in ranking of the jobs
   C. an individual rater who is unsure of himself is ranking the jobs
   D. a group of raters is having difficulty reaching unanimity with respect to ranking a certain job

9. A comparison of the various rating systems as described in the above passage shows that
   A. the ranking system is not as appropriate for general use as a properly validated point system
   B. the point system is the same as the Factor Comparison Plan except that it places greater emphasis on money

4 (#1)

C. no system is capable of combining the point system and the Factor Comparison Plan
D. the point system will be discontinued last when used in combination with the Factor comparison System

10. The above passage implies that the PRINCIPAL reason for creating job evaluation and rating systems was to help 10.____
   A. overcome union opposition to existing salary plans
   B. base wage determination on a more objective and orderly foundation
   C. eliminate personal bias on the part of the trained scientific job evaluators
   D. management determine if it was overpricing the various jobs in the organizational hierarchy

Questions 11-13.

DIRECTIONS: Questions 11 through 13 are to be answered SOLELY on the basis of the following passage.

The common sense character of the merit system seems so natural to most Americans that many people wonder why it should ever have been inoperative. After all, the American economic system, the most phenomenal the world has ever known, is also founded on a rugged selective process which emphasizes the personal qualities of capacity, industriousness, and productivity. The criteria may not have always been appropriate and competition has not always been fair, but competition there was, and the responsibilities and the rewards—with exceptions, of course—have gone to those who could measure up in terms of intelligence, knowledge, or perseverance. This has been true not only in the economic area, in the money-making process, but also in achievement in the professions and other walks of life.

11. According to the above passage, economic rewards in the United State have 11.____
    A. always been based on appropriate, fair criteria
    B. only recently been based on a competitive system
    C. not going to people who compete too ruggedly
    D. usually gone to those people with intelligence, knowledge, and perseverance

12. According to the above passage, a merit system is 12.____
    A. an unfair criterion on which to base rewards
    B. unnatural to anyone who is not American
    C. based only on common sense
    D. based on the same principles as the American economic system

13. According to the above passage, it is MOST accurate to say that 13.____
    A. the United States has always had a civil service merit system
    B. civil service employees are very rugged
    C. the American economic system has always been based on a merit objective
    D. competition is unique to the American way of life

Questions 14-15.

DIRECTIONS: Questions 14 and 15 are to be answered SOLELY on the basis of the following passage.

In-basket tests are often used to assess managerial potential. The exercise consists of a set of papers that would be likely to be found in the in-basket of an administrator or manager at any given time, and requires the individuals participating in the examination to indicate how they would dispose of each item found in the in-basket. In order to handle the in-basket effectively, they must successfully manage their time, refer and assign some work to subordinates, juggle potentially conflicting appointments and meetings, and arrange for follow-up of problems generated by the items in the in-basket. In other words, the in-basket test is attempting to evaluate the participants' abilities to organize their work, set priorities, delegate, control, and make decisions.

14. According to the above passage, to succeed in an in-basket test, an administrator must
    A. be able to read very quickly
    B. have a great deal of technical knowledge
    C. know when to delegate work
    D. arrange a lot of appointments and meetings

14.____

15. According to the above passage, all of the following abilities are indications of managerial potential EXCEPT the ability to
    A. organize and control   B. manage time
    C. write effective reports   D. make appropriate decisions

15.____

Questions 16-19.

DIRECTIONS: Questions 16 through 19 are to be answered SOLELY on the basis of the following passage.

A personnel researcher has at his disposal various approaches for obtaining information, analyzing it, and arriving at conclusions that have value in predicting and affecting the behavior of people at work. The type of method to be used depends on such factors as the nature of the research problem, the available data, and the attitudes of those people being studied to the various kinds of approaches. While the experimental approach, with its use of control groups, is the most refined type of study, there are others that are often found useful in personnel research. Surveys, in which the researcher obtains facts on a problem from a variety of sources, are employed in research on wages, fringe benefits, and labor relations. Historical studies are used to trace the development of problems in order to understand them better and to isolate possible causative factors. Case studies are generally developed to explore all the details of a particular problem that is representative of other similar problems. A researcher chooses the most appropriate form of study for the problem he is investigating. He should recognize, however, that the experimental method, commonly referred to as the scientific method, if used validly and reliably, gives the most conclusive results.

16. The above passage discusses several approaches used to obtain information on particular problems.
    Which of the following may be MOST reasonably concluded from the passage?
    A(n)
    A. historical study cannot determine causative factors
    B. survey is often used in research on fringe benefits
    C. case study is usually used to explore a problem that is unique and unrelated to other problems
    D. experimental study is used when the scientific approach to a problem fails

17. According to the above passage, all of the following are factors that may determine the type of approach a researcher uses EXCEPT
    A. the attitudes of people toward being used in control groups
    B. the number of available sources
    C. his desire to isolate possible causative factors
    D. the degree of accuracy he requires

18. The words *scientific method*, as used in the last sentence of the above passage, refer to a type of study which, according to the above passage
    A. uses a variety of sources
    B. traces the development of problems
    C. uses control groups
    D. analyzes the details of a representative problem

19. Which of the following can be MOST reasonably concluded from the above passage?
    In obtaining and analyzing information on a particular problem, a researcher employs the method which is the
    A. most accurate   B. most suitable
    C. least expensive   D. least time-consuming

Questions 20-25.

DIRECTIONS: Questions 20 through 25 are to be answered SOLELY on the basis of the following passage.

The quality of the voice of a worker is an important factor in conveying to clients and co-workers his attitude and, to some degree, his character. The human voice, when not consciously disguised, may reflect a person's mood, temper, and personality. It has been shown in several experiments that certain character traits can be assessed with better than chance accuracy through listening to the voice of an unknown person who cannot be seen.

Since one of the objectives of the worker is to put clients at ease and to present an encouraging and comfortable atmosphere, a harsh, shrill, or loud voice could have a negative effect. A client who displays emotions of anger or resentment would probably be provoked even further by a caustic tone. In a face-to-face situation, an unpleasant voice may be compensated for, to some degree, by a concerned and kind facial expression. However, when one speaks on the telephone, the expression on one's face cannot be seen by the listener. A supervising clerk who wishes to represent himself effectively to clients should try to eliminate as many faults as possible in striving to develop desirable voice qualities.

20. If a worker uses a sarcastic tone while interviewing a resentful client, the client, according to the above passage, would MOST likely
    A. avoid the face-to-face problem
    B. be ashamed of his behavior
    C. become more resentful
    D. be provoked to violence

21. According to the passage, experiments comparing voice and character traits have demonstrated that
    A. prospects for improving an unpleasant voice through training are better than chance
    B. the voice can be altered to project many different psychological characteristics
    C. the quality of the human voice reveals more about the speaker than his words do
    D. the speaker's voice tells the hearer something about the speaker's personality

22. Which of the following, according to the above passage, is a person's voice MOST likely to reveal?
    His
    A. prejudices
    B. intelligence
    C. social awareness
    D. temperament

23. It may be MOST reasonably concluded from the above passage that an interested and sympathetic expression on the face of a worker
    A. may induce a client to feel certain he will receive welfare benefits
    B. will eliminate the need for pleasant vocal qualities in the interviewer
    C. may help to make up for an unpleasant voice in the interviewer
    D. is desirable as the interviewer speaks on the telephone to a client

24. Of the following, the MOST reasonable implication of the above paragraph is that a worker should, when speaking to a client, control and use his voice to
    A. simulate a feeling of interest in the problems of the client
    B. express his emotions directly and adequately
    C. help produce in the client a sense of comfort and security
    D. reflect his own true personality

25. It may be concluded from the above passage that the PARTICULAR reason for a worker to pay special attention to modulating her voice when talking on the phone to a client is that, during a telephone conversation
    A. there is a necessity to compensate for the way in which a telephone distorts the voice
    B. the voice of the worker is a reflection of her mood and character
    C. the client can react only on the basis of the voice and words she hears
    D. the client may have difficulty getting a clear understanding over the telephone

KEY (CORRECT ANSWERS)

1.	D	11.	D
2.	B	12.	D
3.	B	13.	C
4.	B	14.	C
5.	C	15.	C
6.	A	16.	B
7.	D	17.	D
8.	D	18.	C
9.	A	19.	B
10.	B	20.	C

21.	D
22.	D
23.	C
24.	C
25.	C

TEST 2

DIRECTIONS: Each question or incomplete statement is followed by several suggested answers or completions. Select the one that BEST answers the question or completes the statement. *PRINT THE LETTER OF THE CORRECT ANSWER IN THE SPACE AT THE RIGHT.*

Questions 1-3.

DIRECTIONS: Questions 1 through 3 are to be answered SOLELY on the basis of the following paragraph.

Suppose you are given the job of printing, collating, and stapling 8,000 copies of a ten-page booklet as soon as possible. You have available one photo-offset machine, a collator with an automatic stapler, and the personnel to operate these machines. All will be available for however long the job takes to complete. The photo-offset machine prints 5,000 impressions an hour, and it takes about 15 minutes to set up a plate. The collator, including time for insertion of pages and stapling, can process about 2,000 booklets an hour. (Answers should be based on the assumption that there are no breakdowns or delays.)

1. Assuming that all the printing is finished before the collating is started, if the job is given to you late Monday and your section can begin work the next day and is able to devote seven hours a day, Monday through Friday, to the job until it is finished, what is the BEST estimate of when the job will be finished?
    A. Wednesday afternoon of the same week
    B. Thursday morning of the same week
    C. Friday morning of the same week
    D. Monday morning of the next week

1.____

2. An operator suggests to you that instead of completing all the printing and then beginning collating and stapling, you first print all the pages for 4,000 booklets, so that they can be collated and stapled while the last 4,000 pages are being printed.
   If you accepted this suggestion, the job would be completed
    A. sooner but would require more man-hours
    B at the same time using either method
    C. later and would require more man-hours
    D. sooner but there would be more wear and tear on the plates

2.____

3. Assume that you have the same assignment and equipment as described above, but 16,000 copies of the booklet are needed instead of 8,000.
   If you decided to print 8,000 complete booklets, then collate and staple them while you started printing the next 8,000 booklets, which of the following statements would MOST accurately describe the relationship between this new method and your original method of printing all the booklets at one time, and then collating and stapling them? The
    A. job would be completed at the same time regardless of the method used
    B. new method would result in the job's being completed 3½ hours earlier
    C. original method would result in the job's being completed an hour later
    D. new method would result in the job's being completed 1½ hours earlier

3.____

Questions 4-6.

DIRECTIONS: Questions 4 through 6 are to be answered SOLELY on the basis of the following passage.

When using words like company, association, council, committee, and board in place of the full official name, the writer should not capitalize these short forms unless he intends them to invoke the full force of the institution's authority. In legal contracts, in minutes, or in formal correspondence where one is speaking formally and officially on behalf of the company, the term Company is usually capitalized, but in ordinary usage, where it is not essential to load the short form with this significance, capitalization would be excessive. (Example: The company will have many good openings for graduates this June.)

The treatment recommended for short forms of place names is essentially the same as that recommended for short forms of organizational names. In general, we capitalize the full form but not the short form. If Park Avenue is referred to in one sentence, then the *avenue* is sufficient in subsequent references. The same is true with words like building, hotel, station, and airport, which are capitalized when part of a proper name changed (Pan Am Building, Hotel Plaza, Union Station, O'Hare Airport), but are simply lower-cased when replacing these specific names.

4. The above passage states that USUALLY the short forms of names of organizations
   A. and places should not be capitalized
   B. and places should be capitalized
   C. should not be capitalized, but the short forms of names of places should be capitalized
   D. should be capitalized, but the short forms of names of places should not be capitalized

5. The above passage states that in legal contracts, in minutes, and in formal correspondence, the short forms of names of organizations should
   A. usually not be capitalized
   B. usually be capitalized
   C. usually not be used
   D. never be used

6. It can be inferred from the above passage that decisions regarding when to capitalize certain words
   A. should be left to the discretion of the writer
   B. should be based on generally accepted rules
   C. depend on the total number of words capitalized
   D. are of minor importance

Questions 7-10.

DIRECTIONS: Questions 7 through 10 are to be answered SOLELY on the basis of the following passage.

Use of the systems and procedures approach to office management is revolutionizing the supervision of office work. This approach views an enterprise as an entity which seeks to fulfill definite objectives. Systems and procedures help to organize repetitive work into a routine, thus reducing the amount of decision making required for its accomplishment. As a result, employees are guided in their efforts and perform only necessary work. Supervisors are relieved of any details of execution and are free to attend to more important work. Establishing work guides which require that identical tasks be performed the same way each time permits standardization of forms, machine operations, work methods, and controls. This approach also reduces the probability of errors. Any error committed is usually discovered quickly because the incorrect work does not meet the requirement of the work guides. Errors are also reduced through work specialization, which allows each employee to become thoroughly proficient in a particular type of work. Such proficiency also tends to improve the morale of the employees.

7. The above passage states that the accuracy of an employee's work is INCREASED by
    A. using the work specialization approach
    B. employing a probability sample
    C. requiring him to shift at one time into different types of tasks
    D. having his supervisor check each detail of work execution

8. Of the following, which one BEST expresses the main theme of the above passage? The
    A. advantages and disadvantages of the systems and procedures approach to office management
    B. effectiveness of the systems and procedures approach to office management in developing skills
    C. systems and procedures approach to office management as it relates to office costs
    D. advantages of the systems and procedures approach to office management for supervisors and office workers

9. Work guides are LEAST likely to be used when
    A. standardized forms are used
    B. a particular office task is distinct and different from all others
    C. identical tasks are to be performed in identical ways
    D. similar work methods are expected from each employee

10. According to the above passage, when an employee makes a work error, it USUALLY
    A. is quickly corrected by the supervisor
    B. necessitates a change in the work guides
    C. can be detected quickly if work guides are in use
    D. increases the probability of further errors by that employee

Questions 11-12.

DIRECTIONS: Questions 11 and 12 are to be answered SOLELY on the basis of the following passage.

The coordination of the many activities of a large public agency is absolutely essential. Coordination, as an administrative principle, must be distinguished from and is independent of cooperation. Coordination can be of either the horizontal or the vertical type. In large organizations, the objectives of vertical coordination are achieved by the transmission of orders and statements of policy down through the various levels of authority. It is an accepted generalization that the more authoritarian the organization, the more easily may vertical coordination be accomplished. Horizontal coordination is arrived through staff work, administrative management, and conferences of administrators of equal rank. It is obvious that of the two types of coordination, the vertical kind is more important, for at best horizontal coordination only supplements the coordination effected up and down the line,

11. According to the above passage, the ease with which vertical coordination is achieved in a large agency depends upon
    A. the extent to which control is firmly exercised from above
    B. the objectives that have been established for the agency
    C. the importance attached by employees to the orders and statements of policy transmitted through the agency
    D. the cooperation obtained at the various levels of authority

11.____

12. According to the above passage,
    A. vertical coordination is dependent for its success upon horizontal coordination
    B. one type of coordination may work in opposition to the other
    C. similar methods may be used to achieve both types of coordination
    D. horizontal coordination is at most an addition to vertical coordination

12.____

Questions 13-17.

DIRECTIONS: Questions 13 through 17 are to be answered SOLELY on the basis of the following situation.

Assume that you are a newly appointed supervisor in the same unit in which you have been acting as a provisional for some time. You have in your unit the following workers:

WORKER I: He has always been an efficient worker. In a number of his cases, the clients have recently begun to complain that they cannot manage on the departmental budget.

WORKER II: He has been under selective supervision for some time as an experienced, competent worker. He now begins to be late for his supervisory conferences and to stress how much work he has to do.

WORKER III: He has been making considerable improvement in his ability to handle the details of his job. He now tells you, during an individual conference, that he does not need such close supervision and that he wants to operate more independently. He says that Worker II is always available when he needs a little information or help but, in general, he can manage very well by himself.

5 (#2)

WORKER IV: He brings you a complex case for decision as to eligibility. Discussion of the case brings out the fact that he has failed to consider all the available resources adequately but has stressed the family's needs to include every extra item in the budget. This is the third case of a similar nature that his worker has brought to you recently. This worker and Worker I work in adjacent territory and are rather friendly.

In the following questions, select the option that describes the method of dealing with these workers that illustrate BEST supervisory practice.

13. With respect to supervision of Worker I, the assistant supervisor should
    A. discuss with the worker, in an individual conference, any problems that he may be having due to the increase in the cost of living
    B. plan a group conference for the unit around budgeting, as both Workers I and IV seem to be having budgetary difficulties
    C. discuss with Workers I and IV together the meaning of money as acceptance or rejection to the clients
    D. discuss with Worker I the budgetary data in each case in relation to each client's situation

13.____

14. With respect to supervision of Worker II, the supervisory should
    A. move slowly with this worker and give him time to learn that the supervisor's official appointment has not changed his attitudes or methods of supervision
    B. discuss the worker's change of attitude and asks him to analyze the reasons for his change in behavior
    C. take time to show the worker how he is avoiding his responsibility in the supervisor-worker relationship and that he is resisting supervision
    D. hold an evaluatory conference with the worker and show him how he is taking over responsibilities that are not his by providing supervision for Worker III

14.____

15. With respect to supervision of Worker III, the supervisor should discuss with this worker
    A. why he would rather have supervision from Worker II than from the supervisor
    B. the necessity for further improvement before he can go on selective supervision
    C. an analysis of the improvement that has been made and the extent to which the worker is able to handle the total job for which he is responsible
    D. the responsibility of the supervisor to see that clients receive adequate service

15.____

16. With respect to supervision of Worker IV, the supervisor should
    A. show the worker that resources figures are incomplete but that even if they were complete, the family would probably be eligible for assistance
    B. ask the worker why he is so protective of these families since there are three cases so similar

16.____

C. discuss with the worker all three cases at the same time so that the worker may see his own role in the three situations
D. discuss with the worker the reasons for departmental policies and procedures around budgeting

17. With respect to supervision of Workers I and IV, since these two workers are friends and would seem to be influencing each other, the supervisor should

17.____

　　A. hold a joint conference with them both, pointing out how they should clear with the supervisor and not make their own rules together
　　B. handle the problems of each separately in individual conferences
　　C. separate them by transferring one to another territory or another unit
　　D. take up the problem of workers asking help of each other rather than from the supervisor in a group meeting

Questions 18-20.

DIRECTIONS: Questions 18 through 20 are to be answered SOLELY on the basis of the following passage.

　　One of the key supervisory problems in a large municipal recreation department is that many leaders are assigned to isolated playgrounds or small centers, where it is difficult to observe their work regularly. Often their facilities are extremely limited. In such settings, as well as in larger recreation centers, where many recreation leaders tend to have other jobs as well, there tends to be a low level of morale and incentive. Still, it is the supervisor's task to help recreation personnel to develop pride in their work and to maintain a high level of performance. With isolated leaders, the supervisor may give advice or assistance. Leaders may be assigned to different tasks or settings during the year to maximize their productivity and provide new challenges. When it is clear that leaders are no willing to make a real effort to contribute to the department, the possibility of penalties must be considered, within the scope of departmental policy and the union contract. However, the supervisor should be constructive, encourage and assist workers to take a greater interest in their work, be innovative, and try to raise morale and to improve performance in positive ways.

18. The one of the following that would the MOST appropriate title for the above passage is

18.____

　　A. Small Community Centers – Pro and Con
　　B. Planning Better Recreation Programs
　　C. The Supervisor's Task in Upgrading Personnel Performance
　　D. The Supervisor and the Municipal Union – Rights and Obligations

19. The above passage makes clear that recreation leadership performance in all recreation playgrounds and centers throughout a large city is

19.____

　　A. generally above average, with good morale on the part of most recreation leaders
　　B. beyond description since no one has ever observed or evaluated recreation leaders

C. a key test of the personnel department's effort to develop more effective hiring standards
D. of mixed quality, with many recreation leaders having poor morale and a low level of achievement

20. According to the above passage, the supervisor's role is to 20.____
    A. use disciplinary action as his major tool in upgrading performance
    B. tolerate the lack of effort of individual employees since they are assigned to isolated playgrounds or small centers
    C. employ encouragement, advice, and, when appropriate, disciplinary action to improve performance
    D. inform the county supervisor whenever malfeasance or idleness is detected

Questions 21-25.

DIRECTIONS: Questions 21 through 25 are to be answered SOLELY on the basis of the following passage.

EMPLOYEE LEAVE REGULATIONS

Peter Smith, as a full-time permanent city employee under the Career and Salary Plan, earns an *annual leave allowance*. This consists of a certain number of days off a year with pay and may be used for vacation, personal business, and for observing religious holidays. As a newly appointed employee, during his first 8 years of city service, he will earn an annual leave allowance of 20 days off a year (an average of $1^2/_3$ days off a month). After he has finished 8 full years of working for the city, he will begin earning an additional 5 days off a year. His annual leave allowance, therefore, will then be 25 days a year and will remain at this amount for seven full years. He will begin earning an additional two days off a year at this amount for seven full years. He will begin earning an additional two days off a year after he has completed a total of 15 years of city employment. Therefore, in his sixteenth year of working for the city, Mr. Smith will be earning 27 days off a year as his annual leave allowance (an average of $2¼$ days off a month).

A *sick leave allowance* of one day a month is also given to Mr. Smith, but it can be used only in cases of actual illness. When Mr. Smith returns to work after using sick leave allowance, he must have a doctor's note if the absence is for a total of more than 3 days, but he may also be required to show a doctor's note for absences of 1, 2, or 3 days.

21. According to the above passage, Mr. Smith's annual leave allowance consists 21.____
    of a certain number of days off a year which he
    A. does not get paid for
    B. gets paid for at time and a half
    C. may use for personal business
    D. may not use for observing religious holidays

22. According to the above passage, after Mr. Smith has been working for the city 22.____
    for 9 years, his annual leave allowance will be _____ days a year.
    A. 20   B. 25   C. 27   D. 37

8 (#2)

23. According to the above passage, Mr. Smith will begin earning an average of 2 days off a month as his annual leave allowance after he has worked for the city for _____ full years.
    A. 7   B. 8   C. 15   D. 17

23._____

24. According to the above passage, Mr. Smith is given a sick leave allowance of
    A. 1 day every 2 months   B. 1 day per month
    C. $1^2/_3$ days per month   D. 2¼ days a month

24._____

25. According to the above passage, when he uses sick leave allowance, Mr. Smith may be required to show a doctor's note
    A. even if his absence is for only 1 day
    B. only if his absence is for more than 2 days
    C. only if his absence is for more than 3 days
    D. only if his absence is for 3 days or more

25._____

KEY (CORRECT ANSWERS)

1.	C	11.	A
2.	C	12.	D
3.	D	13.	D
4.	A	14.	A
5.	B	15.	C
6.	B	16.	C
7.	A	17.	B
8.	D	18.	C
9.	B	19.	D
10.	C	20.	C

21.	C
22.	B
23.	C
24.	B
25.	A

TEST 3

DIRECTIONS: Each question or incomplete statement is followed by several suggested answers or completions. Select the one that BEST answers the question or completes the statement. *PRINT THE LETTER OF THE CORRECT ANSWER IN THE SPACE AT THE RIGHT.*

Questions 1-6.

DIRECTIONS: Questions 1 through 6 are to be answered SOLELY on the basis of the following passage.

    A folder is made of a sheet of heavy paper (manila, kraft, pressboard, or red rope stock) that has been folded once so that the back is about one-half inch higher than the front. Folders are larger than the papers they contain in order to protect them. Two standard folder sizes are *letter size* for papers that are 8½" x 11" and *legal cap* for papers that are 8½" x 13".
    Folders are cut across the top in two ways: so that the back is straight (straight-cut) or so that the back has a tab that projects above the top of the folder. Such tabs bear captions that identify the contents of each folder. Tabs vary in width and position. The tabs of a set of folders that are *one-half cut* are half the width of the folder and have only two positions.
    One-third cut folders have three positions, each tab occupying a third of the width of the folder. Another standard tabbing is *one-fifth cut*, which has five positions. There are also folders with *two-fifths cut*, with the tabs in the third and fourth or fourth and fifth positions.

1. Of the following, the BEST title for the above passage is 1.____
   A. Filing Folders
   B. Standard Folder Sizes
   C. The Uses of the Folder
   D. The Use of Tabs

2. According to the above passage, one of the standard folder sizes is called 2.____
   A. Kraft cut
   B. legal cap
   C. one-half cut
   D. straight-cut

3. According to the above passage, tabs are GENERALLY placed along the ____ of the folder. 3.____
   A. back   B. front   C. left side   D. right side

4. According to the above passage, a tab is GENERALLY used to 4.____
   A. distinguish between standard folder sizes
   B. identify the contents of a folder
   C. increase the size of the folder
   D. protect the papers within the folder

5. According to the above passage, a folder that is two-fifths cut has ____ tabs. 5.____
   A. no   B. two   C. three   D. five

6. According to the above passage, one reason for making folders larger than the papers they contain is that
   A. only a certain size folder can be made from heavy paper
   B. they will protect the papers
   C. they will aid in setting up a tab system
   D. the back of the folder must be higher than the front

6.____

Questions 7-15.

DIRECTIONS: Questions 7 through 15 are to be answered SOLELY on the basis of the following passage.

The City University of New York traces its origins to 1847, when the Free Academy, which later became City College, was founded as the first tuition-free municipal college. City and Hunter Colleges were placed under the direction of the Board of Higher Education in 1926, and Brooklyn and Queens Colleges were subsequently added to the system of municipal colleges. In 1955, Staten Island Community College, the first of the two-year colleges sponsored by the Board of Higher Education under the program of the State University of New York, joined the system.

In 1961, the four senior colleges and three community colleges then under the jurisdiction of the Board of Higher Education became the City University of New York, and a University Graduate Division was organized to offer programs leading to the Ph.D. Since then, the university has undergone even more rapid growth. Today, it consists of nine senior colleges, an upper division college which admits students at the junior level, eight community colleges, a graduate division, and an affiliated medical center.

In the summer of 1969, the Board of Higher Education resolved that the time had come to commit the resources of the university to meeting an urgent social need—unrestricted access to higher education for all youths of the City. Determined to prevent the waste of human potential represented by the thousands of high school graduates whose limited educational opportunities left them unable to meet existing admission standards, the Board moved to adopt a policy of Open Admissions. It was their judgment that the best way of determining whether a potential student can benefit from college work is to admit him to college, provide him with the learning assistance he needs, and then evaluate his performance.

Beginning with the class of June 1970, every New York City resident who received a high school diploma from a public or private high school was guaranteed a place in one of the colleges of City University.

7. Of the following, the BEST title for the above passage is
   A. A Brief History of the City University
   B. High Schools and the City University
   C. The Components of the University
   D. Tuition-free Colleges

7.____

8. According to the above passage, which one of the following colleges of the City University was ORIGINALLY called the Free Academy?
   A. Brooklyn College   B. City College
   C. Hunter College   D. Queens College

8.____

9. According to the above passage, the system of municipal colleges became the City University of New York in
   A. 1926 B. 1955 C. 1961 D. 1969

9.____

10. According to the above passage, Staten Island Community College came under the jurisdiction of the Board of Higher Education
    A. 6 years after a Graduate Division was organized
    B. 8 years before the adoption of the Open Admissions Policy
    C. 29 years after Brooklyn and Queens Colleges
    D. 29 years after City and Hunter Colleges

10.____

11. According to the above passage, the Staten Island Community College is
    A. a graduate division center
    B. a senior college
    C. a two-year college
    D. an upper division college

11.____

12. According to the above passage, the TOTAL number of colleges, divisions, and affiliated branches of the City University is
    A. 18 B. 19 C. 20 D. 21

12.____

13. According to the above passage, the Open Admissions Policy is designed to determine whether a potential student will benefit from college by PRIMARILY
    A. discouraging competition for placement in the City University among high school students
    B. evaluating his performance after entry into college
    C. lowering admission standards
    D. providing learning assistance before entry into college

13.____

14. According to the above passage, the FIRST class to be affected by the Open Admissions Policy was the
    A. high school class which graduated in January 1970
    B. City University class which graduated in June 1970
    C. high school class when graduated in June 1970
    D. City University class when graduated in June 1970

14.____

15. According to the above passage, one of the reasons that the Board of Higher Education initiated the policy of Open Admission was to
    A. enable high school graduates with a background of limited educational opportunities to enter college
    B. expand the growth of the City University so as to increase the number and variety of degrees offered
    C. provide a social resource to the qualified youth of the City
    D. revise admission standards to meet the needs of the City

15.____

Questions 16-18.

DIRECTIONS: Questions 16 through 18 are to be answered SOLELY on the basis of the following passage.

Hereafter, all probationary students interested in transferring to community college career programs (associate degrees) from liberal arts programs in senior colleges (bachelor degrees) will be eligible for such transfers if they have completed no more than three semesters.

For students with averages 1.5 or above, transfer will be automatic. Those with 1.0 to 1.5 averages can transfer provisionally and will be required to make substantial progress during the first semester in the career program. Once transfer has taken place, only those courses in which passing grades were received will be computed in the community college grade-point average.

No request for transfer will be accepted from probationary students wishing to enter the liberal arts programs at the community college.

16. According to the above passage, the one of the following which is the BEST statement concerning the transfer of probationary students is that a probationary student
    A. may transfer to a career program at the end of one semester
    B. must complete three semester hours before he is eligible for transfer
    C. is not eligible to transfer to a career program
    D. is eligible to transfer to a liberal arts program

17. Which of the following is the BEST statement of academic evaluation for transfer purposes in the case of probationary students?
    A. No probationary student with an average under 1.5 may transfer.
    B. A probationary student with an average of 1.3 may not transfer.
    C. A probationary student with an average of 1.6 may transfer.
    D. A probationary student with an average of .8 may transfer on a provisional basis.

18. It is MOST likely that, of the following, the next degree sought by one who already holds the Associate in Science degree would be a(n) _____ degree.
    A. Assistantship in Science   B. Associate in Applied Science
    C. Bachelor of Science   D. Doctor of Philosophy

Questions 19-20.

DIRECTIONS: Questions 19 and 20 are to be answered SOLELY on the basis of the following passage.

Auto: Auto travel requires prior approval by the President and/or appropriate Dean and must be indicated in the *Request for Travel Authorization* form. Employees authorized to use personal autos on official College business will be reimbursed at the rate of 28¢ per mile for the first 500 miles driven and 18¢ per mile for mileage driven in excess of 500 mile. The Comptroller's Office may limit the amount of reimbursement to the expenditure that would have been made if a less expensive mode of transportation (railroad, airplane, bus, etc.) had been utilized. If this occurs, the traveler will have to pick up the excess expenditure as a personal expense.

Tolls, Parking Fees, and Parking Meter Fees are not reimbursable and many not be claimed.

19. Suppose that Professor T gives the office assistant the following memorandum: 19.____
Used car for official trip to Albany, New York, and return. Distance from New York to Albany is 148 miles. Tolls were $3.50 each way. Parking garage cost $3.00. When preparing the Travel Expense Voucher for Professor T, the figure which should be claimed for transportation is
    A. $120.88   B. $113.88   C. $82.88   D. $51.44

20. Suppose that Professor V gives the office assistant the following memorandum: 20.____
Used car for official trip to Pittsburgh, Pennsylvania, and return. Distance from New York to Pittsburgh is 350 miles. Tolls were $3.30, $11.40 going, and $3.30, $2.00 returning.
When preparing the Travel Expense Voucher for Professor V, the figure which should be claimed for transportation is
    A. $225.40   B. $176.00   C. $127.40   D. $98.00

Questions 21-25.

DIRECTIONS: Questions 21 through 25 are to be answered SOLELY on the basis of the following passage.

For a period of nearly fifteen years, beginning in the mid-1950's, higher education sustained a phenomenal rate of growth. The factor principally responsible were continuing improvement in the rate of college entrance by high school graduates, a 50 percent increase in the size of the college-age (eighteen to twenty-one) group and—until about 1967—a rapid expansion of university research activity supported by the Federal government.

Today, as one looks ahead to the year 2010, it is apparent that each of these favorable stimuli will either be abated or turn into a negative factor. The rate of growth of the college-age group has already diminished; and from 2000 to 2005, the size of the college-age group has shrunk annually almost as fast as it grew from 1965 to 1970. From 2005 to 2010, this annual decrease will slow down so that by 2010 the age group will be about the same size as it was in 2009. This substantial net decrease in the size of the college-age group (from 1995 to 2010) will dramatically affect college enrollments since, currently, 83 percent of undergraduates are twenty-one and under, and another 11 percent are twenty-to to twenty-four.

21. Which one of the following factors is NOT mentioned in the above passage as contributing to the high rate of growth of higher education? 21.____
    A. A large increase in the size of the eighteen to twenty-one age group
    B. The equalization of educational opportunities among socio-economic groups
    C. The Federal budget impact on research and development spending in the higher education sector
    D. The increasing rate at which high school graduates enter college

22. Based on the information in the above passage, the size of the college-age group in 2010 will be
    A. larger than it was in 2009
    B. larger than it was in 1995
    C. smaller than it was in 2005
    D. about the same as it was in 2000

23. According to the above passage, the tremendous rate of growth of higher education started around
    A. 1950   B. 1955   C. 1960   D. 1965

24. The percentage of undergraduates who are over age 24 is MOST NEARLY
    A. 6%   B. 8%   C. 11%   D. 17%

25. Which one of the following conclusions can be substantiated by the information given in the above passage?
    A. The college-age group was about the same size in 2000 as it was in 1965.
    B. The annual decrease in the size of the college-age group from 2000 to 2005 is about the same as the annual increase from 1965 to 1970.
    C. The overall decrease in the size of the college-age group from 2000 to 2005 will be followed by an overall increase in its size from 2005 to 2010.
    D. The size of the college-age group is decreasing at a fairly constant rate from 1995 to 2010.

KEY (CORRECT ANSWERS)

1.	A		11.	C
2.	B		12.	C
3.	A		13.	B
4.	B		14.	C
5.	B		15.	A
6.	B		16.	A
7.	A		17.	C
8.	B		18.	C
9.	C		19.	C
10.	D		20.	B

21. B
22. C
23. B
24. A
25. B

WORD MEANING

EXAMINATION SECTION

TEST 1

DIRECTIONS: Select the letter of the word or expression that MOST NEARLY expresses the meaning of the capitalized word in the group. *PRINT THE LETTER OF THE CORRECT ANSWER IN THE SPACE AT THE RIGHT.*

1. INTRICATE
   - A. complicated
   - B. fascinating
   - C. medium
   - D. human
   - E. original

   1.____

2. GENIAL
   - A. particular
   - B. difficult
   - C. imaginary
   - D. oversized
   - E. cheerful

   2.____

3. EVASIVE
   - A. penetrating
   - B. blotting
   - C. shifty
   - D. broad
   - E. unsympathetic

   3.____

4. POMP
   - A. magnificence
   - B. aid
   - C. thoughtfulness
   - D. timeliness
   - E. scarcity

   4.____

5. PHASE
   - A. expression
   - B. concern
   - C. adolescence
   - D. aspect
   - E. embarrassment

   5.____

6. ASSERTION
   - A. declaration
   - B. abandonment
   - C. agreement
   - D. decoding
   - E. appraisal

   6.____

7. DENOUNCE
   - A. abdicate
   - B. accuse
   - C. execute
   - D. displace
   - E. recite

   7.____

8. EXONERATE
   - A. free from blame
   - B. object
   - C. expel
   - D. prepare for action
   - E. meet secretly

   8.____

9. JOSTLE
   - A. entertain
   - B. travel afar
   - C. crowd
   - D. ride horseback
   - E. deceive

   9.____

10. PREROGATIVE
    - A. privilege
    - B. inferiority
    - C. redemption
    - D. naval command
    - E. combination

    10.____

KEY (CORRECT ANSWERS)

1. A 6. A
2. E 7. B
3. C 8. A
4. A 9. C
5. D 10. A

TEST 2

DIRECTIONS: Select the letter of the word or expression that MOST NEARLY expresses the meaning of the capitalized word in the group. *PRINT THE LETTER OF THE CORRECT ANSWER IN THE SPACE AT THE RIGHT.*

1. ACCELERATE
   A. surpass B. cheer C. quicken
   D. impede E. transport

   1.____

2. FRAUDULENT
   A. deceptive B. erosive C. horrifying
   D. demanding E. joking

   2.____

3. HUMDRUM
   A. monotonous B. noisy C. misleading
   D. distinguished E. moist

   3.____

4. LETHAL
   A. belated B. deadly C. neglectful
   D. devout E. oblivious

   4.____

5. IMPAIR
   A. consume B. control C. design
   D. damage E. restrain

   5.____

6. OVATION
   A. eggshell B. circumference C. opening
   D. slyness E. homage

   6.____

7. RAVAGE
   A. lay waste B. complain C. talk wildly
   D. rush about E. admire

   7.____

8. ENSUE
   A. ascertain B. follow C. trap
   D. envelop E. plead

   8.____

9. DETACHMENT
   A. liking B. chance C. activity
   D. secrecy E. aloofness

   9.____

10. CARICATURE
    A. famine B. exaggeration C. list
    D. consideration E. expense

    10.____

KEY (CORRECT ANSWERS)

1.	C	6.	E
2.	A	7.	A
3.	A	8.	B
4.	B	9.	E
5.	D	10.	B

TEST 3

DIRECTIONS: Select the letter of the word or expression that MOST NEARLY expresses the meaning of the capitalized word in the group. *PRINT THE LETTER OF THE CORRECT ANSWER IN THE SPACE AT THE RIGHT.*

1. DEADLOCK
   - A. useless material
   - B. fatigue
   - C. will
   - D. fixed limit
   - E. state of inaction

   1.____

2. DEPUTY
   - A. arranger
   - B. detective
   - C. fugitive
   - D. substitute
   - E. cleanser

   2.____

3. OPPRESS
   - A. conclude
   - B. crush
   - C. branch out
   - D. alter
   - E. stay within

   3.____

4. REVELATION
   - A. respect
   - B. disclosure
   - C. repetition
   - D. suitability
   - E. remainder

   4.____

5. IRKSOME
   - A. unreasonable
   - B. unclean
   - C. related
   - D. aglow
   - E. tedious

   5.____

6. SALLOW
   - A. yellowish
   - B. external
   - C. healing
   - D. quiet
   - E. vague

   6.____

7. IMPERIOUS
   - A. large
   - B. surprising
   - C. overbearing
   - D. mischievous
   - E. healthy

   7.____

8. STRINGENT
   - A. rigid
   - B. threaded
   - C. musty
   - D. obtainable
   - E. avoided

   8.____

9. ATTRIBUTE
   - A. characteristic
   - B. donation
   - C. friction
   - D. vengeance
   - E. dress

   9.____

10. WRANGLE
    - A. dispute
    - B. come to grips
    - C. squirm
    - D. expel moisture
    - E. plead

    10.____

KEY (CORRECT ANSWERS)

1.	E	6.	A
2.	D	7.	C
3.	B	8.	A
4.	B	9.	A
5.	E	10.	A

TEST 4

DIRECTIONS: Select the letter of the word or expression that MOST NEARLY expresses the meaning of the capitalized word in the group. *PRINT THE LETTER OF THE CORRECT ANSWER IN THE SPACE AT THE RIGHT.*

1. COMMEND
   - A. begin
   - B. praise
   - C. remark
   - D. graduate
   - E. plead

   1.____

2. PLACID
   - A. public
   - B. watered
   - C. quiet
   - D. established
   - E. colorless

   2.____

3. SEGREGATE
   - A. multiply
   - B. encircle
   - C. conform
   - D. isolate
   - E. deny

   3.____

4. DERIDE
   - A. plead
   - B. mock
   - C. appeal
   - D. surprise
   - E. obligate

   4.____

5. GUILE
   - A. blame
   - B. market
   - C. direction
   - D. deceit
   - E. throat

   5.____

6. PRUDENT
   - A. critical
   - B. cautious
   - C. bluish
   - D. unfinished
   - E. outrageous

   6.____

7. ORNATE
   - A. proper
   - B. insincere
   - C. stubborn
   - D. birdlike
   - E. adorned

   7.____

8. DISDAINFUL
   - A. scornful
   - B. disgraceful
   - C. willful
   - D. ungrateful
   - E. unhealthful

   8.____

9. PURGE
   - A. knit
   - B. chase
   - C. pucker
   - D. elope
   - E. cleanse

   9.____

10. AGGRAVATE
    - A. accuse
    - B. consider
    - C. grieve
    - D. intensify
    - E. engrave

    10.____

KEY (CORRECT ANSWERS)

1. B   6. B
2. C   7. E
3. D   8. A
4. B   9. E
5. D   10. D

———

TEST 5

DIRECTIONS: Select the letter of the word or expression that MOST NEARLY expresses the meaning of the capitalized word in the group. *PRINT THE LETTER OF THE CORRECT ANSWER IN THE SPACE AT THE RIGHT.*

1. ULTIMATUM
   - A. shrewd plan
   - B. final terms
   - C. first defeat
   - D. dominant leader
   - E. electric motor

   1._____

2. GIRD
   - A. surround
   - B. appeal
   - C. request
   - D. break
   - E. glance

   2._____

3. WANGLE
   - A. moan
   - B. mutilate
   - C. exasperate
   - D. manipulate
   - E. triumph

   3._____

4. PROCUREMENT
   - A. acquisition
   - B. resolution
   - C. healing
   - D. importance
   - E. miracle

   4._____

5. CULMINATION
   - A. rebellion
   - B. lighting system
   - C. climax
   - D. destruction
   - E. mystery

   5._____

6. INSUPERABLE
   - A. incomprehensible
   - B. elaborate
   - C. unusual
   - D. indigestible
   - E. unconquerable

   6._____

7. CLICHÉ
   - A. summary argument
   - B. new information
   - C. new hat
   - D. trite phrase
   - E. lock device

   7._____

8. CONCESSION
   - A. nourishment
   - B. plea
   - C. restoration
   - D. similarity
   - E. acknowledgment

   8._____

9. INSIPID
   - A. disrespectful
   - B. uninteresting
   - C. persistent
   - D. whole
   - E. stimulating

   9._____

10. REPRISAL
    - A. retaliation
    - B. drawing
    - C. capture
    - D. release
    - E. suspicion

    10._____

KEY (CORRECT ANSWERS)

1. B
2. A
3. D
4. A
5. C
6. E
7. D
8. E
9. B
10. A

TEST 6

DIRECTIONS: Select the letter of the word or expression that MOST NEARLY expresses the meaning of the capitalized word in the group. *PRINT THE LETTER OF THE CORRECT ANSWER IN THE SPACE AT THE RIGHT.*

1. DUBIOUS
   - A. economical
   - B. well-groomed
   - C. boring
   - D. discouraged
   - E. uncertain

   1.____

2. ATROCIOUS
   - A. brutal
   - B. innocent
   - C. shrunken
   - D. yellowish
   - E. unsound

   2.____

3. BLITHE
   - A. wicked
   - B. criminal
   - C. merry
   - D. unintelligible
   - E. substantial

   3.____

4. PRESTIGE
   - A. speed
   - B. influence
   - C. omen
   - D. pride
   - E. excuse

   4.____

5. TRITE
   - A. brilliant
   - B. unusual
   - C. funny
   - D. stiff
   - E. commonplace

   5.____

6. VINDICATE
   - A. outrage
   - B. waver
   - C. enliven
   - D. justify
   - E. fuse

   6.____

7. EXUDE
   - A. accuse
   - B. discharge
   - C. inflict
   - D. appropriate
   - E. distress

   7.____

8. LIVID
   - A. burned
   - B. patient
   - C. hurt
   - D. salted
   - E. discolored

   8.____

9. FACTION
   - A. clique
   - B. judgment
   - C. truth
   - D. type of architecture
   - E. health

   9.____

10. INCLEMENT
    - A. merciful
    - B. sloping
    - C. harsh
    - D. disastrous
    - E. personal

    10.____

KEY (CORRECT ANSWERS)

1. E
2. A
3. C
4. B
5. E
6. D
7. B
8. E
9. A
10. C

TEST 7

DIRECTIONS: Select the letter of the word or expression that MOST NEARLY expresses the meaning of the capitalized word in the group. *PRINT THE LETTER OF THE CORRECT ANSWER IN THE SPACE AT THE RIGHT.*

1. RELUCTANT
   A. displeased B. stern C. conclusive
   D. voluntary E. unwilling

   1.____

2. WARY
   A. dangerous B. cautious C. clear
   D. warm E. exciting

   2.____

3. INTERLOPER
   A. alien B. intruder C. questioner
   D. magician E. rainmaker

   3.____

4. INCONSISTENT
   A. insane B. senatorial C. undeviating
   D. contradictory E. faithful

   4.____

5. VULNERABLE
   A. usually harmless B. slyly greedy C. poisonous
   D. deeply religious E. open to attack

   5.____

6. INDIGNATION
   A. poverty B. anger C. exaggeration
   D. mercy E. publicity

   6.____

7. ABATE
   A. strike out B. catch C. diminish
   D. embarrass E. wound

   7.____

8. SUSTENANCE
   A. nourishment B. overabundance C. anxiety
   D. equality E. alertness

   8.____

9. BULWARK
   A. target B. grass C. safeguard
   D. tail E. compartment

   9.____

10. DEMEANOR
    A. bearing B. expenditure C. irritability
    D. questionnaire E. death

    10.____

97

KEY (CORRECT ANSWERS)

1.	E	6.	B
2.	B	7.	C
3.	B	8.	A
4.	D	9.	C
5.	E	10.	A

TEST 8

DIRECTIONS: Select the letter of the word or expression that MOST NEARLY expresses the meaning of the capitalized word in the group. *PRINT THE LETTER OF THE CORRECT ANSWER IN THE SPACE AT THE RIGHT.*

1. CURRENTLY
    A. at the present time
    B. swiftly
    C. commendably
    D. smoothly
    E. electrically

    1.____

2. PARTICIPANT
    A. a form of the verb
    B. haste
    C. sharer
    D. weak player
    E. very steep hill

    2.____

3. INEVITABLE
    A. not subject to evil
    B. obscure
    C. probable
    D. unavoidable
    E. harmful

    3.____

4. INVINCIBLE
    A. unable to be defended
    B. undeniable
    C. past help
    D. unable to be conquered
    E. very sharp

    4.____

5. TENACITY
    A. laziness
    B. misfortune
    C. persistency
    D. poise
    E. stability

    5.____

6. FANATICISM
    A. perplexity
    B. endurance
    C. remarkable power
    D. idleness
    E. excessive enthusiasm

    6.____

7. CREVICE
    A. scouting party
    B. difficult travel
    C. a tight squeeze
    D. fissure
    E. implement for digging

    7.____

8. SAGELY
    A. carelessly
    B. mildly
    C. tastefully
    D. bitterly
    E. wisely

    8.____

9. CONCERTED
    A. accompanied by music
    B. disturbed
    C. arranged by mutual consent
    D. handled with care

    9.____

10. OSTENSIBLY
    A. professedly
    B. meekly
    C. cruelly
    D. bravely
    E. with hostility

    10.____

KEY (CORRECT ANSWERS)

1.	A	6.	E
2.	C	7.	D
3.	D	8.	E
4.	D	9.	C
5.	C	10.	A

TEST 9

DIRECTIONS: Select the letter of the word or expression that MOST NEARLY expresses the meaning of the capitalized word in the group. *PRINT THE LETTER OF THE CORRECT ANSWER IN THE SPACE AT THE RIGHT.*

1. UNCOMPROMISING
   A. capable
   B. unsuccessful
   C. unwilling to make concessions
   D. arranged in a conference
   E. lacking in courage

   1.____

2. COLLATERAL
   A. something given as security
   B. profitable enterprise
   C. unnecessary help
   D. steep slope
   E. very wide board

   2.____

3. CONSERVATIVE
   A. exact
   B. moderate
   C. natural
   D. unusual
   E. deceptive

   3.____

4. RETROSPECT
   A. special kind of telescope
   B. microscope
   C. prism
   D. review of the past
   E. forecast of future events

   4.____

5. DEVIATE
   A. speak evil of
   B. sap the life out of
   C. turn from a course
   D. turn upside down
   E. injure

   5.____

6. DESPICABLE
   A. contemptible
   B. poverty-stricken
   C. destructible
   D. peace-loving
   E. without intelligence

   6.____

7. INCITEMENT
   A. commotion
   B. exception
   C. stimulation
   D. duration
   E. emotion

   7.____

8. INCONTROVERTIBLE
   A. not advisable
   B. not accepted
   C. steadfast
   D. difficult to understand
   E. not to be disputed

   8.____

9. PROLETARIAN
   A. politician
   B. day laborer
   C. cruel tyrant
   D. soldier
   E. stupid fellow

   9.____

10. COMPLEMENT
    A. flattery
    B. contempt
    C. remuneration
    D. tool
    E. completing part

    10.____

KEY (CORRECT ANSWERS)

1. C
2. A
3. B
4. D
5. C
6. A
7. C
8. E
9. B
10. E

TEST 10

DIRECTIONS: Select the letter of the word or expression that MOST NEARLY expresses the meaning of the capitalized word in the group. *PRINT THE LETTER OF THE CORRECT ANSWER IN THE SPACE AT THE RIGHT.*

1. INCESSANTLY
   A. uncertainly   B. continually   C. incidentally
   D. universally   E. quickly

2. INACCESSIBLE
   A. involved   B. erect   C. remote
   D. unjust   E. ignorant

3. DISSENTING
   A. agreeing   B. fooling   C. withholding approval
   D. annoying   E. removing odor

4. REFUTE
   A. disobey
   B. remove to a far point
   C. offend
   D. disprove
   E. strike

5. POTENT
   A. lacking strength   B. making a request   C. having power
   D. soothing   E. perfumed

6. COMPLACENT
   A. businesslike   B. obedient   C. self-satisfied
   D. dishonest   E. careless

7. CYNICAL
   A. poisonous   B. sneering   C. pleasure-loving
   D. doubtful   E. careless

8. DISPARAGE
   A. belittle   B. declare unequal   C. separate
   D. divide   E. dismiss

9. ANARCHY
   A. government by one man   B. government by the rich
   C. government by the poor   D. absence of government
   E. hostility

10. PAYEE
    A. one who becomes wealthy   B. debtor
    C. banker   D. savage rodent
    E. one to whom money is paid

KEY (CORRECT ANSWERS)

1.	B	6.	C
2.	C	7.	D
3.	C	8.	A
4.	D	9.	D
5.	C	10.	E

EXAMINATION SECTION

TEST 1

DIRECTIONS: The questions that follow the paragraphs below are designed to test your appreciation of correctness and effectiveness of expression in English. The paragraphs are presented first in full so that you may read it through for sense. Disregard the errors you find as you will be asked to correct them in the questions that follow. The paragraphs are then presented sentence by sentence with portions underlined and numbered. At the end of this material, you will find numbers corresponding to those below the underlined portions, each followed by five alternatives lettered A, B, C, D, and E. In every case, the usage in the alternative lettered A is the same as that in the original paragraph and is followed by four possible usages. Choose the usage that you consider BEST in each case. *PRINT THE LETTER OF THE CORRECT ANSWER IN THE SPACE AT THE RIGHT.*

The use of the machine produced up to the present time outstanding changes in our modern world. One of the most significant of these changes have been the marked decreases in the length of the working day and the working week. The fourteen-hour day not only has been reduced to one of ten hours but also, in some lines of work, to one of eight or even six. The trend toward a decrease is further evidenced in the longer weekend already given to employees in many business establishment. There seems also to be a trend toward shorter working weeks and longer summer vacations. An important feature of this development is that leisure is no longer the privilege of the wealthy few,—it has become the common right of most people. Using it wisely, leisure promotes health, efficiency and happiness, for there is time for each individual to live their own "more abundant life" and having opportunities for needed recreation.

Recreation, like the name implies, is a process of revitalization. In giving expression to the play instincts of the human race, new vigor and effectiveness are afforded by recreation to the body and to the mind. Of course not all forms of amusement, by no means constitute recreation. Furthermore, an activity that provides recreation for one person may prove exhausting for another. Today, however, play among adults, as well as children, is regarded as a vital necessity of modern life. Play being recognized as an important factor in improving mental and physical health and thereby reducing human misery and poverty.

Among the most important form of amusement available at the present time are the automobile, the moving picture, the radio, television, and organized sports. The automobile, especially, has been a boon to the American people, since it has been the chief means of them getting out into the open. The motion picture, the radio and television have tremendous opportunities to supply whole-some recreation and to promote cultural advancement. A criticism often leveled against organized sports as a means of recreation is because they make passive spectators of too many people. It has been said "that the American public is afflicted with "spectatoritis," but there is some recreational advantages to be gained even from being a spectator at organized games. Such sports afford a release from the monotony of daily toil, get people outdoors and also provide an exhilaration that is tonic in its effect.

2 (#1)

The chief concern, of course, should be to eliminate those forms of amusement that are socially undesirable. There are, however, far too many people who, we know, do not use their leisure to the best advantage. Sometime leisure leads to idleness, and idleness may lead to demoralization. The value of leisure both to the individual and to society will depend on the uses made of it.

The use of the machine <u>produced</u> up to the
                                                          1

1.   A. produced   B. produces   C. has produced   1.____
      D. had produced   E. will have produced

present time many outstanding changes in our modern world. One of the most significant of these changes <u>have been</u> the marked
                                              2

2.   A. have been   B. was   C. were   2.____
      D. has been   E. will be

decreases in the length of the working day and the working week. <u>The fourteen-hour day not only has been reduced</u> to one of ten hours but also, in some lines of work, to one of eight or
                3
even six.

3.   A. The fourteen-hour day not only has been reduced   3.____
      B. Not only the fourteen-hour day has been reduced
      C. Not the fourteen-hour day only has been reduced
      D. The fourteen-hour day has not only been reduced

The trend toward a decrease is further evidenced in the longer week-end <u>already</u> given

4.   A. already   B. all ready   C. allready   4.____
      D. ready   E. all in all

to employees in many business establishments. There seems also to be a trend toward shorter working weeks and longer summer vacations. An important feature of this development is that leisure is no longer the privilege of the wealthy few<u>, —it</u> has become the common right of most people.

5.   A. , —it   B. : it   C. ; it   5.____
      D. ...it   E. omit punctuation

<u>Using it wisely</u>, leisure promotes health, efficiency, and happiness, for there is time for each
      6
individual to live <u>their</u> own "more abundant life" and <u>having</u> opportunities for needed recreation
                 7   8

6.   A. Using it wisely   B. If used wisely   6.____
      C. Having used it wisely   D. Because of its wise use
      E. Because of usefulness

3 (#1)

7. A. their B. his C. its D. our E. your   7.____

8. A. having B. having had C. to have   8.____
   D. to have had E. had

Recreation, <u>like</u> the name implies, is a
　　　　　　9

9. A. like B. since C. through D. for E. as   9.____

process of revitalization. In giving expression to the play instincts of the human race, <u>new vigor and effectiveness are afforded by creation to the body and to the mind.</u>
　　　　　　　　　　　　　　　　　　　　10

10. A. new vigor and effectiveness are afforded by recreation to the body and to   10.____
       the mind
    B. recreation affords new vigor and effectiveness to the body and to the mind
    C. there are afforded new vigor and effectiveness to the body and to the mind
    D. by recreation the body and mind are afforded new vigor and effectiveness
    E. the body and the mind afford new vigor and effectiveness to themselves by
       recreation

Of course not all forms of amusement, <u>by no means,</u> constitute recreation. Furthermore, an
　　　　　　　　　　　　　　　　　　　　11
activity that provides recreation for one person may prove exhausting for another. Today, however, play among adults, as well as children is regarded as a vital necessity of modern life.

11. A. by no means B. by those means C. by some means   11.____
    D. by every means E. by any means

<u>Play being recognized</u> as an important factor in improving mental and physical health and
　　　　12
thereby reducing human misery and poverty.

12. A. . Play being recognized as B. , by their recognizing play as   12.____
    C. . They recognizing play as D. . Recognition of it being
    E. , for play is recognized as

Among the most important forms of amusement available at the present time are the automobile, the moving picture, the radio, television, and organized sports. The automobile, especially, has been a boon to the American people, since it has been the chief means of <u>them</u>
　　13
getting out into the open. The motion picture, the radio and television have tremendous opportunities to supply wholesome recreation and to promote cultural advancement. A criticism often leveled against organized

13. A. them B. their C. his D. our E. the people   13.____

sports as a means of recreation is <u>because</u> they make passive spectators of too many people.
                                      14

14. A. because   B. since   C. as   D. that   E. why   14._____

it has been said <u>"that</u> the American public is afflicted with "spectatoritis," but there <u>is</u> some
                    15   16
recreational advantages to be gained even from being a spectator at organized games.

15. A. "that   B. "that"   C. that"   D. 'that   E. that   15._____

16. A. is   B. was   C. are   D. were   E. will be   16._____

Such sports afford a release from the monotony of daily toil, get people outdoors and also provide an exhilaration that is tonic in its effect. The chief concern, of course, should be to eliminate those forms of amusement that are socially undesirable. There are, however, far too many people <u>who,</u> we know, do not use their leisure to the best advantage. Sometimes leisure
                 17
leads to idleness, and idleness may lead to demoralization. The value of leisure both to the individual and to society will depend on the uses made of it.

17. A. who   B. whom   C. which   D. such as   E. that which   17._____

KEY (CORRECT ANSWERS)

1.	C	11.	E
2.	D	12.	E
3.	E	13.	B
4.	A	14.	D
5.	C	15.	E
6.	B	16.	C
7.	B	17.	A
8.	C		
9.	E		
10.	B		

TEST 2

DIRECTIONS: The questions that follow the paragraphs below are designed to test your appreciation of correctness and effectiveness of expression in English. The paragraphs are presented first in full so that you may read it through for sense. Disregard the errors you find as you will be asked to correct them in the questions that follow. The paragraphs are then presented sentence by sentence with portions underlined and numbered. At the end of this material, you will find numbers corresponding to those below the underlined portions, each followed by five alternatives lettered A, B, C, D, and E. In every case, the usage in the alternative lettered A is the same as that in the original paragraph and is followed by four possible usages. Choose the usage that you consider BEST in each case. *PRINT THE LETTER OF THE CORRECT ANSWER IN THE SPACE AT THE RIGHT.*

When this war is over, no nation will either be isolated in war or peace. Each will be within trading distance of all the others and will be able to strike them. Every nation will be most as dependent on the rest for the maintainance of peace as is any of our own American states on all the others. The world that we have known was a world made up of individual nations, each of which had the privilege of doing about as they pleased without being embarassed by outside interference. The world has dissolved before the impact of an invention, the airplane has done to our world what gunpowder did to the feudal world. Whether the coming century will be a period of further tragedy or one of peace and progress depend very largely on the wisdom and skill with which the present generation adjusts their thinking to the problems immediately at hand. Examining the principal movements sweeping through the world, it can be seen that they are being accelerated by the war. There is undoubtedly many of these whose courses will be affected for good or ill by the settlements that will follow the war. The United States will share the responsibility of these settlements with Russia, England and China. The influence of the United States, however, will be great. This country is likely to emerge from the war stronger than any other nation. Having benefitted by the absence of actual hostilities on our own soil, we shall probably be less exhausted that our allies and better able than them to help restore the devastated areas. However many mistakes have been made in our past, the tradition of America, not only the champion of freedom but also fair play, still lives among millions who can see light and hope scarcely nowhere else.

When this war is over, no nation will <u>either be isolated in war or peace.</u>
                                                          1

1. A. either be isolated in war or peace
   B. be either isolated in war or peace
   C. be isolated in neither war nor peace
   D. be isolated either in war or in peace
   E. be isolated neither in war or peace

1.____

<u>Each</u> will be
 2

2. A. Each   B. It   C. Some   D. They   E. A nation

2.____

2 (#2)

within trading distance of all others and will be able to strike them.
                                     3

3. A. within trading distance of all the others and will be able to strike them   3.____
    B. near enough to trade with and strike all the others
    C. trading and striking the others
    D. within trading and striking distance of all the others
    E. able to strike and trade with all the others

Every nation will be most as dependent on

4. A. most   B. wholly   C. much   D. mostly   E. almost   4.____

the rest for the maintainance of peace as is
                  5

5. A. maintainance   B. maintainence   C. maintenence   5.____
    D. maintenance   E. maintanence

any of our own American states on all the others. The world that we have known as a world made up of individual nations, each
                                                                                    6

6. A. nations, each   B. nations. Each   C. nations: each   6.____
    D. nations; each   E. nations each

of which had the priviledge of doing about as
                    7

7. A. priviledge   B. priveledge   C. privelege   7.____
    D. privalege   E. privilege

they pleased without being
 8

8. A. they   B. it   C. they individually   8.____
    D. he   E. the nations

embarassed by outside interference. That
    9

9. A. embarassed   B. embarrased   C. embaressed   9.____
    D. embarrased   E. embarrassed

world has dissolved before the impact of an invention, the airplane has done to our world what
                                                 10
gunpowder did to the feudal world. Whether the coming century will be a period of further tragedy or one of peace and

3 (#2)

10. A. invention, the   B. invention but the   C. invention: the   10.____
    D. invention. The   E. invention and the

progress <u>depend</u> very largely on the wisdom and skill with which the present generation
             11

11. A. depend   B. will have depended   C. depends   11.____
    D. depended   E. shall depend

<u>adjusts their</u> thinking to the problems immediately at hand.
    12

12. A. adjusts their   B. adjusts there   C. adjusts its   12.____
    D. adjust our   E. adjust it's

<u>Examining the principal movements sweeping through the world, it can be seen</u>
                              13

13. A. Examining the principal movements sweeping through the world, it can be   13.____
    seen
    B. Having examined the principal movements sweeping through the world, it
    can be seen
    C. Examining the principal movements sweeping through the world can be
    seen
    D. Examining the principal movements sweeping through the world, we can
    see
    E. It can be seen examining the principal movements sweeping through the
    world

that they are being <u>accelerated</u> by the war.
                      14

14. A. accelerated   B. acelerated   C. accelerated   14.____
    D. acellerated   E. accelerated

There <u>is</u> undoubtedly many of these whose courses will be affected for good or ill by the
      15
settlements that will follow the war. The United States will share the responsibility of these
settlements with Russia, England and China. The influence of the United

15. A. is   B. were   C. was   D. are   E. might be

States, <u>however</u>, will be great. This country is likely to emerge from the war stronger than any
       16
other nation.

16. A. , however,   B. however,   C. , however   16.____
    D. however   E. ; however,

4 (#2)

Having <u>benefitted</u> by the absence of actual hostilities on our own soil, we shall probably be
       17
less exhausted

17. A. benefitted   B. beniffited   C. benefited   17.____
     D. benifited   E. benafitted

than our allies and better able than <u>them</u> to help restore the devastated areas. However many
                                   18
mistakes have been made in our past, the tradition of America,

18. A. them   B. themselves   C. they   18.____
     D. the world   E. the nations

<u>not only the champion of freedom but also fair play,</u> still lives among millions who can
                  19

19. A. not only the champion of freedom but also fair play,   19.____
     B. the champion of not only freedom but also of fair play,
     C. the champion not only of freedom but also of fair play,
     D. not only the champion but also freedom and fair play,
     E. not the champion of freedom only, but also fair play,

see light and hope <u>scarcely nowhere else.</u>
                  20

20. A. scarcely nowhere else   B. elsewhere   20.____
     C. nowhere   D. scarcely anywhere else
     E. anywhere

KEY (CORRECT ANSWERS)

1.	D	11.	C
2.	A	12.	C
3.	D	13.	D
4.	E	14.	A
5.	D	15.	D
6.	A	16.	A
7.	E	17.	C
8.	B	18.	C
9.	B	19.	C
10.	D	20.	D

WRITTEN ENGLISH EXPRESSION
EXAMINATION SECTION
TEST 1

DIRECTIONS: In each of the sentences below, four portions are underlined and lettered. Read each sentence and decide whether any of the UNDERLINED parts contains an error in spelling, punctuation, or capitalization, or employs grammatical usage which would be inappropriate for carefully written English. If so, note the letter printed under the unacceptable form and indicate this choice in the space at the right. If all four of the underlined portions are acceptable as they stand, select the answer E. (No sentence contains more than ONE unacceptable form.)

1. The revised <u>procedure</u> was <u>quite</u> different <u>than</u> the one which <u>was</u> employed up
                A   B   C   D
 to that time. <u>No error</u>
                E

 1.____

2. <u>Blinded</u> by the storm that <u>surrounded</u> him, his plane <u>kept going</u> in <u>circles</u>.
     A   B   C   D
 <u>No error</u>
   E

 2.____

3. They <u>should</u> give the book to <u>whoever</u> <u>they</u> think deserves <u>it</u>. <u>No error</u>
         A   B   C   D   E

 3.____

4. The <u>government</u> will not consent to your <u>firm</u> <u>sending</u> that package as
         A   B   C
 <u>second class</u> matter. <u>No error</u>
     D   E

 4.____

5. She <u>would have</u> avoided all the trouble <u>that</u> followed if she <u>would have</u> waited
         A   B   C
 ten minutes <u>longer</u>. <u>No error</u>
             D   E

 5.____

6. <u>His</u> poetry, <u>when</u> it was carefully examined, showed <u>characteristics</u> not unlike
  A   B   C
 <u>Wordsworth</u>. <u>No error</u>
     D   E

 6.____

7. <u>In my opinion</u>, based upon long years of research, <u>I think</u> the plan offered by
     A   B
 my opponent is <u>unsound</u>, because it is not <u>founded</u> on true facts. <u>No error</u>
                 C   D   E

 7.____

8. The soldiers of <u>Washington's</u> army at Valley Forge <u>were</u> men ragged in
                        A   B
   <u>appearance</u> but <u>who were</u> noble in character. <u>No error</u>
        C   D   E

9. Rabbits <u>have a distrust</u> of man <u>due to</u> the fact <u>that</u> they are <u>so often</u> shot.
                A   B   C   D
   <u>No error</u>
        E

10. <u>This</u> is the man <u>who</u> I believe <u>is</u> best <u>qualified</u> for the position. <u>No error</u>
       A   B   C   D   E

11. Her voice was <u>not only</u> <u>good</u>, but <u>she</u> also very clearly <u>enunciated</u>.
                    A   B   C   D
   <u>No error</u>
        E

12. <u>Today he</u> is wearing a <u>different</u> suit <u>than</u> the <u>one</u> he wore yesterday. <u>No error</u>
        A   B   C   D   E

13. Our work <u>is</u> to improve the club; if anybody <u>must</u> resign, let it <u>not</u> be you or <u>I</u>.
              A   B   C   D
   <u>No error</u>
        E

14. There was so much talking <u>in back of</u> me <u>as</u> I <u>could</u> not <u>enjoy</u> the music.
                                 A   B   C   D
   <u>No error</u>
        E

15. <u>Being that</u> he is that <u>kind of</u> <u>boy</u>, he cannot be blamed <u>for</u> the mistake.
        A   B   C   D
   <u>No error</u>
        E

16. The king, <u>having read</u> the speech, <u>he</u> and the <u>queen</u> <u>departed</u>. <u>No error</u>
                   A   B   C   D   E

17. I <u>am</u> <u>so tired</u> I <u>can't</u> <u>scarcely</u> stand. <u>No error</u>
      A   B   C   D   E

18. We are <u>mailing bills</u> to our customers <u>in Canada</u>, and, <u>being</u> eager to
                 A   B   C
   clear our books before the new season opens, it is <u>to be hoped</u> they will
                                                            D
   send their remittances promptly. <u>No error</u>
                                          E

19. I reluctantly acquiesced to the proposal. No error   19.____
    A   B   C   D   E

20. It had lain out in the rain all night. No error   20.____
    A   B   C   D   E

21. If he would have gone there, he would have seen a marvelous sight.   21.____
         A   B   C   D
    No error
       E

22. The climate of Asia Minor is somewhat like Utah. No error   22.____
                 A   B   C   D   E

23. If everybody did unto others as they would wish others to do unto them, this   23.____
       A   B   C   D
    world would be a paradise. No error
                                   E

24. This was the jockey whom I saw was most likely to win the race. No error   24.____
    A   B   C   D   E

25. The only food the general demanded was potatoes. No error   25.____
        A   B   C   D   E

KEY (CORRECT ANSWERS)

1.	C		11.	C
2.	A		12.	C
3.	B		13.	D
4.	B		14.	B
5.	C		15.	A
6.	D		16.	A
7.	B		17.	C
8.	D		18.	C
9.	B		19.	E
10.	E		20.	E

21. A
22. D
23. D
24. B
25. E

TEST 2

DIRECTIONS: In each of the sentences below, four portions are underlined and lettered. Read each sentence and decide whether any of the UNDERLINED parts contains an error in spelling, punctuation, or capitalization, or employs grammatical usage which would be inappropriate for carefully written English. If so, note the letter printed under the unacceptable form and indicate this choice in the space at the right. If all four of the underlined portions are acceptable as they stand, select the answer E. (No sentence contains more than ONE unacceptable form.)

1. A party <u>like</u> <u>that</u> <u>only</u> <u>comes</u> once a year. <u>No error</u> 1.____
            A   B   C   D   E

2. <u>Our's</u> <u>is</u> <u>a</u> <u>swift moving</u> age. <u>No error</u> 2.____
     A   B C   D   E

3. The <u>healthy</u> climate soon <u>restored</u> him <u>to</u> his <u>accustomed</u> vigor. <u>No error</u> 3.____
         A   B   C   D   E

4. <u>They</u> needed six typists and hoped that <u>only</u> that <u>many</u> <u>would</u> apply for the position. <u>No error</u> 4.____
    A   B   C   D
                E

5. He <u>interviewed</u> people <u>whom</u> he thought had <u>something</u> <u>to impart</u>. <u>No error</u> 5.____
          A   B   C   D   E

6. <u>Neither</u> of his three sisters <u>is</u> older <u>than</u> <u>he</u>. <u>No error</u> 6.____
     A   B   C D E

7. <u>Since</u> he is <u>that</u> <u>kind</u> of <u>a</u> boy, he cannot be expected to cooperate with us. <u>No error</u> 7.____
    A   B   C   D
   E

8. <u>When passing</u> <u>through</u> the tunnel, the air pressure <u>affected</u> <u>our</u> years. <u>No error</u> 8.____
       A   B   C   D   E

9. <u>The story having</u> a sad ending, <u>it</u> never <u>achieved</u> popularity <u>among</u> the students. <u>No error</u> 9.____
        A   B   C   D
           E

10. <u>Since</u> we are both hungry, <u>shall</u> we go <u>somewhere</u> for lunch? <u>No error</u> 10.____
     A   B   C   D E

2 (#2)

11. <u>Will</u> you please <u>bring</u> this book <u>down to</u> the library and give it to my friend<u>,</u>   11._____
      A   B   C   D
    who is waiting for it? <u>No error</u>
                              E

12. You <u>may</u> <u>have</u> the book; I <u>am</u> finished <u>with</u> it. <u>No error</u>   12._____
         A   B   C   D   E

13. I <u>don't</u> know <u>if</u> I <u>should</u> mention <u>it</u> to her or not. <u>No error</u>   13._____
        A   B   C   D   E

14. Philosophy is not <u>a subject</u> <u>which</u> <u>has to do</u> with philosophers and   14._____
                              A   B   C
    mathematics <u>only</u>. <u>No error</u>
                  D   E

15. The thoughts of the scholar <u>in his library</u> are little different <u>than</u> the old woman   15._____
                                    A   B
    who first said, "<u>It's</u> no use crying over spilt milk<u>.</u>" <u>No error</u>
                 C   D   E

16. A complete <u>system</u> of philosophical ideas <u>are</u> <u>implied</u> in many simple   16._____
                  A   B   C
    <u>utterances.</u> <u>No error</u>
        D   E

17. Even <u>if</u> one has never put <u>them</u> into words, <u>his</u> ideas <u>compose</u> a kind of a   17._____
          A   B   C   D
    philosophy. <u>No error</u>
                E

18. Perhaps it <u>is</u> <u>well enough</u> that most <u>people</u> do not attempt this <u>formulation.</u>   18._____
             A   B   C   D
    <u>No error</u>
    E

19. <u>Leading their</u> ordered lives, this <u>confused</u> <u>body</u> of ideas and feelings <u>is</u>   19._____
         A   B   C   D
    sufficient. <u>No error</u>
                   E

20. Why <u>should</u> we <u>insist upon</u> <u>them</u> <u>formulating</u> it? <u>No error</u>   20._____
           A   B   C   D   E

21. <u>Since</u> it includes <u>something</u> of the wisdom of the ages, it is <u>adequate</u> for the   21._____
       A   B   C
    <u>purposes</u> of ordinary life. <u>No error</u>
        D   E

22. Therefore, I <u>have sought</u> to make a pattern <u>of mine,</u> <u>and so</u> there were, early   22.____
         A   B   C
moments of <u>my trying</u> to find out what were the elements with which I had to
              D
deal. <u>No error</u>
           E

23. I <u>wanted</u> <u>to get</u> <u>what</u> knowledge I <u>could</u> about the general structure of the   23.____
       A   B   C   D
universe. <u>No error</u>
                E

24. I wanted to <u>know</u> <u>if</u> life <u>per se</u> had any meaning or <u>whether</u> I must strive to give   24.____
                 A   B   C   D
it one. <u>No error</u>
              E

25. <u>So,</u> in a <u>desultory</u> way, I <u>began</u> <u>to read</u>. <u>No error</u>   25.____
     A   B   C   D   E

KEY (CORRECT ANSWERS)

1.	C		11.	B
2.	A		12.	C
3.	A		13.	B
4.	C		14.	D
5.	B		15.	B
6.	A		16.	B
7.	D		17.	A
8.	A		18.	C
9.	A		19.	A
10.	E		20.	D

21. E
22. C
23. C
24. B
25. E

EXAMINATION SECTION
TEST 1

DIRECTIONS: In the following questions, you are given a complete sentence which you are to rewrite in your mind, starting with the words given just below it. Make whatever changes the new sentence plan requires, but no others; do not change the overall meaning of the sentence. (Note that you are not correcting a mistake in the original sentence; you are simply changing the construction. The revised sentence should be grammatically correct, but it need not necessarily be a better way of expressing the meaning. There may be more than one way of recasting the sentence but only one will enable you to answer the question.) Read the directions for each question carefully. They may specify that the missing word or expression appear somewhere in the rewritten sentence; they may ask for the next word in the rewritten sentence, the word following a specific word, etc. *PRINT THE LETTER OF THE CORRECT ANSWER IN THE SPACE AT THE RIGHT.*

1. *As a literary genre, the messianic drama falls into the category of myth or romance, for its central figure conforms to the definitions supplied by Northrup Frye, in THE ANATOMY OF CRITICISM, of the mythic hero.*
   REWRITTEN:
   Because its central figure conforms to the definitions of the mythic hero supplied by Northrup Frye, in THE ANATOMY OF CRITICISM, the messianic drama is....

   The NEXT WORD in the rewritten sentence is
   A. into	B. literary	C. categorized
   D. categorically	E. a

2. *In THE EMPEROR JULIAN, the second part of the drama, Ibsen reveals Julian to be a false Messiah.*
   REWRITTEN:
   Julian is....

   Somewhere in the part of the rewritten sentence indicated by dots is the word
   A. reveals	B. by	C. falsified
   D. in which	E. messianic

3. *More interesting, because more subtly hidden, is Chekhov's use of melodrama.*
   REWRITTEN:
   Because it is more....

   The NEXT WORD in the rewritten sentence is
   A. subtly	B. interesting	C. melodramatic
   D. used	E. hidden

4. *Shaw's response to this is to withdraw, partially, from his pubic concerns into a more personal, private, and poetic form of expression.*
   REWRITTEN:
   Shaw responded to this with a ....

   Somewhere in the part of the rewritten sentence indicated by dots is the word
   A. partially B. is to C. withdraws
   D. publicly E withdrawal

   4.____

5. *But life draws him back again, against his will, in the form of uncontrollable instinct.*
   REWRITTEN:
   He is....

   The NEXT WORD in the rewritten sentence is
   A. uncontrollable B. instinctive C. back
   D. drawn E. willful

   5.____

6. *Such destructive criticism accounts, in part, for the unpopularity of this drama, for the modern world wants affirmations.*
   REWRITTEN:
   This drama is

   The NEXT WORD in the rewritten sentence is
   A. unpopular B. accounted C. criticized
   D. in part E. destructive

   6.____

7. *Shaw is just as unable to accept the concept of a malevolent or determined man as to accept the concept of a determined and mindless universe.*
   REWRITTEN:
   It is equally difficult....

   Somewhere in the part of the rewritten sentence indicated by dots is(are) the word(s)
   A. unable B. for him C. just
   D. to conceive E. to understand

   7.____

8. *We know from his descriptions that Leeuwenhoek saw both plant and animal microorganisms and that among them may have been some bacteria.*
   REWRITTEN:
   Among the plant and animal microorganisms which we....

   The nEXT WORD in the rewritten sentence is
   A. saw B. described C. know
   D. assume E. discovered

   8.____

9. *The Japanese quickly overcame the Russian fleet and then landed troops on the mainland of Asia.*
   REWRITTEN:
   The Russian fleet....

   Somewhere in the part of the rewritten sentence indicated by dots is(are) the word(s)
   A. overcame   B. and then   C. defeated
   D. retreated   E. who

10. *Napoleon would not tolerate such an arrangement and sent an army of twenty thousand men to suppress the movement.*
    REWRITTEN:
    The movement....

    The NEXT WORD in the rewritten sentence is
    A. was   B. suppressed   C. would
    D. sent   E. of

11. *To have the program succeed, Marx realized he would need the united support of workingmen all over the world.*
    REWRITTEN:
    Marx realized that the success....

    Somewhere in the part of the rewritten sentence indicated by dots is the word
    A. he   B. would   C. have   D. required   E. to

12. *His beautiful descriptions of nature reflect the poet's deep belief in the closeness of nature to the human soul.*
    REWRITTEN:
    One reflection of....

    The NEXT WORD(S) in the rewritten sentence is(are)
    A. beauty   B. the poet's   C. poetry
    D. the descriptions   E. closeness

13. *The extraordinary play is a chronicle of O'Neill's own spiritual metamorphosis from a messianic into an existential rebel.*
    REWRITTEN:
    O'Neill had undergone....

    The NEXT WORD in the rewritten sentence is
    A. extraordinary   B. existentialism   C. rebelliousness
    D. spirituality   E. a

14. *Considering its great influence, Europe is surprisingly small.*
    REWRITTEN:
    The smallness of Europe is surprising when one....

4 (#1)

The NEXT WORD in the rewritten sentence is
A. influences   B. is   C. considers
D. knows   E. consideration

15. *Until late in the 1800's we knew nothing of a remarkable civilization which was old when the Greeks arrived.*
REWRITTEN:
One remarkable civilization which was old when the Greeks arrived....

Somewhere in the part of the rewritten sentence indicated by dots if the word
A. we   B. unknown   C. knew
D. nothing   E. of

15._____

16. *Our knowledge of Aegean civilization comes largely from the work of two men.*
REWRITTEN:
The work of two men....

The NEXT WORD in the rewritten sentence is
A. comes   B. teaches   C. acknowledges
D. enhances   E. contributes

16._____

17. *Twelve of the most important deities formed a council, which was supposed to meet on snowcapped Mount Olympus, in northern Thessaly.*
REWRITTEN:
Mount Olympus, in northern Thessaly, was supposed to be the....

The NEXT WORD(S) in the rewritten sentence is(are)
A. meeting place   B. council   C. most important
D. epitome   E. deities'

17._____

18. *In the United States the states and local governments regulate the public schools and supply them with funds.*
REWRITTEN:
Public schools in the United States are....

Somewhere in the part of the rewritten sentence indicated by dots is the word
A. them   B. regulate   C. subsidized
D. governed   E. supplied

18._____

19. *The obstacle of distance was partly overcome by the invention of the steamship and the building of the Suez Canal.*
REWRITTEN:
The invention of the steamship and the building of the Suez Canal helped....

Somewhere in the part of the rewritten sentence indicated by dots is the word
A. was   B. overcoming   C. overcome
D. partly   E. shorten

19._____

20. *Although cotton has been used for cloth since ancient times, it was not known in England until the seventeenth century when the East India Company brought "calico" (named for Calicut) from India.*
REWRITTEN:
When the East India Company brought "calico" (named for Calicut) from India in the seventeenth century, it was England's first....

Somewhere in the part of the rewritten sentence indicated by dots is the word
A. known   B. knowledge   C. was
D. although   E. until

21. *In the eighteenth century weaving was still done on the hand loom.*
REWRITTEN:
The hand loom....

Somewhere in the part of the rewritten sentence indicated by dots is the word
A. done   B. on   C. for
D. remained   E. weaves

22. *When rubbed with wool, amber accumulates a charge of static electricity and will then attract small pieces of pith or paper.*
REWRITTEN:
Small pieces of pith or paper can....

The NEXT WORD in the rewritten sentence is
A. accumulate   B. be   C. attract
D. charge   E. then

23. *As a result of the Second World War, cities were devastated and millions were left homeless.*
REWRITTEN:
The Second World War resulted....

Somewhere in the part of the rewritten sentence indicated by dots is(are) the word(s)
A. leaving   B. devastating   C. were
D. deprivation   E. devastated

24. *With the growing urbanization and mechanization of modern life has come increasing recognition of the evils of drunkenness.*
REWRITTEN:
The evils of drunkenness have become....

Somewhere in the part of the rewritten sentence indicated by dots is the word
A. recognition   B. recognized   C. come
D. increasing   E. increased

25. *Chekhov dilutes the melodramatic pathos by qualifying our sympathy for the victims.*
    REWRITTEN:
    The result of Chekhov's....

    The NEXT WORD in the rewritten sentence is
    A. dilution
    B. diluting
    C. melodramatic
    D. qualification
    E. qualifying

    25.____

KEY (CORRECT ANSWERS)

1.	C	11.	D
2.	B	12.	B
3.	A	13.	E
4.	E	14.	C
5.	D	15.	B
6.	A	16.	E
7.	B	17.	A
8.	C	18.	E
9.	E	19.	C
10.	A	20.	D

21. C
22. B
23. A
24. B
25. E

7 (#1)

SOLUTIONS TO PROBLEMS

1. Because its central figure conforms to the definitions of the mythic hero supplied by Northrup Frye, in THE ANATOMY OF CRITICISM, the messianic drama is <u>categorized</u> in the literary genre of myth or romance.

2. Julian is revealed <u>by</u> Ibsen to be a false Messiah, in THE EMPEROR JULIAN, the second part of the drama.

3. Because it is more <u>subtly</u> hidden, Chekhov's use of melodrama is more interesting.

4. Shaw responded to this with a partial <u>withdrawal</u> from his public concerns into a more personal, private, and poetic form of expression.

5. He is <u>drawn</u> back again by life, against his will, in the form of uncontrollable instinct.

6. This drama is <u>unpopular</u> partly because it receives such destructive criticism when the modern world wants affirmations.

7. It is equally difficult for Shaw to accept the concept of a malevolent or determined man as it is <u>for him</u> to accept the concept of a determined and mindless universe.

8. Among the plant and animal microorganisms which we <u>know</u> that Leeuwenhoek saw because of his descriptions, there may have been some bacteria.

9. The Russian fleet was quickly overcome by the Japanese <u>who</u> then landed troops on the mainland of Asia.

10. The movement <u>was</u> suppressed by an army of twenty thousand men sent by Napoleon who would not tolerate such an arrangement.

11. Marx realized that the success of the program <u>required</u> the united support of workingmen all over the world

12. One reflection of <u>the poet's</u> deep belief in the closeness of nature to the human soul can be found in his beautiful descriptions of nature.

13. O'Neill had undergone <u>a</u> spiritual metamorphosis from a messianic into an existential rebel, of which this play is an extraordinary chronicle.

14. The smallness of Europe is surprising when one <u>considers</u> its great influence.

15. One remarkable civilization which was old when the Greeks arrived was <u>unknown</u> to us until late in the 1800's.

16. The work of two men <u>contributes</u> largely to our knowledge of Aegean civilization.

17. Snowcapped Mount Olympus, in northern Thessaly, was supposed to be the meeting place for a council formed by twelve of its most important deities.

18. Public schools in the United States are regulated and supplied with funds by the states and local government.

19. The invention of the steamship and the building of the Suez Canal helped to overcome the obstacle of distance.

20. When the East India Company brought "calico" (named for Calicut) from India in the seventeenth century, it was England's first introduction to cotton, although it has been used for cloth since ancient times.

21. The hand loom was still used for weaving in the eighteenth century.

22. Small pieces of pith or paper can be attracted by amber if it has been rubbed into wool to accumulate a charge of static electricity.

23. The Second World War resulted in the devastation of cities and the leaving homeless of millions.

24. The evils of drunkenness have become increasingly recognized with the growing urbanization and mechanization of modern life.

25. The result of Chekhov's qualifying our sympathy for the victims if the dilution of the melodramatic pathos.

TEST 2

DIRECTIONS: In the following questions, you are given a complete sentence which you are to rewrite in your mind, starting with the words given just below it. Make whatever changes the new sentence plan requires, but no others; do not change the overall meaning of the sentence. (Note that you are not correcting a mistake in the original sentence; you are simply changing the construction. The revised sentence should be grammatically correct, but it need not necessarily be a better way of expressing the meaning. There may be more than one way of recasting the sentence but only one will enable you to answer the question.) Read the directions for each question carefully. They may specify that the missing word or expression appear somewhere in the rewritten sentence; they may ask for the next word in the rewritten sentence, the word following a specific word, etc. *PRINT THE LETTER OF THE CORRECT ANSWER IN THE SPACE AT THE RIGHT.*

1. *While gazing through his microscope at a drop of water, he saw many kinds of creatures with one or a few cells, which wriggled about and devoured food.*
   BEGIN THE SENTENCE WITH:
   Many kinds of creatures with one or a few cells wriggling about….

   Somewhere in the part of the rewritten sentence indicated by dots is(are) the word(s)
   A. he saw
   B. and devoured
   C. which
   D. by him
   E. while gazing

   1.____

2. *The worship of ancestors in China must have arisen in prehistoric times, judging from the references to it in the most ancient Chinese literature.*
   SUBSTITUTE:
   …since the most ancient Chinese literature for judging

   The NEXT WORDS in the rewritten sentence are
   A. the references
   B. is judged
   C. refers it
   D. refers to
   E. from the

   2.____

3. *She divided the bread among them, without considering a share for herself.*
   BEGIN THE SENTENCE WITH:
   She did not….

   Somewhere in the part of the rewritten sentence indicated by dots is(are) the word(s)
   A. divided
   B. when she
   C. without
   D. considering
   E. dividing

   3.____

4. *Since Smith has been a resident here for twenty years, we should give serious consideration to his suggestions.*
   SUBSTITUTE:
   …seriously for give serious

   4.____

127

2 (#2)

The NEXT WORD(S) in the rewritten sentence is(are)
  A. to   B. consideration   C. consider
  D. give consideration   E. would

5. *In the fight for women's suffrage, one judge's decision had little effect, for the most part, upon the ladies' determination.*
   CHANGE:
   effect to effected

   Somewhere in the part of the rewritten sentence indicated by dots is(are) the word(s)
     A. had   B. upon   C. part, upon
     D. had, for   E. part, very little

5.____

6. *His approach to the committee was certainly not conducive to a cordial reception of his proposals, which were, at best, of doubtful validity.*
   BEGIN THE SENTENCE WITH:
   He approached….

   Somewhere in the part of the rewritten sentence indicated by dots is(are) the word(s)
     A. was certainly   B. which was   C. to the
     D. his   E. committee was

6.____

7. *When the thirsty horse had drunk its fill, it trotted briskly down the road.*
   BEGIN THE SENTENCE WITH:
   The thirsty horse….

   The NEXT WORD(S) in the rewritten sentence is(are)
     A. having   B. it trotted   C. when
     D. had   E. had trotted

7.____

8. *This country must either set up flood controls or be prepared to lose billions of dollars annually.*
   BEGIN THE SENTENCE WITH:
   If….

   Somewhere in the part of the rewritten sentence indicated by dots is(are) the word(s)
     A. either   B. must set   C. does not
     D. or   E. country must

8.____

9. *They are not in Boston now, but I think they're going to that city next week.*
   BEGIN THE SENTENCE WITH:
   I think….

9.____

Somewhere in the part of the rewritten sentence indicated by dots is(are) the word(s)
- A. but I
- B. in Boston
- C. to Boston
- D. to that
- E. now, but

10. *Mt. Kinley, in Alaska, is higher than any other mountain in North America.*
INSERT THE WORD:
the after is....

The NEXT WORD in the rewritten sentence is
- A. highest
- B. other
- C. any
- D. than
- E. higher

10._____

11. *As a result of the Industrial Revolution, cities grew very rapidly and the demand for food and raw materials increased.*
BEGIN THE SENTENCE WITH:
A result....

Somewhere in the part of the rewritten sentence indicated by dots is(are) the word(s)
- A. grew
- B. rapidly
- C. the demand
- D. materials increased
- E. increased demand

11._____

12. *Since the late eighteenth century, when the American and French revolutions took place, democracy has had a slow but persistent growth.*
SUBSTITUTE:
After for Since....

Somewhere in the part of the rewritten sentence indicated by dots is(are) the] word(s)
- A. slow
- B. has had
- C. persistently
- D. growth
- E. slow but persistent

12._____

13. *The Treaty of Versailles placed the entire blame for World War I on Germany and her allies.*
BEGIN THE SENTENCE WITH:
Germany....

Somewhere in the part of the rewritten sentence indicated by dots is the word
- A. placed
- B. on
- C. blame
- D. were
- E. entire

13._____

14. *A few years after Harvey's death, other scientists began to study the blood vessels with the aid of microscopes.*
BEGIN THE SENTENCE WITH:
Blood vessels....

Somewhere in the part of the rewritten sentence indicated by dots is(are) the word(s)
- A. by
- B. began
- C. study
- D. to
- E. the study

14._____

15. *This pamphlet is in response to requests of various groups for a more permanent and usable form of this material.*
BEGIN THE SENTENCE WITH:
To provide....

Somewhere in the part of the rewritten sentence indicated by dots is(are) the word(s)
   A. responding to   B. as a response to   C. requested
   D. in response to   E. requesting

15.____

16. *The space science events chosen for development illustrate types of experiences in which mathematics and science have a mutually enhancing effect on each other.*
SUBSTITUTE:
....<u>are illustrated by</u> for <u>illustrate</u>

Somewhere in the part of the rewritten sentence indicated by dots is(are) the word(s)
   A. have had   B. have
   C. had had   D. may be shown to have
   E. has

16.____

17. *The criteria will be useful throughout the course in setting up specific objectives, providing learning experiences, and making periodic evaluations.*
SUBSTITUTE:
<u>course</u>....

The NEXT WORD in the rewritten sentence is
   A. in   B. for   C. to   D. with   E. by

17.____

18. *The objectives of a training program are achieved by learning experiences designed to help the trainees develop those behaviors and abilities designated in the objectives.*
BEGIN THE SENTENCE WITH:
To achieve....

Somewhere in the part of the rewritten sentence indicated by dots is(are) the word(s)
   A. employ   B. to use   C. it will be useful
   D. create   E. to create

18.____

19. *Because all of the suggested facilities will not be available in every community, it remains for the teacher to modify or supplement the following suggestions.*
BEGIN THE SENTENCE WITH:
The teacher....

The word that occurs immediately before the word *modify* is
   A. could   B. might   C. would   D. must   E. should

19.____

20. *Although teachers differ in their ways of organizing and coordinating important parts of their presentations, they agree that the purpose of a lesson is effective and meaningful classroom instruction.*
BEGIN THE SENTENCE WITH:
Although teachers agree....

The FIRST WORD of the main clause in the rewritten sentence is
  A. the   B. teachers   C. they   D. differing   E. it

21. *Many common physical quantities such as temperature, the speed of a moving object, or the displacement of a ship can be expressed as a certain number of units.*
BEGIN THE SENTENCE WITH:
One can express....

The NEXT WORD(S) in the rewritten sentence is(are)
  A. as   B. many   C. in   D. a ship's   E. the

22. *A parallel-tuned circuit, on the other hand, offers a very high impedance to currents of its natural, or resonant, frequency and a relatively low impedance to others.*
BEGIN THE SENTENCE WITH:
A very high impedance....

The NEXT WORDS in the rewritten sentence are
  A. is offered to   B. others to   C. is offered for
  D. is offered by   E. on the other hand

23. *As the term implies, a voltage feedback amplifier transfers a voltage from the output of the amplifier back to its input.*
CHANGE:
....transfers to is transferred

The FIRST WORDS of the rewritten sentence are
  A. A voltage   B. Back to its input
  C. A voltage feedback amplifier   D. In accordance with the term
  E. From the output

24. *Unemployment among youth is a serious problem now, and unless the economy grows much more rapidly in the future than it has during the past decade, today's youngsters will feel the sharp pinch of declining ratios of new employment opportunities to persons seeking work.*
BEGIN THE SENTENCE WITH:
Unless the economy grows, ...

The LAST CLAUSE in the rewritten sentence begins with
  A. today's   B. unemployment   C. and unless
  D. now   E. since

25. *In a great society, talents are evoked and realized, creative minds probe the frontiers of knowledge, expectations of excellence are widely shared.*
BEGIN THE SENTENCE WITH:
A great society....

The NEXT WORDS in the rewritten sentence are
   A. evokes and realizes
   B. talents, creative minds, and expectations of excellence
   C. features
   D. is characterized by
   E. in one in which

25.____

KEY (CORRECT ANSWERS)

1.	D		11.	E
2.	D		12.	C
3.	B		13.	D
4.	C		14.	A
5.	E		15.	D
6.	B		16.	B
7.	A		17.	C
8.	C		18.	A
9.	C		19.	E
10.	A		20.	C

21.	A
22.	E
23.	A
24.	E
25.	E

7 (#2)
SOLUTIONS TO PROBLEMS

1. Many kinds of creatures with one or a few cells, wriggling about and devouring food, were seen <u>by him</u> while he was gazing through his microscope at a drop of water.

2. The worship of ancestors in China must have arisen in prehistoric times since the most ancient Chinese literature <u>refers to</u> it.

3. She did not consider a share for herself <u>when she</u> divided the bread among them.

4. Since Smith has been a resident here for twenty years, we should seriously <u>consider</u> his suggestions.

5. In the fight for women's suffrage, one judge's decision affected the ladies' decision, for the most <u>part, very little</u>.

6. He approached the community in a way <u>which was</u> certainly not conducive to a cordial reception of his proposals, which were, at best, of doubtful validity.

7. The thirsty horse, having drunk its fill, trotted briskly down the road.

8. If this country <u>does not</u> set up flood controls, it must be prepared to lose billions of dollars annually.

9. I think they're going <u>to Boston</u> next week, though they're not in that city now.

10. Mr. Kinley, in Alaska, is the <u>highest</u> mountain in North America.

11. A result of the Industrial Revolution was the very rapid growth of cities and the <u>increased demand</u> for food and raw materials.

12. After the late eighteenth century, when the American and French revolutions took place, democracy grew slowly, but <u>persistently</u>.

13. Germany and her allies <u>were</u> blamed entirely for World War I by the Treaty of Versailles.

14. Blood vessels were studied <u>by</u> other scientists, with the aid of microscopes, a few years after Harvey's death.

15. To provide a more permanent and usable form of this material, <u>in response to</u> the requests of various groups, this pamphlet has been written.

16. The space scientist events chosen for development are illustrated by types of experiences in which mathematics and science <u>have</u> a mutually enhancing effect on each other.

17. Use the criteria throughout the course <u>to</u> set up specific objectives, provide learning experiences, and make periodic evaluations.

18. To achieve the objectives of a training program, <u>employ</u> learning experiences designed to help the trainees develop those behaviors and abilities designated in the objectives.

19. The teacher <u>should</u> modify or supplement the following suggestions because all of the suggested facilities will not be available in every community.

20. Although teachers agree that the purpose of a lesson is effective and meaningful classroom instruction, <u>they</u> differ in their ways of organizing and coordinating important parts of their presentations.]

21. One can express <u>as</u> a certain number of units many common physical quantities such as temperature, the speed of a moving object, or the displacement of a ship.

22. A very high impedance, <u>on the other hand</u>, is offered by a parallel-tuned circuit to currents of its natural, or resonant, frequency and a relatively low impedance to others.

23. <u>A voltage</u> is transferred from the output of the amplifier back to its input by a voltage feedback amplifier, as its name implies.

24. Unless the economy grows much more rapidly in the future than it has during the past decade, today's youngsters will feel the sharp pinch of declining ratios of new employment opportunities to persons seeking work <u>since</u> unemployment among youth is a serious problem now.

25. A great society <u>is one in which</u> talents are evoked and realized, creative minds probe the frontiers of knowledge, expectations of excellence are widely shared.

WRITTEN ENGLISH EXPRESSION
EXAMINATION SECTION
TEST 1

DIRECTIONS: The questions that follow the paragraph below are designed to test your appreciation of correctness and effectiveness of expression in English. The paragraph is presented first in full so that you may read it through for sense. Disregard the errors you find, as you will be asked to correct them in the questions that follow. The paragraph is then presented sentence by sentence with portions underlined and numbered. At the end of this material, you will find numbers corresponding to those below the underlined portions, each followed by five alternatives lettered A to E. In every case, the usage in the alternative lettered A is the same as that in the original paragraph and is followed by four possible usages. Choose the usage you consider BEST in each case. *PRINT THE LETTER OF THE CORRECT ANSWER IN THE SPACE AT THE RIGHT.*

    When this war is over, no nation will either be isolated in war or peace. Each will be within trading distance of all the others and will be able to strike them. Every nation will be most as dependent on the rest for the maintainance of peace as is any of our own American states on all the others. The world that we have known was a world made up of individual nations, each of which has the priviledge of doing about as they pleased without being embarassed by outside interference. The world has dissolved before the impact of an invention, the airplane has done to our world what gunpowder did to the feudal world. Whether the coming century will be a period of further tragedy or one of peace and progress depend very largely on the wisdom and skill with which the present generation adjusts their thinking to the problems immediately at hand. Examining the principal movements sweeping through the world, it can be seen that they are being accelerated by the war. There is undoubtedly many of these whose courses will be affected for good or ill by the settlement that will follow the war. The United States will share the responsibility of these settlements with Russia, England and China. The influence of the United States, however, will be great. This country is likely to emerge from the war stronger than any other nation. Having benefitted by the absence of actual hostilities on our own soil, we shall probably be less exhausted than our allies and better able to help restore the devastated areas. However many mistakes have been made in our past, the tradition of America, not only the champion of freedom but also fair play, still lives among millions who can see light and hope scarcely nowhere else.

1. When this war is over, no nation will <u>either be isolated in war or peace</u>. 1.____
   - A. either be isolated in war or peace
   - B. be either isolated in war or peace
   - C. be isolated in neither war nor peace
   - D. be isolated either in war or in peace
   - E. be isolated neither in war or peace

2. <u>Each</u> 2.____
      A. Each   B. It   C. Some   D. They   E. A nation

2 (#1)

3. within trading distance of all the others and will be able to strike them. 3.____
   A. within trading distance of all the others and will be able to strike them.
   B. near enough to trade with and strike all the others.
   C. trading and striking the others.
   D. within trading and striking distance of all the others.
   E. able to strike and trade with all the others,

4. Every nation will be most as dependent on 4.____
   A. most   B. wholly   C. much   D. mostly   E. almost

5. the rest for the maintainance of peace as is 5.____
   A. maintainance   B. maintainence   C. maintenence
   D. maintenance   E. maintanance

6. any of our own American states on all the others. The world that we have 6.____
   known was a world made up of individual nations, each
   A. nations, each   B. nations. Each   C. nations: each
   D. nations; each   E. nations each

7. of which had the priviledge of doing about as 7.____
   A. priviledge   B. priveledge   C. privelege
   D. privalege   E. privilege

8. they pleased without being 8.____
   A. they   B. it   C. they individually
   D. he   E. the nations

9. embarassed by outside interference. That 9.____
   A. embarassed   B. embarrassed   C. embaressed
   D. embarrased   E. embarressed

10. world has dissolved before the impact of an invention, the airplane has done 10.____
    to our world what gunpowder did to the feudal world. Whether the coming
    century will be a period of further tragedy or one of peace and
    A. invention, the   B. invention but the   C. invention: the
    D. invention. The   E. invention and the

11. progress depend very largely on the wisdom and skill with which the present 11.____
    generation
    A. depend   B. will have depended   C. depends
    D. depended   E. shall depend

12. adjusts their thinking to the problems immediately at hand. 12.____
    A. adjusts their   B. adjusts there   C. adjusts its
    D. adjust our   E. adjust it's

13. Examining the principal movements sweeping through the world, it can be seen   13.____
    A. Examining the principal movements sweeping through the world, it can be seen
    B. Having examined the principal movements sweeping through the world, it can be seen
    C. Examining the principal movements sweeping through the world can be seen
    D. Examining the principal movements sweeping through the world, we can see
    E. It can be seen examining the principal movements sweeping through the world

14. that they are being accelerated by the war.   14.____
    A. accelerated   B. acelerated   C. accelerated
    D. acellerated   E. acelerrated

15. There is undoubtedly many of these whose courses will be affected for good or   15.____
    ill by the settlements that will follow the war. The United States will share the responsibility of these settlements with Russia, England and China. The influence of the United
    A. is   B. were   C. was   D. are   E. might be

16. States, however, will be great. This country is likely to emerge from the war   16.____
    stronger than any other nation.
    A. , however,   B. however,   C. , however
    D. however   E. ; however

17. Having benefitted by the absence of actual hostilities on our own soil, we shall   17.____
    probably be less exhausted
    A. benefitted   B. benifitted   C. benefited
    D. benifited   E. benafitted

18. than our allies and better able than them to help restore the devastated   18.____
    areas. However many mistakes have been made in our past, the tradition of American,
    A. them   B. themselves   C. they
    D. the world   E. the nations

19. not only the champion of freedom but also fair play, still lives among millions   19.____
    who can
    A. not only the champion of freedom but also fair play,
    B. the champion of not only freedom but also of fair play,
    C. the champion not only of freedom but also of fair play,
    D. not only the champion but also freedom and fair play,
    E. not the champion of freedom only, but also fair play,

20. see light and hope <u>scarcely nowhere else.</u> 20.____
    A. scarcely nowhere else
    B. elsewhere
    C. nowhere
    D. scarcely anywhere else
    E. anywhere

KEY (CORRECT ANSWERS)

1.	D	11.	C
2.	A	12.	C
3.	D	13.	D
4.	E	14.	A
5.	D	15.	D
6.	A	16.	A
7.	E	17.	C
8.	B	18.	C
9.	B	19.	C
10.	D	20.	D

TEST 2

DIRECTIONS: The questions that follow the paragraph below are designed to test your appreciation of correctness and effectiveness of expression in English. The paragraph is presented first in full so that you may read it through for sense. Disregard the errors you find, as you will be asked to correct them in the questions that follow. The paragraph is then presented sentence by sentence with portions underlined and numbered. At the end of this material, you will find numbers corresponding to those below the underlined portions, each followed by five alternatives lettered A to E. In every case, the usage in the alternative lettered A is the same as that in the original paragraph and is followed by four possible usages. Choose the usage you consider BEST in each case. *PRINT THE LETTER OF THE CORRECT ANSWER IN THE SPACE AT THE RIGHT.*

    The use of the machine produced up to the present time outstanding changes in our modern world. One of the most significant of these changes have been the marked decreases in the length of the working day and the working week. The fourteen-hour day not only has been reduced to one of ten hours but also, in some lines of work, to one of eight or even six. The trend toward a decrease is further evidenced in the longer weekend already given to employees in many business establishments. There seems also to be a trend toward shorter working weeks and longer summer vacations. An important feature of this development is that leisure is no longer the privilege of the wealthy few,—it has become the common right of most people. Using it wisely, leisure promotes health, efficiency, and happiness, for there is time for each individual to live their own "more abundant life" and having opportunities for needed recreation.

    Recreation, like the name implies, is a process of revitalization. In giving expression to the play instincts of the human race, new vigor and effectiveness are afforded by recreation to the body and to the mind. Of course not all forms of amusement, by no means, constitute recreation. Furthermore, an activity that provides recreation for one person may prove exhausting for another. Today, however, play among adults, as well as children, is regarded as a vital necessity of modern life. Play being recognized as an important factor in improving mental and physical health and thereby reducing human misery and poverty,

    Among the most important forms of amusement available at the present time are the automobile, the moving picture, the radio, television, and organized sports. The automobile, especially, has been a boon to the American people, since it has been the chief means of them getting out into the open. The motion picture, the radio and television have tremendous opportunities to supply wholesome recreation and to promote cultural advancement. A criticism often leveled against organized sports as a means of recreation is because they make passive spectators of too many people. It has been said "that the American public is afflicted with "spectatoritis," but there is some recreational advantages to be gained even from being a spectator at organized games. Such sports afford a release from the monotony of daily toil, get people outdoors and also provide an exhilaration that is tonic in its effect.

    The chief concern, of course, should be to eliminate those forms of amusement that are socially undesirable. There are, however, far too many people who, we know, do not use their leisure to the best advantage. Sometimes leisure leads to idleness, and idleness may lead to demoralization. The value of leisure both to the individual and to society will depend on the uses made of it.

2 (#2)

1. The use of the machine <u>produced</u> up to the 1.____
   A. produced B. produces C. has produced
   D. had produced E. will have produced

2. present time many outstanding changes in our modern world. One of the most 2.____
   significant of these changes <u>have been</u> the marked
   A. have been B. was C. were
   D. has been E. will be

3. decreases in the length of the working day and the working week. <u>The fourteen- 3.____
   hour day not only has been reduced</u> to one of ten hour but also, in some line of work, to
   one of eight or even six.
   A. The fourteen-hour day not only has been reduced
   B. Not only the fourteen-hour day has been reduced
   C. Not the fourteen-hour day only has been reduced
   D. The fourteen-hour day has not only been reduced
   E. The fourteen-hour day has been reduced not only

4. The trend toward a decrease is further evidenced in the longer week end <u>already</u> 4.____
   given
   A. already B. all ready C. allready D. ready E. all in all

5. to employees in many business establishments. There seems also to be a trend 5.____
   toward shorter working weeks and longer summer vacations. An important
   feature of this development is that leisure is no longer the privilege of the
   wealthy few,<u>—it</u> has become the common right of people.
   A. ,—it B. : it C. ; it
   D. ...it E. omit punctuation

6. <u>Using it wisely,</u> leisure promotes health, efficiency, and happiness, for there is 6.____
   time for
   A. Using it wisely B. If used wisely
   C. Having used it widely D. Because of its wise use
   E. Because of usefulness

7. each individual to live <u>their</u> own "more abundant life" 7.____
   A. their B. his C. its D. our E. your

8. and <u>having</u> opportunities for needed recreation. 8.____
   A. having B. having had C. to have
   D. to have had E. had

9. Recreation, <u>like</u> the name implies, is a 9.____
   A. like B. since C. through D. for E. as

10. process of revitalization. In giving expression to the play instincts of the human race, <u>new vigor and effectiveness are afforded by recreation to the body and to the mind.</u>
    A. new vigor and effectiveness are afforded by recreation to the body and to the mind.
    B. recreation affords new vigor and effectiveness to the body and to the mind.
    C. there are afforded new vigor and effectiveness to the body and to the mind.
    D. by recreation the body and mind are afforded new vigor and effectiveness.
    E. the body and the mind afford new vigor and effectiveness to themselves by recreation.

11. Of course not all forms of amusement, <u>by no means,</u> constitute recreation. Furthermore, an activity that provides recreation for one person may prove exhausting for another. Today, however, play among adults, as well as children, is regarded as a vital necessity of modern life.
    A. by no means   B. by those means   C. by some means
    D. by every means   E. by any means

12. <u>Play being recognized</u> as an important factor in improving mental and physical health and thereby reducing human misery and poverty.
    A. . Play being recognized as   B. . by their recognizing play as
    C. . They recognizing play as   D. . Recognition of it being
    E. , for play is recognized as

13. Among the most important forms of amusement available at the present time are the automobile, the moving picture, the radio, television, and organized sports. The automobile, especially, has been a boon to the American people, since it has been the chief means of <u>them</u> getting out into the open. The motion picture, the radio, and television have tremendous opportunities to supply wholesome recreation and to promote cultural advancement. A criticism often leveled against organized
    A. them   B. their   C. his   D. our   E. the people

14. sports as a means of recreation is <u>because</u> they make passive spectators of too many people
    A. because   B. since   C. as   D. that   E. why

15. It has been said "<u>that</u> the American public is afflicted with "spectatoritis,"
    A. "that   B. "that"   C. that"   D. 'that   E. that

16. but there <u>is</u> some recreational advantages to be gained even from being a spectator at organized games
    A. is   B. was   C. are   D. were   E. will be

17. Such sports afford a release from the monotony of daily toil, get people outdoors and also provide an exhilaration that is tonic in its effect. The chief concern, of course, should be to eliminate those forms of amusement that are socially undesirable. There are, however, far too many people who, we know, do not use their leisure to the best advantage. Sometimes leisure leads to idleness, and idleness may lead to demoralization. The value of leisure both to the individual and to society will depend on the uses made of it.

   A. who   B. whom   C. which   D. such as   E. that which

17._____

KEY (CORRECT ANSWERS)

1.	C	11.	E
2.	D	12.	E
3.	E	13.	B
4.	A	14.	D
5.	C	15.	E
6.	B	16.	C
7.	B	17.	A
8.	C		
9.	E		
10.	B		

TEST 3

DIRECTIONS: The questions that follow the paragraph below are designed to test your appreciation of correctness and effectiveness of expression in English. The paragraph is presented first in full so that you may read it through for sense. Disregard the errors you find, as you will be asked to correct them in the questions that follow. The paragraph is then presented sentence by sentence with portions underlined and numbered. At the end of this material, you will find numbers corresponding to those below the underlined portions, each followed by five alternatives lettered A to E. In every case, the usage in the alternative lettered A is the same as that in the original paragraph and is followed by four possible usages. Choose the usage you consider BEST in each case. *PRINT THE LETTER OF THE CORRECT ANSWER IN THE SPACE AT THE RIGHT.*

    The process by which the community influence the actions of its members is known as social control. Imitation which takes place when the action of one individual awakens the impulse in each other to attempt the same thing, is one of the means by which society gains this control. When the child acts as other members of his group acts, he receives their approval. There is also adults who seem almost equally imitative. Advertisers of luxuries are careful to convey the idea that important persons use and indorse the merchandise concerned, for most folk will do their utmost to follow the example of those whom they think are the best people.

    Akin to imitation as a means of social control is suggestion. The child is taught to think and feel as do the adults of his community. He is neither encouraged to be critical or to examine all the evidence for his opinion. To be sure, there would be scarcely no time left for other things if school children would have been expected to have considered all sides of every matter on which they hold opinions. It is possible, however and probably very desirable, for pupils of high school age to learn that the point of view accepted in their community is not the only one, and that many widely held opinions may be mistaken. The way in which suggestion operates is illustrated by advertising methods. Depending on skillful suggestion, argument is seldom used in advertising. The words accompanying the picture do not seek to convince the reason but only to intensify the suggestion.

    Some persons are more susceptible to suggestion than others. The ignorant person is more easily moved to action by suggestion than he who is well educated, education developing the habit of criticizing what is read and heard. Whoever would think clearly, freeing himself from emotion and prejudice, must beware of the influence of the crowd or mob. A crowd is a group of people in a highly suggestible condition, each stimulating the feelings of the others until an intense uniform emotion has control of the group. Such a crowd may become irresponsible and anonymous, and whose activity may lead in any direction. The educated person ought to be beyond reach of this kind of appeal, no one may be said to have a real individuality who, at the mercy of the suggestions of others, allow themselves to succumb to "crowd-mindedness."

1.   The process by which the community <u>influence the action of its members</u> is known as social control.   1._____
    A. influence the actions of its members
    B. influences the actions of its members
    C. had influenced the actions of its members
    D. influences the actions of their members
    E. will influence the actions of its members

143

2. Imitation which takes place when the action
   A. which   B. , which   C. —which   D. that   E. what

3. of one individual awakens the impulse in each other to attempt the same thing, is one of the means by which society gains this control.
   A. each other   B. some other   C. one other
   D. another   E. one another

4. When the child acts as other members of his group acts, he receives their approval
   A. acts   B. act   C. has acted
   D. will act   E. will have acted

5. There is also adults who seem almost equally imitative.
   A. is   B. are   C. was   D. were   E. will be

6. Advertisers of luxuries are careful to convey the idea that important persons use and indorse the merchandise concerned, for most folk will do their utmost to follow the example of those whom they think are the best people.
   A. whom   B. what   C. which
   D. who   E. that which

7. Akin to imitation as a means of social control is suggestion. The child is taught to think and feel as do the adults of his community.
   A. do   B. does   C. had   D. may   E. might

8. He is neither encouraged to be critical or to examine all the evidence for his opinions.
   A. neither encouraged to be critical or to examine
   B. neither encouraged to be critical nor to examine
   C. either encouraged to be critical or to examine
   D. encouraged either to be critical nor to examine
   E. not encouraged either to be critical or to examine

9. To be sure, there would be scarcely no time left for other things.
   A. scarcely no   B. hardly no   C. scarcely any
   D. enough   E. but only

10. if school children would have been expected
    A. would have been   B. should have been   C. would have
    D. were   E. will be

11. to have considered all sides of every matter on which they hold opinions
    A. to have considered   B. to be considered
    C. to consider   D. to have been considered
    E. and have considered

12. It is possible, <u>however</u> and probably very desirable, for pupils of high school age to learn that the point of view accepted in their community is not the only one, and that many widely held opinions may be mistaken. The way in which suggestion operates is illustrated by advertising methods.
    A. , however
    B. however,
    C. ; however,
    D. however
    E. , however,

    12.____

13. <u>Depending on skillful suggestion, argument is seldom used in advertising.</u> The words accompanying the picture do not seek to convince the reason but only to intensify the suggestion.
    A. Depending on skillful suggestion, argument is seldom used in advertising.
    B. Argument is seldom used by advertisers, who depend instead on skillful suggestion.
    C. Skillful suggestion is depended on by advertisers instead of argument.
    D. Suggestion, which is more skillful, is used in place of argument by advertisers.
    E. Instead of suggestion, depending on argument is used by skillful advertisers.

    13.____

14. Some persons are more susceptible to suggestion than others. The ignorant person is more easily moved to action by suggestion than he who is well educated, <u>education developing</u> the habit of criticizing what is read and heard. Whoever would think clearly, freeing himself from emotion and prejudice, must beware of the influence of the crowd or mob.
    A. , education developing
    B. , education developed by
    C. , for education develops
    D. . Education will develop
    E. . Education developing

    14.____

15. A crowd is a group of people in a highly suggestible condition, each stimulating the feelings of the others until an intense uniform emotion has control of the group. Such a crowd may become irresponsible and anonymous, <u>and whose</u> activity may lead in any direction. The educated person ought to be beyond reach of this kind of appeal,
    A. and whose
    B. whose
    C. and its
    D. and the
    E. and the crowd's

    15.____

16. <u>no</u> one may be said to have a real individuality who,
    A. , no
    B. : no
    C. —no
    D. . No
    E. omit punctuation

    16.____

17. at the mercy of the suggestions of others, <u>allow themselves</u> to succumb to "crowd-mindedness."
    A. allow themselves
    B. allows themselves
    C. allow himself
    D. allows himself
    E. allow ourselves

    17.____

KEY (CORRECT ANSWERS)

1. B
2. B
3. D
4. B
5. B

6. D
7. A
8. E
9. C
10. D

11. C
12. E
13. B
14. C
15. C

16. D
17. D

TEST 4

DIRECTIONS: The questions that follow are designed to test your appreciation of correctness and effectiveness of expression in English. In each statement, you will find underlined portions. In some cases, the usage in the underlined portion is correct. In other cases, it requires correction. Five (5) alternatives lettered A to E are presented. In every case, the usage in the alternative lettered A (No Change) is the same as that in the original statement and is followed by four (4) other possible usages. Choose the usage you consider BEST in each case. *PRINT THE LETTER OF THE CORRECT ANSWER IN THE SPACE AT THE RIGHT.*

Sample Questions and Answers

Questions
1. John ran home.
   A. No change
   B. run
   C. runned
   D. runed
   E. None right

2. John aint here.
   A. No change
   B. ain't
   C. am not
   D. arre'nt
   E. None right

Answers
1. A
   (The sentence is obviously correctly written. Therefore, the correct answer is A. No change.)

2. E
   (word aint is unacceptable in usage today. The correct answer should be is not or isn't. Since the alternatives offered in A, B, C, and D are all incorrect, the correct answer is, therefore, E. None right.)

1. It takes study to become a lawyer.
   A. No change
   B. before you can become
   C. in becoming
   D. for becoming
   E. None right

2. His novels never concern old people who wished to be young.
   A. No change
   B. concerned old people who wish
   C. concerned old people who had wished
   D. concern old people who wish
   E. None right

3. You people like we boys as much as we. boys like you.
   A. No change
   B. we boys as much as us
   C. us boys as much as us
   D. us boys as much as we
   E. None right

4. Jane and Mary are <u>more poised than he, but Bill is the brighter</u> of all three. 4.____
   A. No change
   B. more poised than he, but Bill is the brightest
   C. more poised than him, but Bill is the brightest
   D. more poised than him, but Bill is the brighter
   E. None right

5. It is a thing of joy, beauty, <u>and containing</u> terror. 5.____
   A. No change   B. and abounding in   C. and of
   D. and contains   E. None right

6. If he <u>was able, he would demand that she return</u> home. 6.____
   A. No change
   B. were able, he would demand that she return
   C. was able, he would demand that she returns
   D. were able, he would demand that she returns
   E. None right

7. He <u>use to visit when he was supposed to.</u> 7.____
   A. No change
   B. use to visit when he was suppose to.
   C. used to visit when he was suppose to.
   D. used to visit when he was supposed to.
   E. None right

8. I saw the <u>seamstress and asked her for a needle, hook and eye,</u> and thimble. 8.____
   A. No change
   B. seamstress, and asked her for a needle, hook and eye
   C. seamstress and asked her for a needle, hook and eye
   D. seamstress, and asked her for a needle, hook and eye
   E. None right

9. A tall, young<u>, man threw the heavy, soggy,</u> ball. 9.____
   A. No change
   B. , young man threw the heavy, soggy
   C. young man threw the heavy, soggy
   D. , young man threw the heavy soggy
   E. None right

10. The week <u>before my sister, thinking of other matters,</u> thrust her hand into the fire. 10.____
    A. No change
    B. before, my sister thinking of other matters
    C. before my sister thinking of other matters
    D. before my sister, thinking of other matters
    E. None right

11. We seldom eat a roast at our house. <u>My</u> wife being a vegetarian. 11.____
    A. No change   B. my   C. , my
    D. ; my   E. None right

3 (#4)

12. I have only one request. <u>That</u> you leave at once. 12.____
    A. No change B. that C. ; that
    D. : that E. None right

13. I admire stimulating conversation and appreciative listening, <u>therefore</u> I talk to myself. 13.____
    A. No change B. , therefore, C. therefore
    D. therefore, E. None right

14. The <u>battle-scarred veteran was as bald as a newlaid egg.</u> 14.____
    A. No change
    B. battlescarred veteran was as bald as a new-laid egg.
    C. battle-scarred veteran was as bald as a new-laid egg.
    D. battle scarred veteran was as bald as a new laid egg.
    E. None right

15. The President's proclamation opened with the following statement: <u>"The intention of the government is,</u> to make the people aware of one of the greatest dangers to the safety of the country." 15.____
    A. No change
    B. , "The intention of the government is
    C. : "The intention of the government is:
    D. : "The intention of the government is
    E. None right

16. I get only a <u>week vacation after two years work.</u> 16.____
    A. No change
    B. week's vacation after two years work.
    C. week's vacation after two years' work.
    D. weeks vacation after two years work.
    E. None right

17. <u>You first</u> wash your brush in turpentine. Then hang it up to dry. 17.____
    A. No change B. First you C. First you should
    D. First E. None right

18. The teacher insisted that you and <u>he were responsible for the mistakes of Joe and me.</u> 18.____
    A. No change
    B. him were responsible for the mistakes of Joe and me.
    C. he were responsible for the mistakes of Joe and I.
    D. him were responsible for the mistakes of Joe and I.
    E. None right

19. <u>He sometimes in a generous mood gave the flowers to others</u> that he had grown in his garden. 19.____
    A. No change
    B. He in a generous mood sometimes gave to others the flowers
    C. In a generous mood he sometimes gave the flowers to others

D. Sometimes in a generous mood he gave to others the flowers
E. None right

20. He is attending college since September.
    A. No change
    B. has attended
    C. was attending
    D. attended
    E. None right

21. He enjoys me hearing him singing.
    A. No change
    B. my hearing him sing
    C. me hearing him sing
    D. me hearing his singing
    E. None right

22. Even patients of anxious temperament occasionally feel an element of primitive pleasure.
    A. No change
    B. temperament occassionally feel an element of primitive
    C. temperment occassionally feel an element of primitive
    D. temperament occasionally feel an element of primitive
    E. None right

23. Undoubtedly even the loneliest patient feels tranquill.
    A. No change
    B. Undoubtably even the loneliest patient feels tranquill.
    C. Undoubtedly even the loneliest patient feels tranquil.
    D. Undouvtably even the loneliest patient feels tranquil.
    E. None right

24. Sophmores taking behavioral psychology must pay a labratory fee.
    A. No change
    B. Sophmores taking behavioral psychology must pay a laboratory
    C. Sophmores taking behavioral psychology must pay a laboratory
    D. Sophomores taking behavioral psychology must pay a laboratory
    E. None right

25. Atheletic heroes often find their studies an unnecessary hinderance.
    A. No change
    B. Athletic heroes often find their studies an unnecessary hinderance.
    C. Athletic heros often find their studies an unnecessary hindrance.
    D. Athletic heroes often find their studies an unnecessary hindrance.
    E. None right

KEY (CORRECT ANSWERS)

1. A
2. D
3. D
4. B
5. E

6. B
7. D
8. D
9. C
10. E

11. C
12. D
13. E
14. C
15. D

16. C
17. D
18. A
19. D
20. B

21. B
22. A
23. E
24. C
25. D

TEST 5

DIRECTIONS: The questions that follow are designed to test your appreciation of correctness and effectiveness of expression in English. In each statement, you will find underlined portions. In some cases, the usage in the underlined portion is correct. In other cases, it requires correction. Five (5) alternatives lettered A to E are presented. In every case, the usage in the alternative lettered A (No Change) is the same as that in the original statement and is followed by four (4) other possible usages. Choose the usage you consider BEST in each case. *PRINT THE LETTER OF THE CORRECT ANSWER IN THE SPACE AT THE RIGHT.*

1. Many of the <u>childrens' games were supervised by students who's</u> interests lay in teaching.
    A. No change
    B. children's games were supervised by students who's
    C. childrens' games were supervised by students whose
    D. children's games were supervised by students whose
    E. None right

2. I told <u>father that a college president</u> was invited to speak.
    A. No change
    B. Father that a college president
    C. father that a College President
    D. Father that a College president
    E. None right

3. One should either <u>be able to read</u> German or French.
    A. No change
    B. be able either to read
    C. be able to either read
    D. be able to read either
    E. None right

4. <u>Twirling around on my piano stool, my head begins to swim.</u>
    A. No change
    B. My head begins to swim, twirling around on my piano stool.
    C. Twirling around on my piano stool, a dizzy spell ensues.
    D. Twirling around on my piano stool, I begin to feel dizzy.
    E. None right

5. As the reverberations of my deep bass voice <u>increase, one of my dogs starts</u> to howl.
    A. No change
    B. increase, one of my dogs start
    C. increases, one of my dogs start
    D. increases, one of my dogs starts
    E. None right

6. Roy bellows at Eve that it is <u>her, not he</u> who shouts.
    A. No change
    B. her, not him
    C. she, not him
    D. she, not he
    E. None right

7. The only man who I think will knock out whoever he fights is Roy.   7._____
   A. No change
   B. who I think will knock out whomever
   C. whom I think will knock out whomever
   D. whom I think will knock out whoever
   E. None right

8. The more prettier of my eyes is the glass one.   8._____
   A. No change   B. most pretty   C. prettier
   D. prettiest   E. None right

9. When a good actress cries, she feels real sad.   9._____
   A. No change   B. feels real sadly
   C. feels really sadly   D. really feels sad
   E. None right

10. I asked the instructor what I should do with this examina-paper. Can you   10._____
    imagine what he said?
    A. No change   B. ? Can you imagine what he said.
    C. ? Can you imagine what he said?   D. . Can you imagine what he said.
    E. None right

11. Not wishing to hurt my friend's feeling, I tell him that I am leaving, because   11._____
    I have a previous engagement.
    A. No change   B. I tell him that I am leaving
    C. , I tell him that I am leaving   D. I tell him that I am leaving,
    E. None right

12. I remember Utopia College where I studied, while I lived abroad, when the   12._____
    world was at peace.
    A. No change
    B. College where I studied, while I lived abroad
    C. College, where I studied while I lived abroad
    D. College, where I studied, while I lived abroad
    E. None right

13. Would Robinson Crusoe have survived if he was less unimaginative?   13._____
    A. No change   B. were   C. had been
    D. would have been   E. None right

14. Neither time nor tide delay either the traveler or the stay-at-home from his   14._____
    pastime.
    A. No change
    B. delays either the traveler or the stay-at-home from his
    C. delay either the traveler or the stay-at-home from their
    D. delays either the traveler or the stay-at-home from their
    E. None right

15. When the committee reports its findings somebody will lose their composure. 15._____
    A. No change
    B. their findings somebody will lose their
    C. their findings somebody will lose his
    D. its findings somebody will lose his
    E. None right

16. The worst one of the problems which is confronting me concern money. 16._____
    A. No change					B. are confronting me concern
    C. is confronting me concerns		D. are confronting me concerns
    E. None right

17. Far in the distance rumble the motors of the convoy, but there's no signs of it yet. 17._____
    A. No change
    B. rumbles the motors of the convoy, but there is
    C. rumbles the motors of the convoy, but there are
    D. rumble the motors of the convoy, but there are
    E. None right

18. Neither of the patients believe that Hansel or Gretel are alive. 18._____
    A. No change					B. believes that Hansel or Gretel are
    C. believe that Hansel or Gretel is	D. believes that Hansel or Gretel is
    E. None right

19. Its in untried emergencies that a man's native metal receives its ultimate test. 19._____
    A. No change
    B. It's in untried emergencies that a man's native metal receives its
    C. It's in untried emergencies that a man's native metal receives its
    D. It's in untried emergencies that a man's native metal receives its'
    E. None right

20. Expecting my friends to be on time, their tardiness seemed almost an insult. 20._____
    A. No change
    B. it seemed that their tardiness was almost an insult.
    C. resentment at their tardiness grew in my mind.
    D. only an accident on the way could account for their tardiness.
    E. None right

21. On first reading "The Wasteland" seems obscure. 21._____
    A. No change
    B. On first reading it, "The Wasteland" seems obscure.
    C. "The Wasteland" seems an obscure poem on first reading it.
    D. On first reading "The Wasteland," it seems an obscure poem.
    E. None right

4 (#5)

22. A special light will be required to inspect the engine.   22.____
    A. No change
    B. To inspect the engine, a special light will be required.
    C. To inspect the engine, you will require a special light.
    D. To inspect the engine, your light must be special.
    E. None right

23. When mixing it, the cake batter must be thoroughly beaten.   23.____
    A. No change   B. mixing   C. being mixed
    D. being mix   E. None right

24. What you say may be different from me.   24.____
    A. No change   B. from what I say C. than me
    D. than mine   E. None right

25. Trumping is playing a trump when another suit has been led.   25.____
    A. No change   B. to play   C. if you play
    D. where one plays   E. None right

KEY (CORRECT ANSWERS)

1.	D	11.	C
2.	A	12.	C
3.	D	13.	C
4.	D	14.	B
5.	A	15.	D
6.	D	16.	D
7.	B	17.	D
8.	C	18.	D
9.	D	19.	B
10.	A	20.	E

21. B
22. B
23. C
24. B
25. A

EXAMINATION SECTION
TEST 1

DIRECTIONS: Each question or incomplete statement is followed by several suggested answers or completions. Select the one that BEST answers the question or completes the statement. *PRINT THE LETTER OF THE CORRECT ANSWER IN THE SPACE AT THE RIGHT.*

Questions 1-10.

DIRECTIONS: Some of the following groups of words make correct, complete sentences. Others contain errors or are not complete sentences. If the group of words makes a correct, complete sentence, indicate 0 (ZERO). If the group of words does not make a correct, complete sentence, indicate the letter of the part which contains the error or which should be changed to make a complete sentence.

1. A. No one
   B. knows
   C. why he came
   D. or where he went.

2. A. What do you
   B. think
   C. is the answer
   D. to the problem?

3. A. What
   B. fun to be
   C. on the
   D. relay team!

4. A. Hope
   B. to win
   C. the next set
   D. of races.

5. A. The class giving
   B. a play
   C. for parents
   D. and friends

6. A. How
   B. exciting
   C. winning
   D. would be!

1.____

2.____

3.____

4.____

5.____

6.____

7. A. Richard
    B. likes
    C. swimming and to water ski
    D. in the summer.   7.____

8. Charles   8.____
    A. has played
    B. football for
    C. three years and
    D. will again next year.

9. He likes   9.____
    A. all sports the coach
    B. says Charles is the best
    C. all-round athlete
    D. the school has ever had.

10. A. Although the weather   10.____
    B. is cold,
    C. we can see
    D. signs of nature's reawakening

Questions 11-25.

DIRECTIONS: In each sentence below, one or more letters are underlined. Indicate C (CORRECT) or W (WRONG) in the space at the right of each sentence in which the letter or letters underlined are CORRECTLY capitalized.

11. Tom learned much about the sea from captain Jones.   11.____

12. Dear sir: 12.____

13. Will you please send us information about tours through the east? I am   13.____
    especially interested in seeing

14. india and the   14.____

15. Taj Mahal.   15.____

16. Yours very sincerely, John Brown   16.____

17. Jeffrey calls his dog Frisker.   17.____

18. He bought the dog from a neighbor who lives a black north of Jeffrey.   18.____

19. He got the dog last Summer.   19.____

20. Once we visited the United States senate.   20.____

3 (#1)

21. Washington Irving wrote "The legend of Sleepy Hollow." 21._____
22. My uncle says that story is one of his favorites. 22._____
23. I shall always remember my drive through the Cumberland Mountains. 23._____
24. "It is early," the guide said, "but we shall be ready to start the tour soon." 24._____
25. "I am glad," Jane replied. "we are very eager to go." 25._____

Questions 26-50.

DIRECTIONS: From the list of choices below, select the punctuation mark which should be used where the parenthesis appear in each sentence. Indicate the letter of the correct answer in the space at the right.

- A. Colon
- B. Comma
- C. Dash
- D. Double quotation marks
- E. Exclamation point
- F. Hyphen
- G. Question mark
- H. Period
- I. Semicolon
- J. Single quotation marks
- K. No punctuation

26. Last night we heard a bird call from the woods near our home(). 26._____
27. We wondered what it could be() 27._____
28. Because we had not heard the call before() we did not recognize it as the song of a whippoorwill. 28._____
29. Are you ready for school now() Nancy? 29._____
30. School does not begin until 8()30. 30._____
31. I want to arrive in time to see Miss Smith() the music teacher. 31._____
32. I should like to join the chorus() but tryouts come during the time when I have band practice. 32._____
33. It is possible() of course() that band practice will be over before the tryouts are. 33._____
34. The snow() covered bushes looked like ghosts huddled together. 34._____
35. On the farm were the following() 35._____
36. cows() pigs() chickens() and geese. 36._____

4 (#1)

37. The farm is near Lincoln() Nebraska.   37._____

38. On our vacation, we traveled in Minnesota() and Wisconsin() and Michigan.   38._____

39. What interesting experiences we had()   39._____

40. Someone said the world would end on August 7() 1987.   40._____

41. Sammy's bright() happy smile made him popular with everyone.   41._____

42. We appreciate your help; however() it is too late to continue.   42._____

43. Da Vinci() who was famous as a painter() was also a scientist and an inventor. 43._____

44. Please mail the package to 412 Park Avenue() Denver.   44._____

45. Mother said the border was three and three() fourths inches wide.   45._____

46. Miss Swanson() our home economics teacher() has taught us to bake bread.   46._____

47. The Home Economics Club is for everyone() who enjoys cooking or sewing.   47._____

48. The path was steep and rough() nevertheless, we did not turn back.   48._____

49. "Father likes to quote the lines, ()He prayeth best who loveth best,()" said Joanne. 49._____

50. "Do you like poetry()" asked James.   50._____

KEY (CORRECT ANSWERS)

1.	0	11.	W	21.	W	31.	B	41.	B
2.	0	12.	W	22.	C	32.	B	42.	B
3.	B	13.	W	23.	C	33.	B	43.	B
4.	A	14.	W	24.	C	34.	F	44.	B
5.	A	15.	C	25.	W	35.	A	45.	F
6.	0	16.	C	26.	H	36.	B	46.	B
7.	C	17.	C	27.	H	37.	B	47.	K
8.	D	18.	C	28.	B	38.	K	48.	I
9.	A	19.	W	29.	B	39.	E	49.	J
10.	0	20.	W	30.	A	40.	B	50.	G

TEST 2

DIRECTIONS: Each question or incomplete statement is followed by several suggested answers or completions. Select the one that BEST answers the question or completes the statement. *PRINT THE LETTER OF THE CORRECT ANSWER IN THE SPACE AT THE RIGHT.*

Questions 1-10.

DIRECTIONS: In answering Questions 1 through 10, indicate the CORRECT answer.

1. Perhaps the jewelry is 1.____
   A. hers   B. her's   C. hers'

2. _____ the best musician in our group. 2.____
   A. You're   B. Your

3. _____ painting did you think was most pleasing? 3.____
   A. Who's   B. Whose

4. The children gave _____ pennies to buy a gift for the sick child. 4.____
   A. there   B. their   C. they're

5. It is _____ too warm for ice fishing. 5..____
   A. all together   B. altogether

6. _____ going to rain soon. 6.____
   A. Its   B. It's

7. The speaker used so many _____ that we found it tiresome to listen to him. 7.____
   A. wells   B. wells'   C. well's

8. _____ eyes were sparkling happily. 8.____
   A. Agneses   B. Agne's   C. Agnes's

9. We faced the mountain and called, but only our _____ answered us. 9.____
   A. echos   B. echoes

10. Alice likes skiing and skating, _____. 10.____
    A. to   B. two   C. too

Questions 11-25.

DIRECTIONS: In answering Questions 11 through 25, indicate which choice makes the sentence CORRECT?

11. Paul _____ hardly started to wade when his foot slipped, and he fell into the water. 11.____
    A. had   B. had not

161

12. _____ across a chair was a beautiful Spanish shawl.   12._____

13. The book had been _____ by some careless child.   13._____
    A. teared   B. tore   C. torn

14. The clown _____ a tattered hat.   14._____
    A. weared   B. wore   C. worn

15. Someone had _____ all of the orange juice.   15._____
    A. drinked   B. drank   C. drunk

16. Our dog _____ like music.   16._____
    A. don't   B. doesn't

17. The child had _____ so softly that we were not sure that we had heard him   17._____
    correctly.
    A. speaked   B. spoke   C. spoken

18. Jim had _____ across the pool twice before I even got started.   18._____
    A. swimmed   B. swam   C. swum

19. The _____ milk   19._____
    A. freezed   B. frozen   C. froze

20. _____ the bottle.   20._____
    A. busted   B. bursted   C. burst

21. _____ are always teasing each other.   21._____
    A. She and Joanne   B. Her and Joanne

22. Where had you _____ the drawings?   22._____
    A. lay   B. laid   C. lain

23. Children were _____ on the stairway.   23._____
    A. sitting   B. setting

24. I have _____ most of the invitations.   24._____
    A. writed   B. wrote   C. written

25. Holding onto a flimsy thread of its web,   25._____
    A. a spider swayed back and forth.
    B. we saw a spider swaying back and forth.

Questions 26-50.

DIRECTIONS: In answering Questions 26 through 50, indicate from the even-numbered items
             that which makes the sentence correct. Select from the odd-numbered choices
             that rule which makes the sentence incorrect.

3 (#2)

26. John is wittier than   26.____
    A. I   B. me   C. myself

27. A. Nominative case, predicate pronoun   27.____
    B. Objective case, object of a preposition
    C. Reflexive pronoun, to refer to the speaker
    D. Nominative case, subject of a verb understood

28. No one could catch Jack and   28.____
    A. I   B. me   C. myself

29. A. Nominative case, predicate pronoun   29.____
    B. Objective case, object of a verb
    C. Objective case, object of a preposition
    D. Reflexive pronoun, to refer to the speaker

30. One of the children _____ an excellent violinist.   30.____
    A. is   B. are

31. A. Singular verb, to agree with One   31.____
    B. Singular verb, to agree with violinist
    C. Plural verb, to agree with children

32. Neither Tom nor his brothers _____ able to play yesterday.   32.____
    A. was   B. were

33. A. Singular verb, to agree with Tom   33.____
    B. Singular verb, to agree with Neither
    C. Plural verb, to agree with brothers
    D. Plural verb, to agree with a compound subject

34. Either the team members or the coach _____ asked to pick up the trophy.   34.____
    A. was   B. were

35. A. Singular verb, to agree with coach   35.____
    B. Singular verb, to agree with team
    C. Plural verb, to agree with members
    D. Plural verb, to agree with a compound object

36. Both of the boys _____ excellent students.   36.____
    A. is   B. are

37. A. Singular verb, to agree with Both   37.____
    B. Plural verb, to agree with Both
    C. Plural verb, to agree with boys

38. Everybody at the party _____ having a good time.   38.____
    A. was   B. were

4 (#2)

39. A. Singular verb, to agree with Everybody
     B. Singular verb, too agree with party
     C. Singular verb, to agree with time
     D. Plural verb, to agree with Everybody

39.____

40. Which of the two dresses do you think is the
    A. prettier   B. prettiest

40.____

41. A. Comparative degree of an adjective
     B. Superlative degree of an adjective
     C. Comparative degree of the adverb

41.____

42. Miss Brown sent Bob and _____ postcards from France.
    A. I   B. me   C. myself

42.____

43. A. Nominative case, predicate pronoun
     B. Objective case, direct object of the verb
     C. Objective case, indirect object of the verb
     D. Reflexive pronoun, to refer to the speaker

43.____

44. Because the gift came from Jerry and _____, we appreciated it very much.
    A. he   B. him

44.____

45. A. Nominative case, predicate pronoun
     B. Objective case, object of the verb
     C. Objective case, object of a preposition

45.____

46. Everyone present had _____ own opinion about the problem.
    A. his   B. their

46.____

47. A. Singular pronoun, to refer to Everyone
     B. Singular pronoun, to refer to problem
     C. Plural pronoun, to refer to Everyone

47.____

48. It is _____ too late to call now.
    A. sure   B. surely

48.____

49. A. Adjective, to modify It
     B. Adverb, to modify is
     C. Adverb, to modify to call

49.____

50. The sunset was _____ beautiful.
    A. real   B. very

50.____

51. A. Adjective, to modify sunset
     B. Adverb, to modify was
     C. Adverb, to modify beautiful

51.____

KEY (CORRECT ANSWERS)

1. A	11. A	21. A	31. A	41. A
2. A	12. A	22. B	32. B	42. B
3. B	13. C	23. A	33. C	43. B
4. B	14. B	24. C	34. A	44. B
5. B	15. C	25. A	35. A	45. C
6. B	16. B	26. A	36. B	46. A
7. A	17. C	27. A	37. B	47. A
8. C	18. C	28. B	38. A	48. B
9. B	19. B	29. B	39. A	49. B
10. C	20. C	30. A	40. A	50. B
				51. C

TEST 3

DIRECTIONS: Each question or incomplete statement is followed by several suggested answers or completions. Select the one that BEST answers the question or completes the statement. *PRINT THE LETTER OF THE CORRECT ANSWER IN THE SPACE AT THE RIGHT.*

Questions 1-14.

DIRECTIONS: In answering Questions 1 through 14, indicate from the even-numbered items that which makes the sentence correct. Select from the odd-numbered choices that rule which makes the sentence incorrect.

1. Velvet feels
   A. soft
   B. softly

2. A. Adjective, to modify Velvet
   B. Adverb, to modify feels
   C. Adjective, to modify feels

3. Jane asked _____ rang the doorbell.
   A. who
   B. whom

4. A. Objective case, object of asked
   B. Objective case, object of rang
   C. Nominative case, subject of rang

5. For _____ did you ask when you telephoned the office?
   A. who
   B. whom

6. A. Nominative case, subject of did ask
   B. Objective case, object of the verb
   C. Objective case, object of a preposition

7. _____ can laugh at himself will probably make an agreeable companion.
   A. Whoever
   B. whomever

8. A. Nominative case, subject of will make
   B. Nominative case, subject of can laugh
   C. Objective case, object of can laugh
   D. Objective case, object of will make

9. Father thinks that _____ tries can succeed.
   A. whoever
   B. whomever

10. A. Nominative case, subject of can succeed
    B. Nominative case, subject of tries
    C. Objective case, object of thinks

11. Our government is run by _____ the people elect.   11._____
    A. whoever   B. whomever

12. A. Objective case, object of a preposition   12._____
    B. Objective case, object of elect
    C. Nominative case, predicate nominative

13. The child speaks   13._____
    A. distinct   B. distinctly

14. A. Adverb, to modify speaks   14._____
    B. Adjective, to modify child
    C. Adjective, to modify speaks

Questions 15-24.

DIRECTIONS: Indicate the letter of the part of speech which correctly describes the use of the word, phrase, or clause in the following sentences. Choose the parts of speech from the column at the right.

                          Parts of Speech

15. Early   A. Adjective   15._____

16. May   B. Adverb   16._____

17. Plains   C. Conjunction   17._____

18. was rising   D. Interjection   18._____

19. of rosy splendor   E. Noun   19._____

20. above   F. Preposition   20._____

21. to be alive and free   G. Pronoun   21._____

22. and   H. Verb   22._____

23. the   23._____

24. we   24._____

Questions 25-34.

DIRECTIONS: Indicate the title of the book which would be alphabetized FIRST among the choices that follow.

25. A. WIND IN THE PINES   B. NIGHT WIND   25._____
    C. IVANHOE   D. KIDNAPED

26. A. VELVET SHOES   B. USES OF COAL   26._____
    C. WONDERLAND   D. YOUNG HEROES

27. A. BUFFALO BILL   B. CARAVAN   27._____
    C. DAYS TO REMEMBER   D. FROM DAWN TO DUSK

28. A. TELEPHONE TALES   B. TELEGRAPHIC CODES   28._____
    C. TEMPEST IN A TEAPOT   D. TELLING SEA TALES

29. A. LEARNING TO SWIM   29._____
    B. THE LAST LEAF
    C. THE SPIDER
    D. THE MAN WITHOUT A COUNTRY

30. A. FOG   B. THE GYPSY   30._____
    C. HOBBIES   D. A PECK OF GOLD

31. A. SKATING   B. SILVER SHIPS   31._____
    C. THE MAN WITH THE MASK D. TIMBER COUNTRY

32. A. WILD ANIMALS I HAVE KNOWN   32._____
    B. FOOL'S GOLD
    C. THE JESTER
    D. UNCLE JAKE'S ADVENTURES WITH A WILDCAT

33. A. PAUL REVERE'S RIDE   B. PRIVATE ZOO   33._____
    C. LOCHINVAR   D. TOP SECRET

34. A. ONCE UPON A STORYTIME   34._____
    B. HEROES OF PROGRESS
    C. HEART, HEALTH, AND HAPPINESS
    D. HENRIETTA HARVEY'S HAVEN

KEY (CORRECT ANSWERS)

1.	A	11.	B	21.	F	31.	C
2.	A	12.	A	22.	C	32.	B
3.	A	13.	B	23.	A	33.	C
4.	C	14.	A	24.	G	34.	C
5.	B	15.	A	25.	C		
6.	C	16.	E	26.	B		
7.	A	17.	E	27.	A		
8.	B	18.	H	28.	B		
9.	A	19.	F	29.	B		
10.	A	20.	A	30.	A		

MATHEMATICS
EXAMINATION SECTION
TEST 1

DIRECTIONS: Each question or incomplete statement is followed by several suggested answers or completions. Select the one that BEST answers the question or completes the statement. *PRINT THE LETTER OF THE CORRECT ANSWER IN THE SPACE AT THE RIGHT.*

Questions 1-60.

DIRECTIONS: For problems 1 through 22, compute an answer for each. For problems 23 through 60, select an answer from among the four choices given.

1. Add: 215
            86
           193

2. From 761, subtract 257.

3. Multiply: 206
              ×57

4. Divide: 25)4175

5. Divide: 408 ÷ 4

6. Multiply: 1/2 × 3/4

7. Add: 3.4 and 1.16

8. Find the product of 3.4 and 7.8.

9. If 12.36 is divided by 6, what is the quotient?

10. What is 2/3 of 300?

11. Subtract: 9.67
              4.85

12. Divide: 8 ÷ 1/3

13. If John spends $6.45, how much change should he receive from a $10 bill?

14. What is the average (mean) of 81, 72, and 78?

15. How many cubic centimeters are in the volume of a rectangular box 6 cm long, 4 cm wide, and 4 cm high?

16. What is the perimeter of a rectangle with length 6 and width 2?

17. A number of test scores are arranged as follows: 58, 65, 65, 75, 85, 85, 99. What is the median score?

18. Solve for x: 4x + 1 = 17.

19. Solve for x: $\frac{6}{10} = \frac{x}{30}$

20. A team lost 40% of its games. If the team played 30 games, how many games were lost?

21. On a map, 1 centimeter represents 12 kilometers. How many kilometers does 2 ½ centimeters on the map represent?

22. What is the area of a square with each side of length 5?

23. ☐ - 186 = 54

    Which number makes this open sentence TRUE?
    A. 132   B. 238   C. 240   D. 250

24. The sum of 3/5 and 2/3 is
    A. 5/8   B. 5/15   C. 19/15   D. 6/8

25. What is he LEAST common denominator of the fractions 1/2, 2/3, and 5/6?
    A. 36   B. 18   C. 12   D. 6

26. Which of the following has the same value as 17/5?
    A. 12   B. 2 2/5   C. 3 2/5   D. 5 2/3

27. When written as a percent, the fraction 3/4 is
    A. 25%   B. 66 2/3%   C. 75%   D. 86 1/2%

28. If 45,534 people were at a football game, what would be the total attendance reported to the nearest thousand?
    A. 40,000   B. 46,000   C. 47,000   D. 50,000

29. Which number represents seventy thousand eight hundred?
    A. 7,080   B. 70,080   C. 70,800   D. 78,000

30. When listed in order from smallest to largest, which fraction would be the FIRST?
    A. 1/5   B. 1/2   C. 1/3   D. 1/4

31. The cost of a telephone call was listed as:
    $1.00 for the first 3 minutes
    $0.30 for each additional minute
    What would be the total cost of a telephone call that was 6 minutes long?
    A. $1.80   B. $1.90   C. $2.00   D. $2.80

32. If A and B are points on the circle, then AB is a(n)
    AB is a(n)
    A. arc
    B. chord
    C. diameter
    D. radius

33. In the triangle ABC, what is the ratio of AB to BC?
    A. 5:6
    B. 5:7
    C. 7:5
    D. 6:5

34. Which number has the GREATEST value?
    A. .0824   B. .1032   C. .125   D. .091

35. Mr. White had a balance of $325.15 in his checking account. If he made a deposit of $75, what would be the amount of the new balance in his checking account?
    A. $250.15   B. $324.40   C. $325.90   D. $400.15

36. The sum of -11 and -8 is
    A. -19   B. -3   C. 3   D. 19

37. One day in March the highest temperature was 8 degrees C and the lowest was -3 degrees C.
    What was the total number of degree difference between the highest and lowest temperatures that day?
    A. 8   B. 11   C. 3   D. 5

38. The expression 10^3 is equal to
    A. -0   B. 300   C. 1,000   D. 10,000

39. On the accompanying graph, point A has coordinates
    A. (0,3)
    B. (1,3)
    C. (3,0)
    D. (3,1)

40. The circle graph to the right shows how each tax dollar is spent in Salt Lake City.
    What is the LARGEST part of the tax dollar spent for?
    A. Repairs
    B. Salaries
    C. Education
    D. Parks

40._____

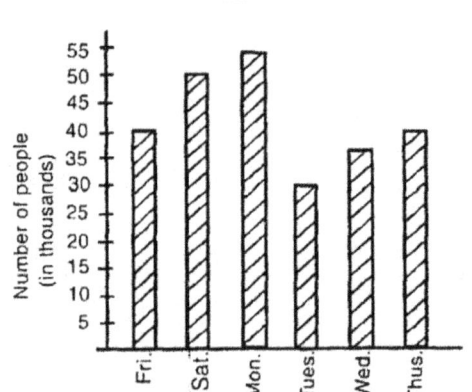

41. The graph to the right shows the number of people attending each game of the World Series one year.
    On which day did the FEWEST number of people attend a World Series game?
    A. Friday
    B. Monday
    C. Tuesday
    D. Thursday

41._____

42. The graph to the right represents the relationship between distance traveled and flying time for a certain airplane.
    How many hours of flying time did the airplane require to travel 450 miles?
    A. 2 1/2
    B. 2
    C. 3
    D. 3 1/2

42._____

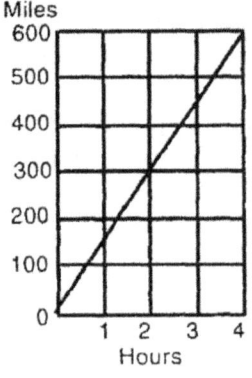

Airplane Travel

43. Which is the prime number?
    A. 21   B. 99   C. 101   D. 125

43._____

44. Mr. Ford bought a t-shirt for $15.00 and had to pay a 7% sales tax.
    If he gave the clerk $20, what should his change be?
    A. $1.05   B. $3.95   C. $4.95   D. $16.05

44._____

45. Of carpeting costs $9.50 a square meter, what is the total cost of carpeting an entire room floor which is 3 meters by 4 meters?
    A. $133   B. $114   C. $85.50   D. $66.50

45._____

46. Ruby buys a television set with a $25 downpayment and 6 installment payments of $20.
    The total cost of the television set is
    A. $95   B. $120   C. $145   D. $150

46._____

47. Carver High School has an enrollment of 50 freshmen, 40 sophomores, 60 juniors, and 30 seniors.
    What is the ratio of the number of juniors to the total enrollment?
    A. 1:6 B. 1:4 C. 2:3 D. 1:3

48. The area pf a circle with a radius of 5 centimeters is
    A. 10π cm² B. 20π cm² C. 25π cm² D. 100π cm²

49. The circumference of a circle with a radius of 4 is
    A. 2π B. 4π C. 8π D. 16π

50. Which of the following is a picture of a cylinder?
    A.   B.   C.   D.

51. A nail is placed against a ruler as shown in the above drawing.
    How many centimeters long is the nail?
    A. 7.0 B. 6.5 C. 6.0 D. 5.5

52. Each race began at 11:00 A.M. The winner ran the course in 2 hours and 19 minutes.
    At what time did the winner cross the finish line?
    A. 8:41 A.M. B. 12:19 P.M. C. 1:19 P.M. D. 2:19 P.M.

53. Each house above represents 10,000 homes.
    What is the total number of homes represented by the figures?
    A. 40,500 B. 45,000 C. 405,000 D. 450,000

54. A radio is sold in a store for $54.50. The same radio can be ordered through the mail for $24.50 plus $1.50 for postage.
    How much would be saved by buying the radio through the mail?
    A. $28.50 B. $30.00 C. $30.50 D. $53.00

55. A stereo which usually sells for $450 is on sale for 1/3 off. 55.____
What is the sale price?

56. Mary has a board 12 1/2 inches long. 56.____
If she cuts 1 1/4 inches off the board, how long will the board be?
   A. 10 1/4 inches B. 11 inches C. 11 1/4 inches D. 11 1/2 inches

57. If 3 cases of canned fruit cost $27, then 1 of these cases would cost 57.____
   A. $81   B. $18   C. $3   D. $9

58. Carlo earns $18 per hour at a part-time job. 58.____
How much does he earn in a day when he works 5 1/2 hours?
   A. $90   B. $99   C. $108   D. $112.50

59. How many kilometers are there in the 10,000 meter run? 59.____
   A. 1   B. 2   C. 10   D. 100

60. What is the probability of obtaining a head when a coin is tossed? 60.____
   A. 1   B. 1/2   C. 1/3   D. 1/4

KEY (CORRECT ANSWERS)

#	Ans	#	Ans	#	Ans	#	Ans	#	Ans	#	Ans
1.	494	11.	4.82	21.	30	31.	B	41.	C	51.	B
2.	504	12.	24	22.	25	32.	B	42.	C	52.	C
3.	11,742	13.	$3.55	23.	C	33.	B	43.	C	53.	B
4.	167	14.	77	24.	C	34.	C	44.	B	54.	A
5.	102	15.	96	25.	D	35.	D	45.	B	55.	C
6.	3/8	16.	16	26.	C	36.	A	46.	C	56.	C
7.	4.56	17.	75	27.	C	37.	B	47.	D	57.	D
8.	26.52	18.	4	28.	C	38.	C	48.	C	58.	B
9.	2.06	19.	18	29.	C	39.	B	49.	C	59.	C
10.	20	20.	12	30.	A	40.	C	50.	A	60.	B

SOLUTIONS TO PROBLEMS

1. 215 + 86 + 193 = 494

2. 761 − 257 = 504

3. (206)(57) = 11,742

4. 4175 ÷ 25 = 167

5. 408 ÷ 4 = 102

6. $(\frac{1}{2})(\frac{3}{4}) = \frac{3}{8}$

7. 3.40 + 1.16 = 4.56

8. (3.4)(7.8) = 26.52

9. 12.36 ÷ 6 = 2.06

10. $\frac{2}{3}(30) = 20$

11. 9.67 − 4.85 = 4.82

12. $8 \div \frac{1}{3} = (8)(\frac{3}{1}) = 24$

13. $10 - $6.45 = $3.55

14. (81+72+78) ÷ 3 = 77

15. Volume = (6)(4)(4) = 96 cubic cen.

16. Perimeter = (2)(6+2) = 16

17. Median = (7+1)/2 = 4th score = 75

18. If 4x + 1 = 17, then 4x = 16. Solving, x = 4

19. If $\frac{6}{10} = \frac{x}{30}$, then 10x = 180. Solving, x = 18

20. (.40)(30) = 12 games lost

21. $(2\frac{1}{2})(12) = 30$ kilometers

22. Area = 5^2 = 25

23. Missing number = 54 + 186 = 240

24. $\frac{3}{5} + \frac{2}{3} = \frac{9}{15} + \frac{10}{15} = \frac{19}{15}$

25. Least common denominator of $\frac{1}{2}, \frac{2}{3}$, and $\frac{5}{6}$ is 6.

26. $\frac{17}{5} = 3\frac{2}{5}$

27. $\frac{3}{4} = (\frac{3}{4})(100)\% = 75\%$

28. 46,534 is 47,000 to the nearest thousand

29. Seventy thousand eight hundred = 70,800

30. $\frac{1}{5}$ is smaller than $\frac{1}{2}, \frac{1}{3}$, and $\frac{1}{4}$

31. Total cost = $1.00 + (3)(.30) = $1.90

32. AB is a chord since it joins 2 points on the circle but does not pass through the center.

33. AB:BC = 5:7

34. .125 is larger than .0824, .1032, and .091

35. New balance = $325.15 + $75 = $400.15

36. (-11) + (-8) = -19

37. 8 – (-3) = 11 degrees difference

38. 10^3 = (10)(10)(10) = 1000

39. Point A has coordinates (1,3)

40. Education represents the largest section.

41. On Tuesday, about 30,000 people attended the World Series. This was the lowest attendance figure in the chart.

42. On the graph, 450 miles corresponds to 3 hours.

43. 101 is prime since it can only be divided evenly by itself and 1.

44. $15 + (.07)($15) = $16.05. Then, $20 - $16.05 = $3.95

45. Total cost = ($9.50)(3)(4) = $114.00

46. Total cost = $25 + (6)($20) = $145

47. Juniors: total enrollment = 60:180 = $\frac{1}{3}$

48. Area = $(\pi)(5cm)^2 = 25\pi$ cm^2

49. Circumference = $(2\pi)(4) = 8\pi$

50. Selection A represents a cylinder. (The other 3 selections are cube, cone, triangular prism.)

51. Length of nail = 6.5 cm

52. 11:00 A.M. + 2 hrs. 19 min. = 1:19 P.M.

53. (10,000)(4.5) = 45,000

54. Amount saved = $54.50 - $24.50 - $1.50 = $28.50

55. Sale price = $450 − ($\frac{1}{3}$)($450) = $300

56. $12\frac{1}{2}$" - $1\frac{1}{4}$" = $11\frac{1}{4}$ inches

57. 1 case costs $27 ÷ 3 = $9

58. ($18)(5 ½) = $99

59. Since 1 km = 1000m, 10 kilometers = 10,000 meters

60. In tossing a coin, the probability of getting a head = $\frac{1}{2}$

BASIC MATHEMATICS
EXAMINATION SECTION
TEST 1

DIRECTIONS: Each question or incomplete statement is followed by several suggested answers or completions. Select the one that BEST answers the question or completes the statement. *PRINT THE LETTER OF THE CORRECT ANSWER IN THE SPACE AT THE RIGHT.*

1. Add: 4,898 + 7 + 361 + 26 1.____
   A. 5,282 B. 5,292 C. 5,382 D. 5,392

2. Subtract: 7,006 − 5,797 2.____
   A. 1,209 B. 1,219 C. 1,309 D. 2,209

3. Multiply: 2,759 3.____
   ×806

   A. 234,274 B. 2,173,754 C. 2,174,754 D. 2,223,754

4. Divide: $87\sqrt{72,732}$ 4.____
   A. 835 B. 836 C. 846 D. 976

5. Combine: (+6)−(−4)+(−3) 5.____
   A. −1 B. +1 C. +7 D. +13

6. Simplify: [(−7) × (−8)] ÷ (−4) 6.____

7. Add: 1 4/9 + 5 3/4 7.____
   A. 6 7/13 B. 6 7/36 C. 7 7/36 D. 7 12/36

8. Subtract: 5 4/7 − 3 3/4 8.____
   A. 1 23/28 B. 2 1/28 C. 2 1/3 D. 2 23/28

9. Multiply: 2 3/4 × 6 1/3 9.____
   A. 12 1/4 B. 13 1/4 C. 17 5/12 D. 18 5/12

10. Divide: 5 1/4 ÷ 1 1/2 10.____
    A. 3/7 B. 3 1/4 C. 3 1/2 D. 7 7/8

11. Add: 536.5 + .03 + 8.209 11.____
    A. .545009 B. .544739 C. 544.739 D. 545.009

12. Subtract: 879.3 − 57.64 12.____
    A. 3.029 B. 30.29 C. 821.66 D. 8216.6

2 (#1)

13. Multiply: 4.87
    ×73.8

    A. 35.8406   B. 35.9406   C. 358.406   D. 359.406

14. Divide: 053√9.858

    A. 18.6   B. 18.7   C. 186   D. 187

15. Add: .5 + 1/4

    A. .075   B. .75   C. 5/4   D. 21/4

16. What is 4.4% of 48?

    A. 2.112   B. 10.90   C. 21.12   D. 211.2

17. 16 is what percent of 8?

    A. 1/2%   B. 5%   C. 50%   D. 200%

18. 24 is 48% of

    A. 2   B. 5   C. 50   D. 500

19. A set of stereo records sells for $26.00. It is discounted 12% for a special sale.
    What is the sale price?

    A. $3.12   B. $12.88   C. $14.00   D. $22.88

20.
TABLE A. ACME MORTGAGE COMPANY
$3200 LOAN – 3/4 OF 1% INTEREST

Month	Payment	Principal Paid/Month	Interest Paid/Month
1	$27.98	$25.58	$2.40
2	27.98	25.77	2.21
3	27.98	25.96	2.02
4	27.98	26.15	1.83
5	27.98	20.35	1.63
6	27.98	26.55	1.43
7	27.98	26.75	1.23
8	27.98	26.95	1.03
9	27.98	27.15	.83
10	27.98	27.35	.63
11	27.98	27.56	.42
12	27.93	27.77	.16
TOTAL	$335.82	$320.00	$15.82

Acme Mortgage Company charges 3/4 of 1% (.0075) on the unpaid balance per month. Bowman Mortgage Company charges 8% per year on the total loan.

Which company charges the MOST amount of interest on a $320 loan held for one year?
A. Bowman charges the most.
B. Acme charges the most.
C. Acme and Bowman charge the same.
D. Insufficient information to determine.

21.
Percent of Auto Insurance Discounts for
High School Students with Certain
Grade Point Averages

Policy Coverage	Grade Point Average Percent of Discount		
	A	B	C
Liability	33 1/3%	33 1/3%	10%
Comprehensive	20%	10%	-
Collision	25%	20%	-

Waldo Brown has an A average. The regular 6-month amounts to be paid for insurance before discounts follow:
  Liability $18.00
  Comprehensive $20.00
  Collision $60.00
  Total $98.00

How much does Waldo pay for insurance for 6 months?
A. $25.00   B. $48.00   C. $73.00   D. $146.00

22. Mrs. Ortiz had a fire in an apartment she owns. Repairing the damage will cost about $800. The apartment is valued at $11,000 and is insured for $10,000. Mrs. Ortiz had paid $28.00 a year for 12 years for her insurance. The insurance company will pay the full amount of the claim ($800).
Which of the following statements are TRUE?
I. The amount of the claim is more than the amount Mrs. Ortiz paid for the insurance.
II. The insurance company should pay $11,000 for this claim.
III. If the house had been completely burned, the insurance company would pay $11,000.
IV. The maximum claim Mrs. Ortiz could collect is $10,000.
The CORRECT answer is:
A. I, IV   B. I, II   C. I, III   D. II, III

23. When two coins are tossed, what is the chance that both will be tails?
1 in ____.
A. 1   B. 2   C. 3   D. 4

4 (#1)

24. If 5 teams are in a football league, how many games are necessary to allow each team to play every team one time?
_____ games.
A. 10   B. 15   C. 20   D. 25

25. Five women agreed to help collect money for the Salvation Army. They collected the following amounts: $43.00, $82.00, $16.00, $139.00, and $75.00. What was the AVERAGE amount collected?
A. $70   B. $71   C. $75   D. $355

26. From the following statements, determine the CORRECT conclusion.
 I. If Joe is a boxer, then Joe is strong.
 II. Joe is not strong.
The CORRECT answer is:
A. Joe is a boxer.
B. Joe is not a boxer.
C. Joe could be a boxer.
D. All boxers are strong.

27. The graph shown at the right represents the distribution of the Rexroth family budget.
How much would the Rexroths have to earn per month if they are to save $1,800 per year.
A. $150
B. $1,650
C. $1,800
D. $21,600

Pie chart: Medical $\frac{1}{12}$, Saving $\frac{1}{12}$, Clothing $\frac{1}{6}$, Rent $\frac{1}{3}$, Food $\frac{1}{3}$

28.

	S	M	T	W	T	F	S
Mr. Tarver	?	8	8	8	8	8	3
Mr. Ramirez	1	8	9	9	8	8	5

Time and one-half is paid on Saturdays and for hours worked beyond 8 hours each day. Double-time is paid for Sunday work.
Mr. Tarver would have to work how many hours on Sunday to earn as much as Mr. Ramirez?
 Regular time: $2.00/hour
 Time and one-half: $3.00/hour
 Double time: $4.00/hour
_____ hour(s).
A. 1   B. 4   C. 5   D. 16

29. Dorothy Cook wrote the following four checks:
 $93.47 for a portable radio
 $113.57 for groceries
 $7.95 for gasoline
 $12.65 for utilities

She deposited $42.96. The balance before the deposit and before the checks were written was $289.54.
After the checks were written and the deposit made, what was her new balance?
  A. $61.90   B. $104.86   C. $227.64   D. $270.60

30. Given the formula I = PRT:
    If I = 27, R = .06, T = 3, find P.
      A. .0067   B. 1.5   C. 4.86   D. 150.00

    30._____

31. Fencing is needed to enclose a piece of land 24 meters on a side.
    How much fencing is needed?
    _____ meters.
      A. 48
      B. 96
      C. 384
      D. 576

    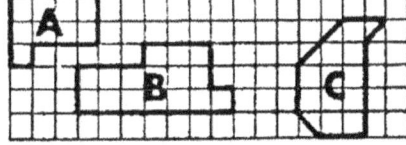

    31._____

32. The area of figure A is 9 square units, and the area of B is 16 square units.
    What is the area of figure C?
    _____ square units.
      A. 12
      B. 12 1/2
      C. 13
      D. 13 1/2

    32._____

33. Using a 3 gallon spray can with a mixture rate of 1 teaspoon insecticide per quart of water and an application rate of 1 gallon of mixture per 100 square feet, how much water and how much insecticide will be needed to spray a 75 feet by 10 feet lawn?
    _____ teaspoons of insecticide and _____ gallons of water.
      A. 30; 7 1/2   B. 30; 10   C. 15; 7 1/2   D. 20; 5

    33._____

34. Frank Silva will carpet his living room which has the following dimensions. If Frank pays $6.00 per square yard for the carpet, how much will it cost to carpet the living room? (9 square feet – 1 square yard)
      A. $126
      B. $150
      C. $1,134
      D. $1,350

    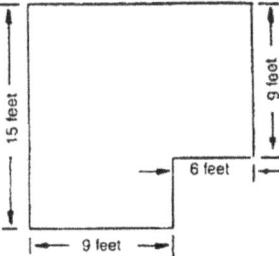

    34._____

35. A cube is painted red and then divided into 27 smaller cubes.
How many of the smaller cubes are painted on three sides only?
   A. 6
   B. 8
   C. 10
   D. 12

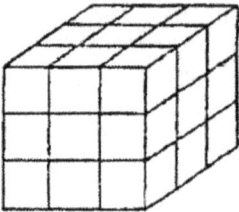

35.____

36. John and Frank wish to pour a cement walk 81 feet long, 4 feet wide, and 3 inches deep.
If ready-mix concrete can be delivered on weekdays for $19.50 a cubic yard and on weekends for $22.50 a cubic yard, how much would be saved on the complete job if they decide to purchase the cement on Wednesday rather than on the weekend? (1 cubic yard = 27 cubic feet)
   A. $3.00   B. $9.00   C. $27.00   D. $58.50

36.____

37. Antifreeze may be purchased in different size containers for different prices
   8 oz. can - 45¢
   10 oz. can - 53¢
   12 oz. can - 64¢
If exactly 15 pints of antifreeze are needed, how many cans of each size are needed for the cost to be minimum? (16 oz. = 1 pint)
   A. 10 – 12 oz. cans and 12 =10 oz. cans
   B. 20 – 12 oz. cans
   C. 24 – 10 oz. cans
   D. 15 – 12 oz. cans and 6 – 10 oz. cans

37.____

38. From the graph shown at the right, assuming the growth rate in the sophomore class is constant, how many students will be in the sophomore class in 2022?
   A. 325
   B. 350
   C. 375
   D. 400

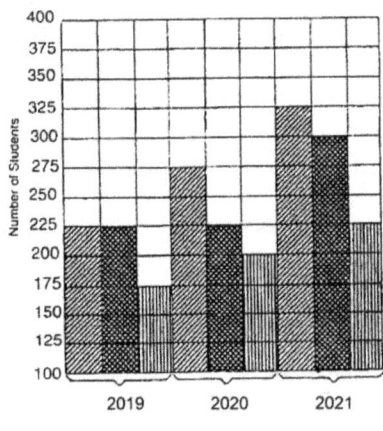

38.____

39.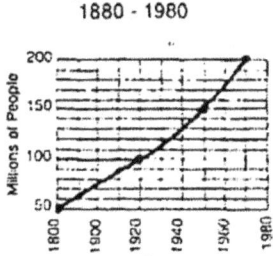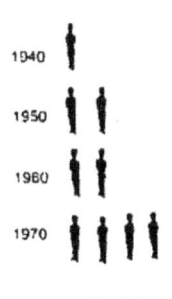

Population in U.S. 1880 - 1980

Percentage of the U.S. Population in College

Key Each ▮ represents 1% of the population

In looking at the two graphs, which of the following conclusions are TRUE?
I. Both graphs cover exactly the same period of time.
II. Both graphs show population growth.
III. In 1950 there were 150 million people in the U.S. and 3 million college students.
IV. In the general population of 200 million in 1970, 8 million students were in college.
V. The percentage of the college students remains the same in the period 1940 to 1970.
VI. In 1920 there were only 1 million college students out of 100 million people.
The CORRECT answer is:
  A. I, II, III   B. II, III, VI   C. II, V, VI   D. II, III, IV

40. Martin Owens owns a mountain cabin that has a market value of $9,000. Its assessed value is 25% of the market value. The tax rate is $11 per $100 of assessed value.
What is the amount of his tax?
  A. $24.75   B. $247.50   C. $495.00   D. $742.50

41. To finance a new state highway system decide to raise the gasoline tax. What information would be MOST helpful in establishing the amount of the raise?
I. The total number of cars in the state
II. The total number of gallons of gasoline sold in the last year
III. The number of drivers under 21 years old
IV. A table showing a rate of increase in gasoline sold from year to year
V. A table showing the average number of miles driven per person
VI. The number of small (4 cylinder) cars in the state
VII. The number of car registrations sold each year
The CORRECT answer is:
  A. III, IV, VI   B. II, V, VII   C. I, V   D. II, IV

42.

INCOME TAX TABLE							
If adjusted gross income is		And the number of exemptions is					
		1	2	3	4	5	6
At least	But less than	Your tax is:					
$2,450	$2,475	$236	$124	$23	$0	0	$0
2,475	2,500	240	128	26	0	0	0
2,500	2,525	244	132	30	0	0	0
2,525	2,550	248	136	33	0	0	0
2,550	2,575	253	139	37	0	0	0
2,575	2,600	257	143	40	0	0	0
2,600	2,625	261	147	44	0	0	0
2,625	2,650	265	151	47	0	0	0
2,650	2,675	270	155	51	0	0	0
2,675	2,700	274	159	54	0	0	0
2,700	2,725	278	163	58	0	0	0
2,725	2,750	282	167	61	0	0	0
2,750	2,775	287	171	65	0	0	0
2,775	2,800	291	175	68	0	0	0
2,800	2,825	295	179	72	0	0	0
2,825	2,850	299	183	76	0	0	0
2,850	2,875	304	187	79	0	0	0

Alvie Ramos earned $2,856.00 during his senior year in high school.
To find his adjusted gross income, he must reduce the amount earned by the standard 10% deduction. He had only one exemption, himself.
How much tax did Alvie pay?
  A. $139   B. $187   C. $253   D. $304

43.

Weight in Ounces	4 oz.	6 oz.	9 oz.	12 oz.	15 oz.
Price	2¢	4¢	7¢	10¢	13¢

Using the above table, predict the price if the weight in ounces is 25.
  A. 23¢   B. 24¢   C. 26¢   D. 27¢

44. Given [(0,3),(1,5),(2,7),...(5,y)]
    What is the value for y?
    A. 9   B. 11   C. 13   D. 15

45. What is 4% of $14,000?
    A. $560   B. $35   C. $56   D. $350

KEY (CORRECT ANSWERS)

1.	B	11.	C	21.	C	31.	B	41.	B
2.	A	12.	C	22.	A	32.	C	42.	C
3.	D	13.	D	23.	D	33.	A	43.	A
4.	B	14.	C	24.	A	34.	A	44.	C
5.	C	15.	B	25.	B	35.	B	45.	A
6.		16.	A	26.	B	36.	B		
7.	C	17.	D	27.	C	37.	C		
8.	A	18.	C	28.	B	38.	C		
9.	C	19.	D	29.	B	39.	D		
10.	C	20.	A	30.	D	40.	B		

10 (#1)

SOLUTIONS TO PROBLEMS

1. 4898 + 7 + 361 + 26 = 5292

2. 7006 − 5797 = 1209

3. (2579)(806) = 2,223,754

4. 72,732 ÷ 87 = 836

5. (-6) − (-4) _ (-3) = 6 + 4 − 3 = +7

6. [(-7)(-8) ÷ (-4) = $\frac{56}{-4}$ = -14

7. 1 4/9 + 5 3/4 = 1 16/36 + 5 27/36 = 6 43/36 = 7 7/36

8. 5 4/7 − 3 3/4 = 5 16/28 − 3 21/28 = 4 44/28 − 3 31/28 = 1 23/28

9. (2 3/4)(6 1/3) = (11/4P)(19/3) = 209/12 = 16 5/12

10. 5 1/4 ÷ 1 1/2 = (21/8)(2/3) = 42/12 = 3 1/2

11. 536.5 + .03 + 8.209 = 544.739

12. 879.3 − 57.64 = 821.66

13. (4.87)(73.8) == 359.406

14. 9.858 ÷ .053 = 186

15. .5 + 1/4 = .5 + .25 = .75

16. (4.4%)(48) = (.044)(48) = 2.112

17. 16/8 = 2 = 200%

18. 24 ÷ 48 = 50

19. $26 − ($26)(.12) = $22.88

20. Acme charges $15.82 in interest, whereas Bowman charges ($320)(.08) = $25.60 in interest. Thus, Bowman charges the most.

21. Total payment = ($18)(66 2/3%) + ($20)(80%) + ($60)(75%) = $73.00

22. Statements I, IV are correct. Note that she paid ($28)(12) = $336 in insurance vs. the amount of the claim ($800). Also, since her house was insured for $10,000, that is the maximum amount she could receive for a claim.

11 (#1)

23. Probability of 2 tails = 1/2 . 1/2 = 1/4 = 1 in 4

24. (5)(4) ÷ 2 = 10 games. This is actually the number of combinations of 5 items taken 2 at a time.

25. ($43 + $82 + $16 + $139 + 75) ÷ 5 = $71

26. The conclusion is *Joe is not a boxer*. Let p = Joe is a boxer, q = Joe is strong. The contrapositive of *If p then q* is *If not q then not p*.

27. Earnings = (12)(savings), so that (12)($1800) = $21,600 earnings per year = $21,600 ÷ 12 = $1800 earnings per month.

28. Mr. Ramirez' earnings = (40)($2) + (7)($3) + (1)($4) = $105. So far, Mr. Tarver has earned ($40)(2) + ($3)(3) = $89

29. New balance = $289.54 + $42.96 - $93.47 - $113.57 - $7.95 - $12.65 = $104.86

30. 27 = (P)(.06)(3), so P = 27 ÷ 18 = 150

31. Fencing needed = (24)(4) = 96 meters

32. Area of C = (4)(5) − (1/2)(2)(2) − (1/2)(1)(1) − 4 1/2 = 13 sq. units

33. (75)(10) ÷ 100 = 7.5 gallons of spray. Since 7.5 gallons = 30 quarts, 30 teaspoons of insecticide and 7 1/2 gallons of water are needed.

34. Area = (15)(15) − (6)(6) = 189 sq.ft. = 21 sq.yds.
    Then, the cost = (21)($6) = $126

35. The cubes which are painted on 3 sides will be the 8 cubes in the corners.

36. Savings = [(27)(1 1/3)(1/12)][$22.50 - $19.50] = $9.00

37. For A: Cost = (10)(.64) + (12)(.53) = $12.76
    For B: Cost = (20)(.64) = $12.80
    For C: Cost = (24)(.53) = $12.72
    For D: Cost = (15)(.64) + (6)(.53) = $12.78
    Option C has the minimum cost.

38. Growth rate = 50 per year. Number of sophomores in 2022 = 325 + 50 = 375

39. Statements II, III, IV are correct. Statement I is wrong since one graph covers 1880-1980, whereas the other graph covers 1940-1970. Statement V is wrong since the percentage of college students increases from 1940 to 1970. Statement VI is unverifiable since the second chart does not include 1920.

40. Assessed value = (.25)($9000) = $2250. The tax = ($11)($2250/$100) = $247.50

12 (#1)

41. The only statements pertinent to gasoline taxes would be II, V, and VII.

42. ($2856)(.90) = $2570.40. This number is found between $2550 and $2575 on the chart. Using the column for 1 exemption, the tax = $253.

43. The price in cents is 2 numbers below the number of ounces. Given 25 ounces, the price = 23 cents.

44. (5,y) corresponds to the sixth point. In the sequence 3, 5, 7,..., the sixth number is 13.

45. (.04)($14,000) = $560

BASIC MATHEMATICS
EXAMINATION SECTION
TEST 1

DIRECTIONS: Each question or incomplete statement is followed by several suggested answers or completions. Select the one that BEST answers the question or completes the statement. *PRINT THE LETTER OF THE CORRECT ANSWER IN THE SPACE AT THE RIGHT.*

1. 534
   18
   +1291

   A. 1733   B. 1743   C. 1833   D. 1843   E. 1853

   1.____

2. (17×23) – 16 + 20 =
   A. 459   B. 427   C. 411   D. 395   E. 355

   2.____

3. 3/7 + 5/11 =
   A. 33/35   B. 4/9   C. 8/18   D. 68/77   E. 15/77

   3.____

4. 4832 ÷ 6 =
   A. 905 1/3   B. 805 1/3   C. 95 1/3   D. 95   E. 85 1/3

   4.____

5. 62.3 – 4.9 =
   A. 5.74   B. 7.4   C. 57.4   D. 58.4   E. 67.4

   5.____

6. 3/5 × 4/9 =
   A. 4/15   B. 7/45   C. 27/20   D. 12/14   E. 15/4

   6.____

7. 14/16 – 5/16 =
   A. 8/16   B. 9/16   C. 11/16   D. 8   E. 9

   7.____

8. 5.03 + 2.7 + 40 =
   A. .570   B. 4.773   C. 5.70   D. 11.73   E. 47.73

   8.____

9. 5.37 × 21.4 =
   A. 11491.8   B. 1149.18   C. 114.918
   D. 11,4918   E. 1.14918

   9.____

10. 5 1/4 + 2 7/8 =
    A. 8 1/4   B. 8 1/8   C. 7 2/3   D. 7 1/4   E. 7 1/8

    10.____

11. -14 + 5 =
    A. -19   B. -9   C. 9   D. 19   E. 70

    11.____

12. 2/7 of 28 =
    A. 98   B. 16   C. 14   D. 8   E. 4

13. 2/5 =
    A. .10   B. .20   C. .25   D. .40   E. .52

14. 20% of _____ is 38.
    A. 7.6   B. 19   C. 76   D. 190   E. 760

15. $\frac{8.4}{400} =$
    A. .0021   B. .021   C. .21   D. 2.1   E. 21

16. $\frac{4}{5} = \frac{?}{60}$
    A. 240   B. 48   C. 20   D. 15   E. 12

17. What is the area of the rectangle shown at the right?
    A. 47 mm²
    B. 94 mm²
    C. 240 mm²
    D. 480 mm²
    E. 960 mm²

18. What number does ▢ represent in the following equation: 25 - ▢ - ▢ - ▢ - ▢ = 13?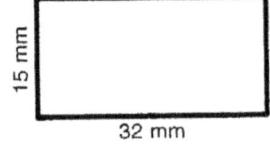
    A. 13   B. 12   C. 7   D. 4   E. 3

19. Approximate lengths are given in the right triangles shown at the right. What does length x equal?
    A. 48
    B. 39
    C. 37
    D. 35
    E. 32

20. What is the perimeter of the triangle shown at the right?
    A. 10 × 15 × 17
    B. 10 + 15 + 17
    C. 1/2 × 10 × 15
    D. 1/2 × 10 × 17
    E. 1/2(10+15+17)

21. Which of the following expressions will give the same answer as 45 × 9?
    A. 5 × 3³   B. (4×9)+(5×9)   C. (40+9) × 5
    D. (45×3) + (45×3)   E. (45×10) − (45×1)

22. Find the average of 19, 21, 21, 22, and 27.
    A. 23   B. 22   C. 21   D. 20   E. 19

22.____

23. In the triangle at the right, how many degrees is <T?
    A. 75°
    B. 85°
    C. 95°
    D. 114°
    E. 180°

23.____

24. About how long is the paper clip?
    A. 5 cm   B. 4 cm   C. 3 cm   D. 2 cm   E. 1 cm

24.____

25. Five stores sell the same size cans of tomato soup. Their prices are listed below.
Which sells the soup for the LOWEST price per can? _____ cans for _____.
    A. 6; 99¢   B. 6; 90¢   C. 5; 93¢   D. 3; 56¢   E. 3; 50¢

25.____

26. Rock star Peter Giles receives $1.97 royalty on each of his albums that is sold. 14,127 albums are sold.
Estimate how much Peter Giles will receive.
    A. $7,000   B. $14,000   C. $20,000   D. $26,000   E. $28,000

26.____

27. An amplifier is advertised for 20% off the list price of $430.
What is the sale price?
    A. $516   B. $454   C. $354   D. $344   E. $215

27.____

28. If 9 dozen eggs cost $3.60, what do 25 dozen eggs cost?
    A. $90.00   B. $10.00   C. $9.00   D. $2.54   E. $40

28.____

29. The distance between New York State and San Antonio is 1,860 miles. If a jet averages 465 miles per hour, how many hours will it take to travel the distance?
    A. 9   B. 5   C. 4   D. 3   E. 2

29.____

30. In a high school homeroom of 32 students, 24 are girls.
What percent are girls?
    A. 3/4%   B. 24%   C. 25%   D. 75%   E. 80%

30.____

31. Which problem could give the answer shown on the calculator?
    A. 2 + .3
    B. 2 × 3/10
    C. 2 × 1/3
    D. 33333 + .2
    E. 7 ÷ 3

32. Cost of Eating at Home
    (One Week)

Age	Male	Female
6-11 yrs.	$14	$14
12-19 yrs.	$19	$15
20-54 yrs.	$20	$16
55 and Up	$14	$14

    According to the above table, how much will it cost in a typical week for the 3 members of the Wright family to eat at home? Mr. Wright is 56 years old; Mrs. Wright, 52; and their son, Harry, 17.
    A. $125   B. $52   C. $49   D. $42   E. $40

33. According to the above table shown in Question 32, how much does it cost in a typical four-week month to feed a 12-year-old girl?
    A. $4   B. $16   C. $48   D. $64   E. $78

34. Reverend Whilhite jogs for 1½ hours each day, 6 days a week. If he burns 800 calories per hour of jogging, how many calories does he burn in a week?
    A. 4800   B. 5600   C. 7200   D. 8400   E. 9000

35. Ground meat costs 90¢ per pound.
    How much does the meat on the scale cost?
    A. $1.80
    B. $1.60
    C. $1.54
    D. $1.44
    E. $.90

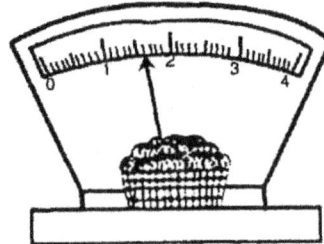

36. According to the graph at the right, about when did the weekly wages for a minimum wage worker go over $100?
    A. 2005
    B. 2010
    C. 2014
    D. 2019
    E. 2020

36._____

37. According to the bar graph at the right, what is the approximate height of the Crystal Beach Comet?
    A. 40 ft.
    B. 90 ft.
    C. 92 ft.
    D. 94 ft.
    E. 98 ft.

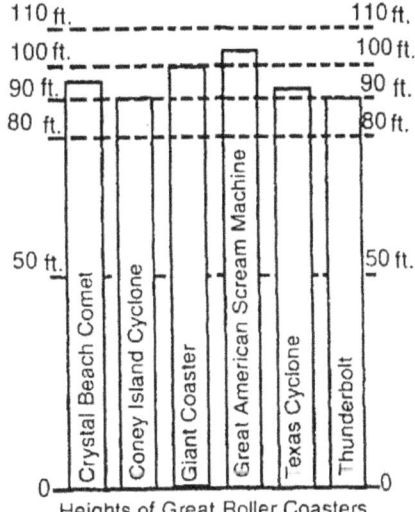

37._____

38. According to the bar graph shown in Question 37, what is the difference in height between the tallest and shortest roller coasters? _____ feet.
    A. 5   B. 10   C. 15   D. 20   E. 50

38._____

39. How much change will you receive from a $10 bill when you buy 4 grapefruits at 90¢ each and 3 apples at 40¢ each?
    A. $6.20   B. $5.20   C. $4.80   D. $4.20   E. $4.00

39._____

40. A medical supplier packages medicine in boxes. The cost of packaging is computed with the flow chart at the right.
What is the cost of packaging medicine in a box that is 30 cm long, 20 cm wide, and 20 cm high?
   A. $.20
   B. $.24
   C. $2.00
   D. $2.40
   E. $3.00

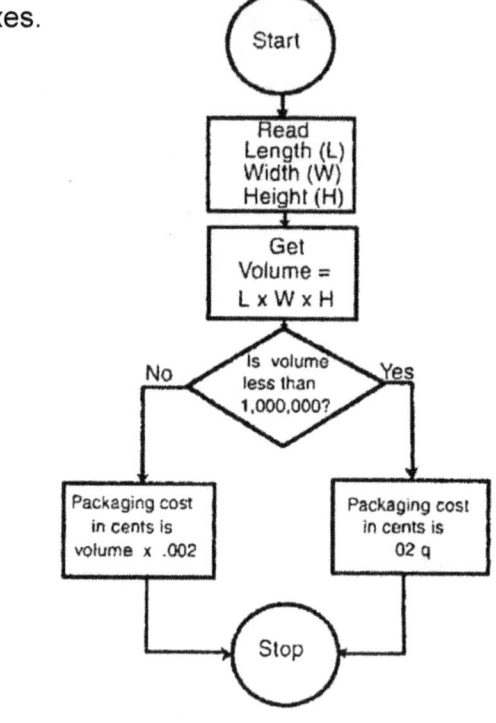

KEY (CORRECT ANSWERS)

1.	D	11.	B	21.	E	31.	E
2.	D	12.	D	22.	B	32.	C
3.	D	13.	D	23.	B	33.	D
4.	B	14.	D	24.	C	34.	C
5.	C	15.	B	25.	B	35.	D
6.	A	16.	B	26.	E	36.	C
7.	B	17.	D	27.	D	37.	D
8.	E	18.	E	28.	B	38.	C
9.	C	19.	A	29.	C	39.	B
10.	B	20.	B	30.	D	40.	A

7 (#1)

SOLUTIONS TO PROBLEMS

1. 534 + 18 + 1291 = 1843

2. (17×23) − 16 + 20 = 391 − 16 + 20 = 395

3. $\frac{3}{7} + \frac{5}{11} = \frac{33}{77} + \frac{35}{77} = \frac{68}{77}$

4. 4832 ÷ 6 = $805\frac{1}{3}$

5. 62.3 − 4.9 = 57.4

6. $\frac{3}{5} \times \frac{4}{9} = \frac{12}{45} = \frac{4}{15}$

7. $\frac{14}{16} \cdot \frac{5}{16} = \frac{9}{16}$

8. 5.03 + 2.7 + 40 = 47.73

9. 5.37 × 21.4 = 114.918

10. $5\frac{1}{4} + 2\frac{7}{8} = 7\frac{9}{8} = 8\frac{1}{8}$

11. -14 + 5 = -9

12. $\frac{2}{7}$ of 28 = $(\frac{2}{7})(\frac{28}{1})$ = 8

13. $\frac{2}{5}$ = .40 as a decimal

14. Let x = missing number. Then, .20x = 38. Solving, x = 190

15. $\frac{84}{400}$ = .021

16. Let x = missing number. Then, $\frac{4}{5} = \frac{x}{60}$. 5x = 240, so x = 48

17. Area = (15)(32) = 480mm^2

18. Let x = ☐. Then, 25 − 4x = 13. So, -4x = -12. Solving, x = 3.

19. $\frac{9}{27} = \frac{16}{x}$. Then, 9x = 432. Solving, x = 48.

20. Perimeter = 17 + 10 + 15 = 42

21. 45 × 9 = 405 = (45×10)-(45×1)

22. 19 + 21 + 21 + 22 + 27 = 110. Then, 110 ÷ 5 = 22

23. ∠T = 180° - 50° - 45° = 85°

24. The paper clip's length is about 5 – 2 = 3 cm.

25. For A: price per can = $\frac{.99}{6}$ = .165
    For B: price per can = $\frac{.90}{6}$ = .15
    For C: price per can = $\frac{.93}{5}$ = 186
    For D: price per can = $\frac{.56}{3}$ = .18$\overline{6}$
    For E: price per can = $\frac{.50}{3}$ = .1$\overline{6}$

    Lowest price is for B.

26. $1.97 = $2.00. Then, ($2.00)(14,127) = $28,254 = $28,000

27. Sale price = ($430)(.80) = $344

28. Let x = cost. Then, 9x = $90, so x = $10.00

29. $\frac{1860}{465}$ = 4 hours

30. $\frac{24}{32}$ = 75%

31. $\frac{7}{3}$ = 2.$\overline{3}$ = 2.33333 on the calculator shown

32. Total cost = $14 + $16 + $19 = $49

33. Cost = ($16)(4) = $64

34. (800)(1$\frac{1}{2}$)(6) = 7200 calories

35. (.90)(1.6) = $1.44

36. Around 2015, the minimum weekly wages exceeded $100.

37. The Crystal Beach Comet's height is about 94 ft.

38. Tallest = 105 ft. and the shortest = 90 ft. Difference = 15 ft.

39. $10 – (3)(.90) – (3)(.40) = $5.20 change.

40. (30)(20)(20) = 12,000 cm³. Since 12,000 < 1,000,000, the price is 20 cents.

ARITHMETICAL REASONING
EXAMINATION SECTION
TEST 1

DIRECTIONS: Each question or incomplete statement is followed by several suggested answers or completions. Select the one that BEST answers the question or completes the statement. *PRINT THE LETTER OF THE CORRECT ANSWER IN THE SPACE AT THE RIGHT.*

1. A unit fraction is one in which the numerator is 1 and the denominator is an integer greater than 1.
   The sum of two unequal unit fractions is
   A. always a proper fraction
   B. sometimes an integer
   C. sometimes an improper fraction
   D. sometimes an irrational number

2. The set of denominators for which 72 is the LEAST common is
   A. 12, 4, 3   B. 4, 8, 12   C. 9, 12, 4   D. 9, 8, 6

3. The product of the highest common factor and the lowest common multiple of the numbers 18 and 27
   A. is less than the product of the numbers by 162
   B. is less than the product of the numbers by 324
   C. equals the product of the numbers
   D. exceeds the product of the numbers by 486

4. In the solution of a certain problem, three numbers of two digits each were added and their sums proved to be a number of two digits.
   It follows, therefore, that
   A. at least two of the addends were less than 50
   B. each addend was less than 50
   C. the addends were not equal
   D. none of the addends exceeded 50

5. The number of grams in one ounce is 28.35. The number of grams in a kilogram is 1,000.
   Therefore, the number of kilograms in one pound is APPROXIMATELY
   A. 2.2   B. 1.0   C. 0.45   D. 4.5

6. The smaller angle between the hand of a clock at 3:30 is
   A. 105°   B. 75°   C. 90°   D. 60°

7. If one-third of the liquid contents of a can evaporates on the first day and three-fourths of the remainder evaporates on the second day, the fractional part of the original contents remaining at the close of the second day is

201

8.

r	3	4	5	6
t	7	10	13	16

The equation expressing the relationship between r and t in the above table is
A. r = 3t − 2   B. t = 2r + 1   C. t − 2 = 3r   D. none of the above

9. The square of a proper fraction is
A. less than the original fraction
B. greater than the original fraction
C. greater than 1
D. not necessarily any of the preceding

10. The formula F = 9/5C+32 shows that when C is increased by 10, F will increase by
A. 18   B. 41   C. 42   D. 122

11. The ACTUAL length represented by 3 1/2 inches on a drawing having a scale of 1/8 inch to the foot is _____ feet.
A. 3.75   B. 28   C. 360   D. 120

12. If one acute angle of a right triangle is 5 times the other, the number of degrees in the SMALLEST angle of the triangle is
A. 18°   B. 30°   C. 75°   D. 15°

13. The single commercial discount which is equivalent to successive discounts of 10%, 10% is
A. 20%   B. 19%   C. 17%   D. 15%

14. The price of an article has been reduced 25%.
In order to restore the original price, the new price must be increased by
A. 20%   B. 25%   C. 33 1/3%   D. 40%

15. A mortgage on a house in the amount of $4,000 provides for quarterly payment of $200 plus interest on the unpaid balance at 44% annually.
The TOTAL second payment to be made is
A. $371.00   B. $285.50   C. $242.75   D. $240.00

16. The number 1729 is the sum of the cubes of two numbers. One of these numbers is 10. The other number is
A. 7   B. 9   C. 13   D. 17

17. Question A of a multiple choice mathematics examination has two possible answers. Question B has three possible answers.
The probability that a student will answer both questions correctly is
A. 1:2   B. 1:3   C. 1:5   D. 1:6

18. The following problem was presented to students for enrichment. A school desk was sold at a 10% discount. A further discount of 10% of the selling price was given for cash payment.
The single discount which is equivalent to the two successive discounts is
A. 11%   B. 15%   C. 19%   D. 21%

18.____

Questions 19-22.

DIRECTIONS: Questions 19 through 22 are to be answered on the basis of the following situation.

A junior high school class has volunteered to redecorate the teachers' cafeteria.

19. In shopping for suitable table covers, the class found on sale a 25 yard roll of plastic material marked down to $19.75 from the regular price of 95 ¢ per yard.
This represented a savings of _____ per yard.
A. 80¢   B. 120¢   C. 16¢   D. 20¢

19.____

20. Each of the tables measured 4 feet by 4 feet.
If the roll of plastic was 6 feet wide, approximately how many tables could be covered if each was to be cut with a 4 inch overhand on all sides?
A. 16   B. 6   C. 7   D. 8

20.____

21. A border strip of contrasting color is to be sewn around each table cover measuring 36" x 76".
Approximately what amount of border strip will be needed for each table?
_____ yards.
A. 5   B. 5 1/2   C. 6   D. 6 1/4

21.____

22. Six colorful pictures, each requiring a frame 18 inches by 12 inches, are to be used for wall decorations. The boys elected to make the frames themselves at a cost of 12¢ per foot of moulding in preference to buying unfinished frames at $1.00 each.
This represented a monetary saving of
A. 30%   B. 40%   C. 50%   D. 60%

22.____

23. A unit of four classes is to share equally a gallon of liquid all-purpose glue. If the liquid is poured into 8-ounce containers, how many containers would each class receive?
A. 2   B. 4   C. 6   D. 8

23.____

24. A slab of clay which weighed 1 lb. 8 oz. when moist weighed 1 lb. 7 oz. when completely dry.
The relative loss of weight is APPROXIMATELY
A. .04%   B. .4%   C. 4%   D. 40%

24.____

25. The wholesale cost of ten pounds of jelly beans is $6.50. Mr. M plans to retail 1/4 pound boxes of the candy at $.30 per box. The boxes for packaging cost one cent each.
The amount of profit on the transaction will be
   A. $5.50   B. $6.50   C. $4.00   D. $5.90

25.____

KEY (CORRECT ANSWERS)

1. A
2. D
3. C
4. A
5. C

6. B
7. C
8. D
9. A
10. A

11. B
12. D
13. B
14. C
15. C

16. B
17. D
18. C
19. C
20. A

21. D
22. B
23. B
24. C
25. D

SOLUTIONS TO PROBLEMS

1. Let $1/x$, $1/y$ represent the unit fractions, where $-x/y$ are positive integers greater than 1. $1/x + = (y+k)/xy$, and since $y + x$ is less than xy, this result is always a proper fraction.

2. 72 is the least common denominator for 9, 8, 6 since no lower number can be divided evenly by all 3 of these.

3. For the numbers 18 and 27, the highest common factor is 9 and the lowest common multiple is 54. Then, $(9)(54) = 486$, which equals $(18)(27)$.

4. Let x, y, z represent the three numbers of 2 digits each. Since $x + y + z < 100$, either (a) one of these addends exceeds 50 while the other two are less than 50, or (b) all three addends are less than 50.

5. 28.35 grams in 1 ounce means $(28.35)(16) = 453.6$ grams in 1 pound. Finally, 453.6 grams = .4536 kilograms or about .45 kilograms.

6. The small hand is halfway between the .3 and 4 when the time is 3:30. The separation between the hands is 2 1/2 digits. Since a separation of 12 digits represents 360°, a separation of 2 1/2 digits is $(360°)(2\ 1/2/12) = 75°$.

7. If 1/3 evaporates after the first day, 2/3 remains. If 3/4 of the 2/3 evaporates after the second day, the amount remaining is $(2/3)(1/4) = 1/6$.

8. Let $t = ar$; a, b constants. By substituting pairs of values, $(3,7)$ and $(4,10)$ for example, we get $7 = 3a + b$ and $10 = 4a + b$. Solving, $a = 3$ and $b = -2$. Thus, $t = 3r - 2$ (none of the given choices).

9. Let x/y represent a proper fraction, so that $x < y$. Then, $(x/y)^2 = x^2/y^2$ which is less than x/y. Example: Given 3/4, $(3/4)^2 = 9/16 < 3/4$.

10. In the formula $F = 9/5C+32$, the ratio 9/5 means that when C increases 5 units, F increases 9 units. By direct proportion, an increase of 10 units for C must correspond to an increase of 18 units for F.

11. $3\ 1/2 \div 1/8 = 28$ ft.

12. Let x = smaller acute angle, $5x$ = larger acute angle. Then, $x + 5x = 90°$. Solving, $x = 15°$.

13. Let x = original price. A single 10% discount results in a price of $.90x$. A second 10% discount results in a price of $(.90)(.90x)$ = Six, which represents a single discount of 19% from the original price.

14. Let x = original price. A reduction of 25% results in a price of $.75x$. In order to raise this back to x, we need an actual increase of $.25x$. But, $.25x \div .75x = 33\ 1/3\%$.

15. 4 1/2% annually = .01125 quarterly. The first payment is $200 + (.01125)($4000), whereas 2nd payment = $200 + (.01125)($3800) = $242.75.

16. $10^3 + x^3 = 1729$, Then, $x^3 = 729$. Solving, $x = 9$.

17. Probability of getting both questions right is (1/2)(1/3) = 1/6 or 1:6.

18. Same solution as #13.

19. The reduced price per yard is $19.75 ÷ 25 = 79 cents. Thus, the savings per yard is 95 cents − 79 cents = 15 cents.

20. Each table requires 4'8" or 4 2/3' of material, including 25 yds. − 75 ft., and 75' ÷ 4 2/3 = 16,07 or 16 tables.

21. 76" = 6'4"   1 yd. × 2 = 2 yd.
    3' = 1 yd.   6'4" × 2 = 12'8" = 4 1/4 approx.
                           2 ++ 4 1/4 = 6 1/4

22. Perimeter of each frame is (2)(18") + (2)(12") = 60" = 5'. At 12 cents per foot, the cost is 60 cents per frame. Since an unfinished frame costs $1.00, the savings is .40, which represents .40/1.00 = 40%.

23. 1 gallon = 128 flluid ounces. 128 ÷ 8 = 16 containers. If this is divided among 4 classes, each class gets 4 containers.

24. Loss of weight = 1 oz. Then, 1/24 ≈ .0417 or about 4% (24 represents, in ounces, 1 lb. 8 oz.)

25. 10 ÷ 1/4 = 40 boxes. The retail value is 40(.30+.01) = $12.40. Thus, the profit is $12.40 = $6.50 = $5.90.

TEST 2

DIRECTIONS: Each question or incomplete statement is followed by several suggested answers or completions. Select the one that BEST answers the question or completes the statement. *PRINT THE LETTER OF THE CORRECT ANSWER IN THE SPACE AT THE RIGHT.*

1. If AB = BC and AD = DE = EC, it follows that
    A. ∠1 = ∠2 = ∠3
    B. ∠2 = (∠1 + ∠3)
    C. ∠1 = ∠3
    D. ∠A is greater than ∠1

    1.____

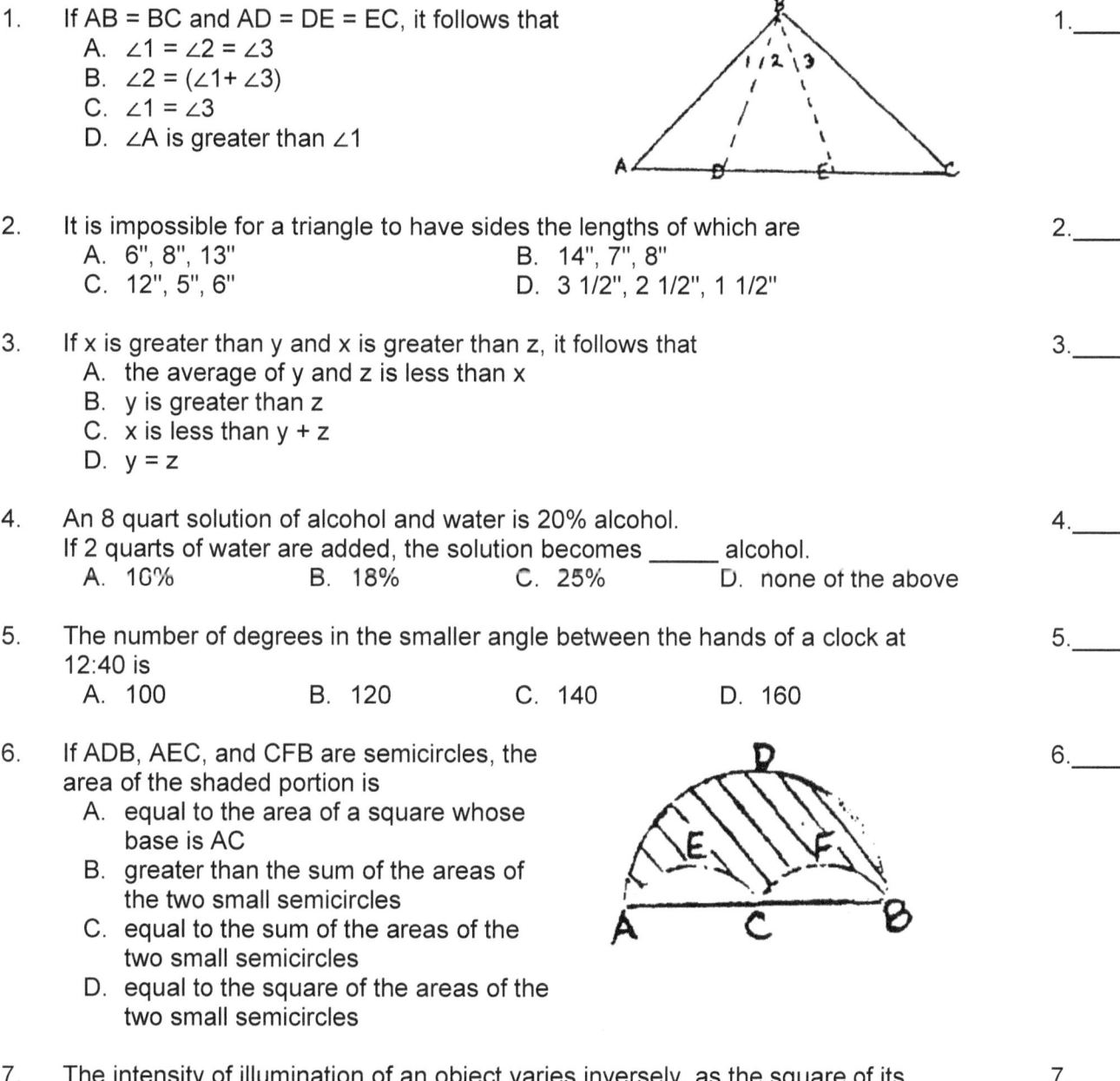

2. It is impossible for a triangle to have sides the lengths of which are
    A. 6", 8", 13"   B. 14", 7", 8"
    C. 12", 5", 6"   D. 3 1/2", 2 1/2", 1 1/2"

    2.____

3. If x is greater than y and x is greater than z, it follows that
    A. the average of y and z is less than x
    B. y is greater than z
    C. x is less than y + z
    D. y = z

    3.____

4. An 8 quart solution of alcohol and water is 20% alcohol.
   If 2 quarts of water are added, the solution becomes ____ alcohol.
    A. 16%   B. 18%   C. 25%   D. none of the above

    4.____

5. The number of degrees in the smaller angle between the hands of a clock at 12:40 is
    A. 100   B. 120   C. 140   D. 160

    5.____

6. If ADB, AEC, and CFB are semicircles, the area of the shaded portion is
    A. equal to the area of a square whose base is AC
    B. greater than the sum of the areas of the two small semicircles
    C. equal to the sum of the areas of the two small semicircles
    D. equal to the square of the areas of the two small semicircles

    6.____

7. The intensity of illumination of an object varies inversely, as the square of its distance from the source of light.
   Accordingly, if the distance of the object from the source of light is multiplied by 9, the intensity of illumination is ____ as great.
    A. 1/81   B. 81 times   C. 1/3   D. 3 times

    7.____

2 (#2)

8. The number of prime integers between 140 and 150 is
   A. 0 B. 1 C. 2 D. 3

9. If an automobile travels 80 miles at the rate of 20 miles per hour and then returns over the same route at the rate of 40 miles per hour, the AVERAGE speed per hour for the entire trip (going and return) is _____ miles.
   A. 30 B. 26 2/3 C. 60 D. 33 1/3

10. The difference between one-tenth of 2000 and one-tenth percent of 2000 is
    A. 0 B. 18 C. 180 D. 198

11. If the radius of a circle is decreased by 5 inches, the resulting decrease in its circumference is _____ inches.
    A. 10π B. 5 C. 10 D. 5π

12. The CLOSEST approximation to $\dfrac{(0.98)^3 \times 1.1.2}{\sqrt{0.26}}$ is
    A. 50 B. 70 C. 100 D. 200

13. Of the following, the one that CANNOT be an even number is the sum of
    A. 2 odd numbers
    B. 3 prime numbers
    C. 2 prime numbers
    D. 3 odd numbers

14. An office manager employs 3 typists at $360 per week, 2 general clerks at $320 per week, and a messenger at $256 per week.
    The AVERAGE weekly wage of these employees is
    A. $300
    B. $312
    C. $329.36
    D. none of the above

15. If x is less than 10, and y is less than 5, it follows that
    A. x is greater than y
    B. x − y = 5
    C. x = 2y
    D. x + y is less than 15

16. A rectangular bin 4 feet long, 3 feet wide, and 2 feet high is solidly packed with bricks whose dimensions are 8 inches, 4 inches, and 2 inches.
    The number of bricks in the bin is
    A. 54
    B. 648
    C. 1,296
    D. none of the above

17. A dealer sells an article at a loss of 50% of the cost.
    Based on the selling price, the loss is
    A. 25%
    B. 50%
    C. 100%
    D. none of the above

18. If 8 men get together at a reunion and each man shakes hands once with each of the others, the TOTAL number of handshakes is
    A. 64 B. 56 C. 49 D. 28

19. The world record for cycling a stretch of 20 kilometers is 26 minutes. This corresponds to an average speed of APPROXIMATELY _____ miles per hour.
    A. 29
    B. 32
    C. 46
    D. none of the above

    19._____

20. The sum, s, of n consecutive integers beginning with 1 can be found by use of the formula $s = \frac{n(n+1)}{2}$.
    The sum of the first 100 consecutive integers is
    A. 5,001
    B. 5,050
    C. 10,000
    D. 10,100

    20._____

21. Of the following, the value of $\frac{\sqrt[3]{64.32}}{\sqrt{0.41}}$ is
    A. 400
    B. 200
    C. 20
    D. 16

    21._____

22. If each edge of a cube is increased by 2 inches, the
    A. volume is increased by 8 cubic inches
    B. diagonal of each face is increased by 2 inches
    C. area of each face is increased by 4 square inches
    D. sum of the edges is increased by 24 inches

    22._____

23. In a school in which 40% of the enrolled students of boys are present on a certain day.
    If 1,152 boys are present, the TOTAL school enrollment is
    A. 1,440
    B. 2,880
    C. 3,600
    D. none of the above

    23._____

24. An agent received a commission of d% of the selling price of a house.
    If the commission amounted to $6,000, the selling price, in dollars, was
    A. $\frac{60,000}{d}$
    B. $\frac{600,000}{d}$
    C. 600d
    D. 6,000d

    24._____

25. A ship sails due north from a position 5°28' South Latitude to a position 6°43' North Latitude.
    Given that one minute of latitude is equivalent to 1 nautical mile, the ship has sailed a distance of _____ nautical miles.
    A. 75
    B. 371
    C. 731
    D. 1,211

    25._____

KEY (CORRECT ANSWERS)

1.	C	11.	A
2.	C	12.	D
3.	A	13.	D
4.	A	14.	C
5.	C	15.	D
6.	C	16.	B
7.	A	17.	C
8.	B	18.	D
9.	B	19.	A
10.	D	20.	B

21.	C
22.	D
23.	B
24.	B
25.	C

5 (#2)

SOLUTIONS TO PROBLEMS

1. ∠1 = ∠3 since ΔBAD is congruent to ΔBCE. However, neither of these two triangles can be proved congruent to ΔBED. So we don't know how ∠2 compares with ∠1.

2. In any triangle, the sum of any two sides must exceed the third side. In choice C, 5" + 6" <12". Thus, this cannot be a triangle.

3. The average of y and z is (y+z)/2. Since y < x, (y+z)/2 < (x+x)/2 = x

4. (.20)(8) = 1.6 quarts of alcohol. By adding 2 quarts of water, the solution has 1.6/10 = 16% alcohol.

5. At 12:40, the small hand is 2/3 of the way between the digits 12 and 1. The hands are then separated by 4 2/3 digits and this converts to (4 2/3/12)(360°) = 140°.

6. Let AB = 8, AC = BC = 4. The areas of semicircles ADB, AEC, and CFB are 8π, 2π, and 2π, respectfully. The area of the shaded portion must be 8π − 2π − 2π = 4π, and this equals the sum of the areas of the two small semicircles. (Any dimensions will prove the result.)

7. The inverse square of 9 is $1/9^2 = 1/81$.

8. The only prime between 140 and 150 is 149, since 149 can only be divided evenly by itself and by 1.

9. Total time is 80/20 + 80/40 = 6 hours. Average speed (m/hr) = total distance ÷ total time = 160/6 = 26 2/3.

10. (2000)(.1) − (2000)(.001) = 198.

11. Let R = original radius. Then, R − 5 is the decreased radius. Difference in circumference is 2πR − 2π(R−5) = 10π.

12. $(.981)^3 ≈ .944$ and $\sqrt{.26} ≈ .5$. So we have the following: (.944)(101.2)/.5 ≈ 191 ≈ 200.

13. The sum of two odd numbers must be an even number. Then, the sum of this even number and another odd number must be an odd number. Thus, the sum of three odd numbers must be odd.

14. Average weekly wage is [(3)($360) + (2)($320) ÷ 6 = $329.33.

15. If x < 10 and y < 5, then x + y < 10 + 5 = 15.

16. Volume of bin is (4)(3)(2) = 24 cu.ft. = (24)(1728) = 41,472 cu.in. The volume of each brick is (8")(4")(2") = 64 cu.in. Then, 41472 ÷ 64 = 648 bricks.

17. Let x = cost, so that .50x = selling price. The loss is x - .50x = 50x and .50x/.50x = 100%.

18. This problem is really the number of combinations of 2 from 8, which is (8)(7)/2 = 28.

19. 1 kilometer ≈ .62 miles, so 20 kilometers ≈ 12.4 miles. Now, 12.4 miles in 26 minutes is (12.4)(60)726 ≈ 29 mph.

20. S = (100)(10)/2 = 5050.

21. $\sqrt[3]{64 \cdot 32} \approx 4$ and $\sqrt{.041} \approx 2$. Then, 4 ÷ 2 = 20.

22. Let x = original edge, x + 2 be the increased edge. Since there are 12 edges to a cube, the sum of the edges of the original cube is 12x. However, the sum of the edges of the new cube is 12x + 24, an increase of 24 inches.

23. School enrollment is 1152 ÷ .40 = 2880.

24. $6000 = d% or D/100 of selling price. Then the selling price = ($6000)(100/d) = 600,000/d.

25. 6°43' − (-5°28') = 11°71' = 12°11' = 731'. Since 1' = t nautical mile, the distance traveled is 731 nautical miles.

TEST 3

DIRECTIONS: Each question or incomplete statement is followed by several suggested answers or completions. Select the one that BEST answers the question or completes the statement. *PRINT THE LETTER OF THE CORRECT ANSWER IN THE SPACE AT THE RIGHT.*

1. Two airplanes leave Chicago, one flying due east and the other due southwest. The smaller angle between the two lines of flight is
    A. 90°   B. 135°   C. 180°   D. 225°

    1.____

2. The arithmetic mean of three numbers is 8.
   If two of these numbers are 4 and 8, the third number must be
    A. 4   B. 6   C. 12   D. 16

    2.____

3. In the expression $\frac{36}{18-\frac{14}{x}}$, the letter x represents a 18 - = x positive whole number.
   If the value of x is doubled, the value of the entire expression is
    A. doubled   B. increased
    C. decreased   D. divided by 2

    3.____

4. When 5 1/3 is divided by 1 5/9, the answer is
    A. 7/24   B. 27/224   C. 3 3/7   D. 8 8/27

    4.____

5. A man bought a briefcase for $15, a billfold for $10, and an overnight bag for $40.
   If the tax on these items is 10%, the TOTAL amount of his bill was
    A. $71.50   B. $69.00   C. $65.00   D. $60.50

    5.____

6. On a map which is drawn to a scale of 1/8" = 10 miles, the distance between two cities is 5 1/2".
   The distance, in miles, between the two cities is
    A. 85   B. 400   C. 440   D. 500

    6.____

7. A man owns a house assessed for $15,000. The real estate tax is $30 per $1,000. Since he paid his tax a month late, he was charged a penalty of 1% on the amount of his tax bill.
   The TOTAL amount to be paid in settling the bill was
    A. $600.00   B. $495.00   C. $454.50   D. $450.00

    7.____

8. The difference, in square feet, between the area of a rectangle 18 feet by 6 feet and the area of a square having the same perimeter is
    A. 36   B. 38   C. 48   D. 52

    8.____

9. Which of the following equations illustrates the associative principle in mathematics?
    A. 4 + 8 = n + 4   B. (2+3) + 5 = .2 + (3+5)
    C. (3×6) = (3×2) + (3×4)   D. 5 + 6 = 11

    9.____

213

10. The CLOSEST approximation to the correct answer for $\sqrt[5]{32 \cdot 076} + (1 \cdot 00017)^3$ is
    A. 1　　　　B. 3　　　　C. 5　　　　D. 9

11. The cube of 1/3 is
    A. 3/9　　　B. 3/27　　　C. 1/81　　　D. 1/27

12. One-fourth percent of 360 is
    A. 0.09　　　B. 0.9　　　C. 9.0　　　D. 90

13. In general, the sum of the squares of two numbers is greater than twice the product of the numbers.
    The pair of numbers for which this generalization is NOT valid is
    A. 8,9　　　B. 9,9　　　C. 9,10　　　D. 8,10

14. A man spent exactly one dollar in the purchase of 3-cent stamps and 5-cent stamps.
    The number of 5-cent stamps which he could NOT have purchased, under the circumstances, is
    A. 5　　　　B. 8　　　　C. 9　　　　D. 11

15. A bicycle was purchased for $50 payable in 60 days or at a discount of 5% for cash.
    If the purchaser pays in 60 days, he is paying interest per annum at an APPROXIMATE rate of
    A. 5%　　　B. 10%　　　C. 15%　　　D. 30%

16. A piece of wire 132 inches long is bent successively in the shape of an equilateral triangle, a square, a regular hexagon, and a circle.
    The plane surface of largest area is included when the wire is bent into the shape of a
    A. circle　　　B. square　　　C. hexagon　　　D. triangle

17. The number missing in the series 2, 5, 10, 17, ____, 37, 50, 65 is
    A. 22　　　B. 24　　　C. 26　　　D. 27

18. Pieces of wire are soldered together so as to form the edges of a cube whose volume is 64 cubic inches.
    The number of inches of wire used is
    A. 24　　　B. 48　　　C. 64　　　D. 96

19. Four quarts of a certain mixture of alcohol and water is at 50% strength.
    To it is added a quart of water.
    The alcohol strength of the new mixture is
    A. 12.5%　　　B. 20%　　　C. 25%　　　D. 40%

20. A is older than B.
    With the passage of time, the
    A. ratio of the ages of A and B remains unchanged
    B. ratio of the ages of A and B increases
    C. ratio of the ages of A and B decreases
    D. difference in their ages varies

21. An illustration in a dictionary is labeled: Scale 1/8.
    A measure of 1 1/2 inches in the illustration corresponds to a real measure of
    A. 3/16 inches   B. 3/8 inches   C. 3/8 feet   D. 1 foot

22. The diagonals of every rectangle
    A. are perpendicular to each other   B. bisect the angles
    C. are equal   D. are oblique to each other

23. If the radius of a circle is increased by 100%, the percent increase of its area is
    A. 100%   B. 200%   C. 300%   D. 400%

24. The distance from City A to City B is 150 miles; from City A to City C, 90 miles.
    Therefore, it is necessarily TRUE that
    A. the distance from B to C is 80 miles
    B. six times the distance from A to B equals 10 times the distance from A to C
    C. the distance from B to C is 240 miles
    D. the distance from A to B exceeds by 30 miles twice the distance from A to C

25. A is 15 years old. B is one-third older.
    The number of years ago when B was twice as old as A is
    A. 3   B. 5   C. 7.5   D. 10

KEY (CORRECT ANSWERS)

1.	B		11.	D
2.	C		12.	B
3.	C		13.	B
4.	C		14.	C
5.	A		15.	D
6.	C		16.	A
7.	C		17.	C
8.	A		18.	B
9.	B		19.	D
10.	B		20.	C

21. D
22. C
23. C
24. B
25. D

5 (#3)

SOLUTIONS TO PROBLEMS

1. From due south to southwest is 45°. Thus, from due east to due southwest is 90° + 45° = 135°.

2. Since the mean of 3 numbers is 8, their sum must be 24. The third number is 24 − 4 − 8 = 12.

3. If x is doubled, 14/x decreases and 18 increases. Finally, 36 ÷ [18 − 14/x] decreases.

4. $5\frac{1}{3} \div 1\frac{5}{9} = (\frac{16}{3})(\frac{9}{14}) = \frac{144}{12} =$ or $3\frac{3}{7}$.

5. ($15+$10) + ($40)(1.10) = $71.50

6. 5 1/2" ÷ 1/8". Then, (44)(10 miles) = 440 miles.

7. ($30)(15) = $450. Then, ($450)(1.01) = $454.50.

8. A rectangle with dimensions of 18' by 6' has a perimeter of 48'. If a square has a perimeter of 48', each side is 12'. The difference in the areas of these two figures is (12')(12') − (18')(6') = 36 sq.ft.

9. (2+3) + 5 = 2 + (3+5) illustrates the associative principle of addition.

10. $\sqrt[5]{32 \cdot 076} \approx 2$ and $(1.00017)^3 \approx 1$, so their sum ≈ 3.

11. Cube of 1/3 = $(1/3)^3$ = 1/27.

12. One-fourth percent of 360 = (.0025)(360) = .9.

13. If the two numbers are equal, such as 9 and 9, $9^2 + 9^2$ is actually equal to (2)(9)(9).

14. He could NOT have purchased 9 5-cent stamps since $1.00 − 9(.05) = .55, and .55 does not divide evenly by .03.

15. A discount of 5% for 60 days is equivalent to a discount per year of about (5%)(365 ÷ 60) or approximately 30%.

16. The greater the number of equal sides, the larger the area. A circle represents the limit of increasing the number of sides and so represents the largest area.

17. The sequence is formed by adding successively 3, 5, 7, 9, 11, 13, and 15. The blank is 17 + 9 = 26.

18. Each edge = $\sqrt[3]{64}$ = 4 inches. The sum of all 12 edges is (12)(4) = 48 inches.

19. Amount of alcohol in either mixture is (.50)(4) = 2 quarts. The alcohol strength in the new mixture is 2/5 = 40%.

20. Although the difference of ages remains constant, the ratio actually decreases. Example: Suppose A is 30 years old and B is 15 years old. The current ratio is 30/15 = 2/1 = 2. In 10 years, the ratio will be 40/25 = 1.6.

21. (1 1/2")(8) = 12" = 1 foot.

22. The diagonals of a rectangle are always equal.

23. Let R = original radius and 2R = increased radius. The area will increase from πR^2 to $4\pi R^2$. This represents an increase of $3\pi R^2$, which corresponds to $3\pi R^2/\pi R^2$ = 3 = 300%.

24. (6)(150) = (10)(90), so choice B is correct.

25. A is 15 years old and B is 15 + (1/3)(15) = 20 years old. Let x = number of years ago when B was twice as old as A. Then, 20 − x = 2(15−x). Simplifying, 20 − x = 30 − 2x. Solving, x = 10.

INTERPRETING STATISTICAL DATA GRAPHS, CHARTS, AND TABLES

EXAMINATION SECTION

TEST 1

DIRECTIONS: Each question or incomplete statement is followed by several suggested answers or completions. Select the one that BEST answers the question or completes the statement. *PRINT THE LETTER OF THE CORRECT ANSWER IN THE SPACE AT THE RIGHT.*

Questions 1-12.

DIRECTIONS: Questions 1 through 12 are to be answered SOLELY on the basis of the information given in the graph and chart below.

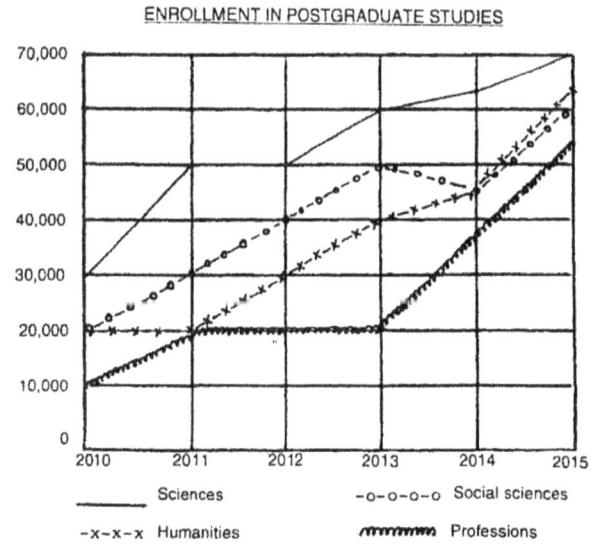

ENROLLMENT IN POSTGRADUATE STUDIES

Fields	Subdivisions	2014	2015
Sciences	Math	10,000	12,000
	Physical Science	22,000	24,000
	Behavioral Science	32,000	35,000
Humanities	Literature	26,000	34,000
	Philosophy	6,000	8,000
	Religion	4,000	6,000
	Arts	10,000	16,000
Social Services	History	36,000	46,000
	Sociology	8,000	14,000
Professions	Law	2,000	2,000
	Medicine	6,000	8,000
	Business	30,000	44,000

219

1. The number of students enrolled in the social sciences and in the humanities was the same in
   A. 2012 and 2014
   B. 2010 and 2014
   C. 2014 and 2015
   D. 2011 and 2014

2. A comparison of the enrollment of students in the various postgraduate studies shows that in every year from 2010 through 2015, there were MORE students enrolled in _____ than in the _____.
   A. professions; sciences
   B. humanities; professions
   C. social sciences, professions
   D. humanities; sciences

3. The number of students enrolled in the humanities was GREATER than the number of students enrolled in the professions by the same amount in _____ of the years.
   A. two
   B. three
   C. four
   D. five

4. The one field of postgraduate study to show a DECREASE in enrollment in one year compared to the year immediately preceding is
   A. humanities
   B. sciences
   C. professions
   D. social sciences

5. If the proportion of arts students to all humanities students was the same in 2012 as in 2015, then the number of arts students in 2012 was
   A. 7,500
   B. 13,000
   C. 15,000
   D. 5,000

6. In which field of postgraduate study did enrollment INCREASE by 20 percent from 2012 to 2013?
   A. Humanities
   B. Professions
   C. Sciences
   D. Social sciences

7. The GREATEST increase in overall enrollment took place between
   A. 2010 and 2011
   B. 2012 and 2013
   C. 2013 and 2014
   D. 2013 and 2015

8. Between 2012 and 2015, the combined enrollment of the sciences and social sciences INCREASED by
   A. 40,000
   B. 48,000
   C. 50,000
   D. 54,000

9. If the enrollment in the social sciences had decreased from 2014 to 2015 at the same rate as from 2013 to 2014, then the social science enrollment in 2015 would have differed from the humanities enrollment in 2015 MOST NEARLY by
   A. 6,000
   B. 8,000
   C. 12,000
   D. 22,000

10. In the humanities, the GREATEST percentage increase in enrollment from 2014 to 2015 was in
    A. literature
    B. philosophy
    C. religion
    D. arts

11. If the proportion of behavioral science students to the total number of students in the sciences was the same in 2011 as in 2014, then the increase in behavioral science enrollment from 2011 to 2015 was
    A. 5,000   B. 7,000   C. 10,000   D. 14,000

11._____

12. If enrollment in the professions increased at the same rate from 2015 to 2016 as from 2014 to 2015, the enrollment in the professions in 2001 would be MOST NEARLY
    A. 85,000   B. 75,000   C. 60,000   D. 55,000

12._____

KEY (CORRECT ANSWERS)

1.	B	7.	D
2.	C	8.	A
3.	B	9.	D
4.	D	10.	D
5.	A	11.	C
6.	C	12.	B

TEST 2

DIRECTIONS: Each question or incomplete statement is followed by several suggested answers or completions. Select the one that BEST answers the question or completes the statement. *PRINT THE LETTER OF THE CORRECT ANSWER IN THE SPACE AT THE RIGHT.*

Questions 1-5.

DIRECTIONS: Questions 1 through 5 involve calculations of annual grade averages for college students who have just completed their junior year. These averages are to be based on the following table showing the number of credit hours for each student during the year at each of the grade levels: A, B, C, D, and F. How these letter grades may be translated into numerical grades is indicated in the first column of the table.

Grade Value	Credit Hours – Junior Year					
	King	Lewis	Martin	Nonkin	Ottly	Perry
A = 95	12	23	9	15	6	3
B = 85	9	12	9	12	18	6
C = 75	6	6	9	3	3	21
D = 65	3	3	3	3	-	-
F = 0	-	-	3	-	-	-

Calculating a grade average for an individual student is a four-step process:
  I. Multiply each grade value by the number of credit hours for which the student received that grade.
  II. Add these multiplication products for each student.
  III. Add the student's total credit hours.
  IV. Divide the multiplication product total by the total number of credit hours.
  V. Round the result, if there is a decimal place, to the nearest whole number. A number ending in .5 would be rounded to the next higher number.

EXAMPLE:
Using student King's grades as an example, his grade average can be calculated by going through the following four steps:

  I. 95 × 12 = 1140
  II. 85 × 9 = 765
  III. 75 × 6 = 450
  IV. 65 × 3 = 195
  V. 0 × 0 = 0

  II. TOTAL = 2550

III. 12
    9
    6
    3
    0
    30 TOTAL CREDIT HOURS

IV. Divide 2550 by 30: $\frac{2550}{30} = 85$.

King's grade average is 85.

1. The grade average of Lewis is
   A. 83   B. 84   C. 85   D. 86

1.____

2 (#2)

2. The grade average of Martin is
   A. 72   B. 73   C. 74   D. 75

   2.____

3. The grade average of Nonkin is
   A. 85   B. 86   C. 87   D. 88

   3.____

4. Student Ottly must attain a grade average of 90 in each of his years in college to be accepted into the graduate school of his choice.
   If, in summer school during his junior year, he takes two three-credit courses and receives a grade of 95 in each one, his grade average for his junior year will then be MOST NEARLY
   A. 87   B. 88   C. 89   D. 90

   4.____

5. If Perry takes an additional three-credit course during the year and receives a grade of 95, his grade average will be increased to APPROXIMATELY
   A. 79   B. 80   C. 81   D. 82

   5.____

KEY (CORRECT ANSWERS)

1. C
2. D
3. C
4. B
5. B

TEST 3

DIRECTIONS: Each question or incomplete statement is followed by several suggested answers or completions. Select the one that BEST answers the question or completes the statement. *PRINT THE LETTER OF THE CORRECT ANSWER IN THE SPACE AT THE RIGHT.*

Questions 1-5.

DIRECTIONS: Questions 1 through 5 are to be answered SOLELY on the basis of the following information and chart.

The following table gives pertinent data for six different applicants with regard to: Grade averages, which are expressed on a scale running from 0 (low) to 4 (high); Scores on qualifying test, which run from 200 (low) to 800 (high); Related work experience, which is expressed in number of months; Personal references, which are related from 1 (low) to 5 (high).

Applicant	Grade Average	Test Score	Work Experience	Reference
Jones	2.2	620	24	3
Perez	3.5	650	0	5
Lowitz	3.2	420	2	4
Uncker	2.1	710	15	2
Farrow	2.8	560	0	3
Shapiro	3.0	560	12	4

An administrative Assistant is in charge of the initial screening process for the program. This process requires classifying applicants into the following four groups:

A. SUPERIOR CANDIDATES: Unless the personal reference rating is lower than 3, all applicants with grade averages of 3.0 or higher and test scores of 600 or higher are classified as superior candidates.

B. GOOD CANDIDATES: Unless the personal reference rating is lower than 3, all applicants with one of the following combinations of grade averages and test scores are classified as good candidates:
   1. Grade average of 2.5 to 2.9 and test score of 600 or higher;
   2. Grade average of 3.0 or higher and test score of 550 to 599.

C. POSSIBLE CANDIDATES: Applicants with one of the following combinations of qualifications are classified as possible candidates:
   1. Grade average of 2.5 to 2.9 and test score of 550 to 599 and a personal reference rating of 3 or higher;
   2. Grade average of 2.0 to 2.4 and test score of 500 or higher and at least 21 months' work experience and a personal reference rating of 3 or higher;
   3. A combination of grade average and test score that would otherwise qualify as superior or good but a personal reference score lower than 3.

D. REJECTED CANDIDATES: Applicants who do not fall in any of the above groups are to be rejected.

EXAMPLE:
Jones' grade average of 2.2 does not meet the standard for either a superior candidate (grade average must be 3.0 or higher) or a good candidate (grade average must be 2.5 to 2.9). Grade average of 2.2 does not qualify Jones as a possible candidate if Jones has a test score of 500 or higher, at least 21 months' work experience, and a personal reference rating of 3 or higher. Since Jones has a test score of 620, 24 months' work experience, and a reference rating of 3, Jones is a possible candidate. The answer is C.

Answer Questions 1 through 5 as explained above, indicating for each whether the applicant should be classified as a
- A. Superior candidate
- B. Good candidate
- C. Possible candidate
- D. Rejected candidate

1. Perez   1.____
2. Lowitz   2.____
3. Uncker   3.____
4. Farrow   4.____
5. Shapiro   5.____

KEY (CORRECT ANSWERS)

1. A
2. D
3. D
4. C
5. B

INTERPRETING STATISTICAL DATA GRAPHS, CHARTS, AND TABLES

EXAMINATION SECTION

TEST 1

DIRECTIONS: Each question or incomplete statement is followed by several suggested answers or completions. Select the one that BEST answers the question or completes the statement. *PRINT THE LETTER OF THE CORRECT ANSWER IN THE SPACE AT THE RIGHT.*

Questions 1-4.

DIRECTIONS: Questions 1 through 4 are to be answered on the basis of the following chart.

	CENSUS DATA TOWNSHIPS IN ROCK COUNTY					
	2015			2020		
Townships	Pop.	% 65 years and over	% under 18 years	Pop.	% 65 years and over	% under 18 years
Smallville	43,095	27	?	45,045	30	?
Bedford	35,600	?	26	37,152	17	30
Hyatt	15,418	30	15	15,398	32	12
Burgess	75,400	21	?	82,504	9	?
Total	?	18	23	180,099	25	21

1. Approximately, what was the average population of the four townships in Rock County in 2015?
   A. 42,378
   B. 42,587
   C. 45,025
   D. Cannot be determined from information given

   1.____

2. Which township experienced the LEAST population growth from 2015 to 2020?
   A. Smallville
   B. Bedford
   C. Burgess
   D. Cannot be determined from information given

   2.____

3. In Rock County, in 2020, two out of every five individuals 18 years of age and over earn less than $32,000 a year.
   Approximately how many individuals are in this category?
   A. 37,821   B. 142,278   C. 56,911   D. 52,040

   3.____

2 (#1)

4. In Rock County, in 2020, 12966 people over 65 receive meals from the Senior Meals program.
If the participation rate is consistent throughout the county, approximately how many people over 65 are receiving meals in the Town of Hyatt?
  A. 1,232
  B. 1,419
  C. 2,879
  D. Cannot be determined from information given

4.____

Questions 5-8.

DIRECTIONS: Questions 5 through 8 are to be answered on the basis of the information shown in the following chart.

THE ECONOMY

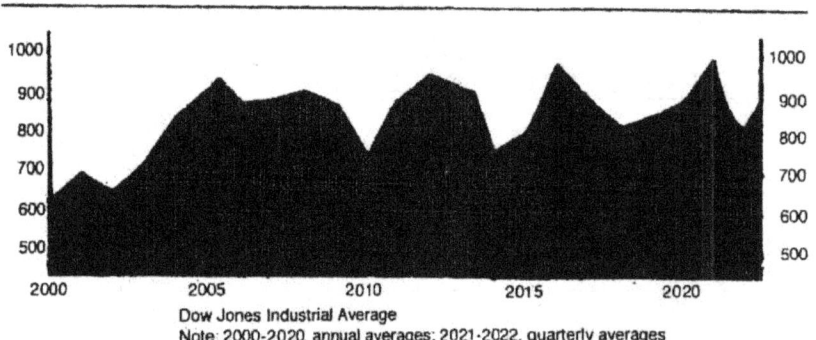

Dow Jones Industrial Average
Note: 2000-2020, annual averages; 2021-2022, quarterly averages

WHAT THE NUMBERS SAY: Both the prime rate and the mortgage interest rate are going down, and inflation is slowing somewhat. Unemployment keeps rising though, faster for Blacks than for Whites.

MONTHLY DATA	9/22	8/22	7/22	9/21	2007
Employment (seasonally adjusted)					
Number of unemployed (millions)	11.260	10.710	11.036	7.966	2.975
Overall unemployment rate	10.1%	8.6?	9.8%	7.5%	3.8%
Black unemployment rate	20.2%	18.8?	18.5%	15.1%	7.4%
Wages					
Average weekly earnings: current dollars	$270.05	$270.69	$269.98	$222.92	$101.84
Average weekly earnings: 2017 dollars	N/A	$168.50	$167.90	$144.94	$184.83
Prices					
All items Consumer Price Index	N/A	292.8	292.2	279.3	100.00
Increase from one year earlier	N/A	5.9%	6.5%	11.0%	2.9%
Food increase from on year earlier	N/A	3.6%	4.5%	6.5%	0.9%
Interest Rates					
Mortgage	14.99	15.68%	15.74%	15.37%	6.50%
Prime Interest Rate	13.50	14.39	16.26%	20.08%	5.61%

3 (#1)

QUARTERLY DATA
(billions of dollars at annual rates,

seasonally adjusted)	2022 2nd	2022 1st	2021 2nd	2007
Gross National Product	3041.1	2995.5	2885.8	796.3
Balance of Trade (exports minus imports)	-20.47	-23.78	-24.9	+3.8
Wages, Salaries, and Benefits	1849.9	1830.8	1752.0	471.9
Corporate Profits	154.9	157.1	190.3	79.3
Gross National Product in 2012 dollars	1475.3	1470.7	1510.4	1007.7

NOTES: N/A means not available. Wages are the average for private sector nonfarm workers; no taxes have been subtracted. SOURCES: Employment, wages, and prices are from the Department of Labor Statistics. Mortgage interest rate is from the Federal Home Loan Bank Board. GNP and its components are from the Department of Commerce, Bureau of Economic Analysis.

5. The average weekly earnings, in 2017 dollars, for August of 2022, compared to the average weekly earnings, in 2017 dollars, for September of 2021, were
   A. $47.77 more
   B. $.60 more
   C. $47.77 less
   D. $23.56 more

6. The average weekly earnings, in current dollars, from September of 2021 increased
   A. 17.4%   B. 21.4%   C. 48%   D. 16%

7. The Balance of Trade from 2007 to the 1st quarter of 2022 had declined approximately
   A. 13.0%   B. 626%   C. 726%   D. 7.26%

8. From 2007 through September of 2022, the one category that has always shown an increase, of the following, is
   A. number of unemployed
   B. mortgage rates
   C. Black unemployment rate
   D. average weekly earnings: current dollars

Questions 9-12.

DIRECTIONS: Questions 9 through 12 are to be answered on the basis of the following chart.

	2009	2010	2011	2012	2013	2014	2015	2016
(Million Dollars)								
Food for development								
School lunch	137.3	106.9	123.3	102.5	79.169		66.3	?
Maternal and preschool feeding	31.4	37.4	51.3	48.8	45.0	54.3	90.5	?
Food for work	52.3	71.4	68.0	64.8	62.2	68.9	102.1	67.1
Total	221.0	215.7	242.6	2151.1	187.3	194.8	258.9	26.4
Emergency & Relief	55.7	47.3	60.2	182.7	?	88.1	57.9	45.3
Total, all programs	276.7	263.0	?	397.8	?	282.9	?	313.7
(Thousand Persons)								
Food for development								
School lunch	35,376	34,437	33,696	35,645	36,584	045	18,940	12,976
Maternal and preschool feeding	10,374	10,932	13,168	10,843	15,621	13,159	11,126	13,849
Food for work	12,884	14,193	10,992	15,260	10,970	8,799	8,481	8,175
Total	58,636	59,562	57,856	61,748	63,175	49,003	38,547	36,000
Emergency & Relief	14,012	18,083	17,467	28,143	23,715	6,406	12,759	4,025
Total, all programs	72,648	77,645	75,323	89,891	?	55,409	51,306	40,025

9. From 2010 to 2016, the value of exports designated for school lunches decreased
   A. 82 million dollars
   B. 56%
   C. 48.5%
   D. 94.4

10. The value of food exported for maternal and pre-school feeding amounted to the GREATEST per person in
    A. 2009   B. 2010   C. 2012   D. 2016

11. If the total value of exports in 2017 decreased from the year before at the same rate as it changed from 2011 to 2012, the 2017 total equals MOST NEARLY _____ million.
    A. 100   B. 413.7   C. 210.2   D. 417.2

12. The value of exported food for emergency and relief was $2.12 greater per person served in 2012 than in 2013.
    What is the APPROXIMATE value of food exported for emergency and relief in 2013? _____ million.
    A. 103.6   B. 204.2   C. 10   D. 91.3

Questions 13-16.

DIRECTIONS: Questions 13 through 16 are to be answered on the basis of the following chart.

THE 2012 BUDGET CUTS
(billions of dollars)

	2012 Original Budget	2012 Projected Outlays Obama Administration	
	Current Services (Outlays)	Amount	Change From Current Services
National Defense	$177.8	$187.5	$2
International Affairs	11.9	11.1	-0.8
General Science, Space & Technology	7.3	6.9	-0.4
Energy	11.8	6.4	-5.4
Natural Resources & Environment	13.8	12.6	-1.2
Agriculture	4.8	8.6	+3.8
Commerce & Housing Credit	5.1	3.3	-1.8
Transportation	21.9	21.2	-0.7
Community & Regional Development	?	8.4	0.8
Education, Training, Employment & Social Services	35.0	27.8	-7.2
Health	75.5	73.4	-2.1
Income Security	259.3	?	-8.4
Veterans Benefits & Services	24.4	24.2	-0.2
Administration of Justice	4.8	4.5	-0.3
General Government	5.2	5.1	-0.1
General Purpose Fiscal Assistance	6.5	6.4	-0.1
Interest	89.9	99.1	?
Contingencies for Other Requirements	-	1.0	-1.0
Allowances for Civilian Agency Pay Raises	3.2	0.4	-2.8
Undistributed Off-setting Receipts	-31.4	-31.6	-0.2
		gains	+22.7
		cuts	-33.5
		net	$?
TOTAL		$?	$725.2 cut

13. By what percent did the 2012 Projected Outlays for National Defense increase from the 2012 original budget?
    A. 9.7%   B. 5.2%   C. 5.5%   D. 52%

13.____

14. What is the difference in outlays for Interest from the 2012 Original Budget to the Projected Outlays?
    A. 1.2 billion dollars
    B. $910,000
    C. 9.2 million dollars
    D. 9,200,000,000

14.____

15. For each dollar spent on Education, Training, Employment, and Social Services, according to the 2012 Original Budget, how much was to have been spent on National Defense?
    A. $2.35   B. $.29   C. $.42   D. $5.08

16. The total change from Current Services is _____ billion dollars.
    A. 736   B. -10.8   C. 10.2   D. 56.2

Questions 17-20.

DIRECTIONS: Questions 17 through 20 are to be answered on the basis of the following chart.

TOWN RECREATION EXPENDITURES 2017-2019
(Hypothetical Data)

	2017	2018	2019
Personnel	$75,000	$82,000	$110,500
Special Events	6,110	6,730	6,860
May Day Festival	2,920	2,530	2,700
Baseball Marathon	3,190	4,200	4,160
Regular Programming	4,770	4,100	4,420
Music in the Park	1,200	1,200	1,350
Children's Theatre	1,580	1,300	1,320
Other	1,990	1,600	1,750
Park Maintenance	5,630	6,070	6,090
Playground Supplies	2,980	3,120	3,090
Landscaping	2,650	2,950	3,000
Total	$91,510	$98,900	$127,870
% Town Budget	3.8%	3.7%	3.6%

17. Of every ten dollars the town spent in 2018, approximately how much was spent on the Regular Programming category?
    A. $0.37
    B. $0.015
    C. $0.255
    D. Cannot be determined from information given

18. Town officials anticipate a 5% greater increase for 2020 personnel expenditures than the increase from 2018 to 2019.
    Approximately what are the estimated 2020 personnel expenditures?
    A. $154,479   B. $43,979   C. $143,979   D. $144,534

19. Approximately what percent of the entire town budget was spent on recreational Special Events in 2019?   19._____
    A. 3.6%
    B. 0.46%
    C. 0.2%
    D. Cannot be determined from information given

20. What area has seen the GREATEST rate of increase in expenditures between 2018 and 2019?   20._____
    A. Personnel
    B. Special Events
    C. Programming
    D. Park Maintenance

Questions 21-24.

DIRECTIONS: Questions 21 through 24 are to be answered on the basis of the following chart.

COMPARISON OF HOURLY WAGE RATES FOR FARMWORKERS
AND PRODUCTION WORKERS IN MANUFACTURING, 2018-2020

	Production Workers in Mfg.			All Hired Farmworkers		Farmworker Wages as a Percentage of Mfg. Wages (In New York
	All Mfg.	Durable Goods	Non-durable Goods			
	NEW YORK			New York	U.S.	
2018						
January	$5.93	$6.46	$5.41	$2.85	$3.18	48%
April	5.99	6.52	5.46	2.71	3.09	45%
July	6.09	6.61	5.54	2.72	2.93	45%
October	6.14	6.77	5.49	2.90	3.18	47%
2019						
January	6.41	6.98	5.78	2.90	3.38	?
April	6.45	7.03	5.82	2.98	3.40	46%
July	6.58	7.17	5.95	2.80	3.23	43%
October	6.71	7.37	6.02	2.85	3.57	42%
2020						
January	6.91	7.50	6.26	3.10	3.69	45%
April	7.02	7.63	6.34	2.95	3.61	42%
July	7.11	7.76	6.42	2.86	3.52	
October	-	-	-	3.54	3.85	-

Farmworkers' piece rates are included in the above-listed figures.

21. For the four months given in 1980, hired farmworkers in the United States earned an average of   21._____
    A. $4.63   B. $3.57   C. $3.50   D. $3.67

22. In New York, in July of 2020, the hourly wage paid farmworkers was what percent of the wage paid production workers in non-durable goods manufacturing?   22._____
    A. 41.3%   B. 44.5%   C. 54.8%   D. 40.2%

23. The average wage for the four months given in 2018 of farmworkers hired in New York, as compared to all those hired in the United States, was
   A. $.30 greater
   B. approximately 90% less
   C. approximately 10% greater
   D. approximately 10% less

23.____

24. The hourly wages of hired farmworkers in New York in January of 2020, compared to the hourly wages of hired farmworkers in New York in October of 2019 increased
   A. 45% B. 42% C. $.25 D. 15%

24.____

Questions 25-28.

DIRECTIONS: Questions 25 through 28 are too be answered on the basis of the following charts.

	MULTIPLE JOBHOLDERS BY SEX, MARITAL STATUS, MAY 2018 COUNTY X							
	Both Sexes			Men			Women		
Characteristics	Total Employed	Multiple Jobholders		Total Employed	Multiple Jobholders		Total Employed	Multiple Jobholders	
		Number	Percent		Number	Percent		Number	Percent
Marital Status									
Single	23,123	1,015	?	13,031	6.16	4.7	10,092	398	3.9
Married, spouse present	61,121	3,142	5.1	38,080	2.356	6.2	23,041	786	3.4
Other marital status	12,565	603	4.8	4,671	237	5.1	7,894	364	?

	MULTIPLE JOBHOLDERS BY TYPE OF INDUSTRY AND CLASS OF WORKER, MAY 2018 COUNTY X								
	Multiple Jobholders			Second Job in Agriculture			Second Job in Nonagriculture		
Primary Job	Total Employed	Number	Percent of Employed	Total	Wage & Salary	Self-employed	Total	Wage & Salary	Self-employed
Total	96,809	4,758	4.9	722	173	549	4,036	3,024	1,012
Agriculture	3,458	180	5.2	?	42	25	113	107	6
Wage & Salary	1,455	67	4.6	44	19	25	23	17	6
Self-employed	1,677	94	5.6	23	23	(1)	71	71	(1)
Unpaid Family	326	20	6.1	0	0	(2)	20	20	(2)
Non-agriculture	93,351	4,578	4.9	?	131	524	3,923	2,917	1,006
Wage & Salary	86,024	4,328	5.0	649	124	524	3,680	2,674	1,006
Self-Employed	6,847	236	3.4	6	6	(1)	229	229	(1)
Unpaid Family	479	?	?	0	0	(2)	?	14	(2)

(1) Self-employed persons with secondary businesses or farms, but no wage or salary jobs, were not counted as multiple jobholders.
(2) Persons whose primary jobs were as unpaid family workers were counted as multiple jobholders only if they also held wage or salary jobs.

25. The ratio of married women with more than one job to all married multiple jobholders is
   A. 1:3 B. 1:4 C. 3:1 D. 1:75

25.____

26. If 50% of those holding a second job in agriculture are men, how many men hold a second job in non-agriculture?
   A. 2,848 B. 3,209 C. 2,488 D. 2,777

26.____

27. The percentage of agricultural workers who are self-employed compared to the percentage of non-agricultural workers who are self-employed is APPROXIMATELY
    A. two times greater
    B. seven times greater
    C. one-third less
    D. four times greater

28. 3.8% of the women and 5.8% of the men in the total labor force were multiple jobholders in May of 2018.
    If, in 2019, the total labor force increased by 10,955, with 40% of the new workers being women, but the percentage of male and female multiple jobholders remaining the same, how many more men than women were multiple jobholders in 2019?
    A. 3,617   B. 6,572   C. 1,891   D. 2,191

Questions 29-32.

DIRECTIONS: Questions 29 through 32 are to be answered on the basis of the following chart.

WORKERS AND DEPENDENTS, 1950-2050 AND BEYOND
CENSUS BUREAU TRENDS AND PROJECTIONS

Year	Percentage of Total Population That is:				Number of Dependents (Non-workers) Per Worker
	0-17	65+	18-64	Working	
1950	9	8.1	60.9	39.8	1.51
1960	35.7	9.2	55.1	37.8	1.65
1970	34.0	9	56.2	39.9	1.51
1979	?	11.2	60.4	44.9	1.23
2000	26.1	12.7	?	45.5	?
2025	24.0	18.2	57.8	43.0	?
2050	23.8	18.5	57.7	?	1.33

29. In the year 2050, dependents per worker is expected to have decreased from the number of dependents per worker in 1960 by
    A. .32 workers
    B. approximately 32%
    C. approximately 2%
    D. approximately 19%

30. If the percentage of the total population that is working in 2060 is 4.4% more than the percentage of the total population working in the year 2000, the percentage of the total population working in 2060 would be
    A. 49.9%   B. 42%   C. 41%   D. 8%

31. If in 1982 the percentage of the total population that was 0-17 years of age had increased by 2% from the 1979 figure for this group, what was the percentage of the total population 0-17 years of age in 1982?

    A. 45.6%
    B. 12.3%
    C. 30.4%
    D. Cannot be determined from information given

31._____

32. In the year 2000, the number of dependents per worker is projected to be
    A. approximately 1.18
    B. approximately 1.20
    C. approximately .83
    D. Cannot be determined from information given

32._____

Questions 33-36.

DIRECTIONS: Questions 33 through 36 are to be answered on the basis of the following chart.

U.S. BALANCE OF TRADE, BY REGION, 2000, 2012, AND 2017
(Billions of Dollars)

	2000	2012	2017	Change From	
				2000-2012	2012-2017
World Total	?	-5.8	-26.7	-11.7	-20.9
Germany	+0.4	-1.4	?	?	+0.2
Other West Europe	+2.6	+1.4	+7.6	?	+6.2
Japan	+0.3	-4.1	-8.1	-4.4	-4.0
Other Developed	-1.1	-2.0	-1.8	-3.1	+0.2
Oil Companies	-0.6	-0.5	?	+0.1	-22.1
Taiwan	+0.5	-1.4	-4.0	?	-2.6
Other Third World	+1.1	+1.7		+0.6	-0.2
Communist Countries	+0.1	?	+1.6	+0.4	?

33. The U.S. Balance of Trade with Taiwan from 2000 to 2017 decreased
    A. 1.9%   B. 2.6 billion dollars
    C. 90%   D. 900%

33._____

34. In 2012, the value of the U.S. Balance of Trade with Communist countries, compared to the value of the U.S. Balance of Trade with the World total, was
    A. 6.3 billion dollars greater
    B. 10% greater
    C. 5.3 billion dollars greater
    D. cannot be determined from information given

34._____

35. If, in 2022, the U.S. Balance of Trade with Germany decreased by 40% from the 2017 figure, the U.S. Balance of Trade with Germany in 2022
    A. decreased 48%   B. was -1.68 billion dollars
    C. was -1.8 billion dollars   D. decreased by .78 billion dollars

35._____

36. If the 2000 World total of the U.S. Balance of Trade was 20% less than the World total of the U.S. Balance of Trade the year before it, then the U.S. Balance of Trade, World total, for 1999 was

    A. +7.080 billion dollars
    B. +6.431 billion dollars
    C. 7.375 billion dollars
    D. cannot be determined from information given

36.____

Questions 37-40.

DIRECTIONS: Questions 37 through 40 are to be answered on the basis of the following chart.

MARKET BASKET COMPARISON (JUNE 1, 2018)				
City	Food Cost	Tax (If Any)	Total	Approximate Difference from U.S. Average
Tampa	$32.58	0-0	$32.58	?
Des Moines	$33.80	0-0	33.80	?
San Diego	$34.02	0-0	$34.02	?
Phoenix	$33.19	?	$34.85	?
Atlanta	$34.60	4%-1.28	$35.98	-2.7%
Cleveland	$36.08	?	$36.08	-2.4%
Dallas	$36.41	0-0	$36.41	-1.5%
New York	$37.72	0-0	$37.72	+2.1%
Portland, Ore.	$38.10	0-0	$38.10	+3.1%
Chicago	$36.47	?	$38.29	+3.4%
Little Rock	$37.36	3%-1.12	$38.48	+4.1%
San Francisco	$38.82	0-0	$38.82	+5.0%
Philadelphia	$38.88	0-0	$38.88	+5.2%
Salt Lake City	$37.12	5%-1.86	$38.98	+5.5%
Washington, D.C.	$38.99	0-0	$38.99	+5.9%
Boston	$39.40	0-0	$39.40	+6.6%
Anchorage	$50.21	0-0	$50.21	+35.9%

37. The percentage of cities in the table that no tax was APPROXIMATELY

    A. 29%   B. 71%   C. 79%   D. 21%

37.____

38. If Portland, Oregon's Food Cost was approximately 3.1% more than the U.S. average, approximately what was the average Food Cost?

    A. $35.70   B. $36.92   C. $37.14   D. $36.95

38.____

39. In Phoenix, the amount of tax on the Food Cost category totaled

    A. 6%
    B. 5%
    C. 4%
    D. cannot be determined from information given

39.____

40. If the Food Cost of a market basket in San Francisco was $59.52 in 2019, then 40.____
the Food Cost in San Francisco in 2019 compared to June 1 of 2018 increased
   A. 20.7%   B. $10.70   C. 53.3%   D. 34.8%

KEY (CORRECT ANSWERS)

1.	A	11.	C	21.	D	31.	C
2.	B	12.	A	22.	B	32.	B
3.	C	13.	C	23.	D	33.	D
4.	B	14.	D	24.	C	34.	A
5.	D	15.	D	25.	B	35.	B
6.	B	16.	B	26.	A	36.	C
7.	C	17.	B	27.	B	37.	B
8.	C	18.	A	28.	C	38.	D
9.	C	19.	C	29.	D	39.	B
10.	D	20.	A	30.	A	40.	C